Thoughts on the Policy of the Crown towards India

Thoughts on the Policy of the Crown towards India

John Malcolm Ludlow

Gian Publishing House

GIAN PUBLISHING HOUSE
PUBLISHERS OF BOOKS ON HUMAN CIVILIZATION
29/6 SHAKTI NAGAR, DELHI-110007

First Reprint in India, 1986

Printed at Goyal Offset Printers, Delhi-110035
and published by Smt. Gayatri Garg
for Gian Publishing House, Delhi-110007

PREFACE.

In the beginning of last year, at the request of a friend, I wrote some letters on "the Indian Government question" in a provincial paper. Some interest was excited by them beyond the natural sphere of the Journal, and I was induced to give greater scope to them, and to treat in particular at some length of the effects of that policy of annexation and absorption of which the late Governor-General of India has been the main exponent. A desire was expressed for the republication of this portion of the series, and I had already prepared it, with considerable additions, for the press, when the appearance of the Queen's Proclamation came to render much of my argument against such a policy superfluous, by sanctioning its leading conclusions. In taking it as my text, I felt I should be best carrying out the purpose which I had in view.*

Many will indeed think, even if they do not say: "We are weary of this subject of India. The poignant interest of the outbreak has passed away. The suspense of the conflict is over. The Lucknow heroes are mostly recruiting their strength at home. There are no more victories to win that we care to hear of. Besides, we

* The form of letters has been retained, though more than half the volume consists of new matter.

have tried to understand the subject, and we cannot. It is so far, so foreign, so complex; we hear such different accounts of it. Where one says black and the other says white, each witness being, for aught we can discover, of equal authority, how can we decide between the two? The last session has seen the fate of a ministry hang on an Indian proclamation and despatch; has seen an India bill passed, the time-honoured administration of the East India Company swept away, the government of India transferred to the Crown, a responsible ministry for India established. At the head of the new Council sits a young statesman, by almost general consent held most fit for his place, if not that to some he seems already fit for one still higher. Is not that enough? We have to think of the Reform Bill at home, of the ferment in Northern Italy, of Napoleonic intrigues, alliances, preparations for war, pacific denials soon denied; of quasi-slave trade complications; of Denmark and the Bund, of Villafranca and the Russians, of Turkey and its rayas, of Servia and her revolution, of the Ionian Isles and Mr. Gladstone abroad. Why cannot we be allowed to forget India, were it only for awhile?"

Much of what is thus said or thought is perfectly true,—all is perfectly natural. Little as I may think of the Derby Cabinet's India Act, I rejoice in the two momentous changes introduced into the Indian administration,—Crown Government and ministerial responsibility. I have hope in Lord Stanley, if not borne down by his Council. I admire the boldness of self-devotion which induced him to undertake, in the midst of a crisis so difficult a task as that of an Indian ministry; I believe that his abilities and industry have hitherto gone far to justify that boldness; I believe him to be actuated by just and generous feelings towards the people of India; I hail with especial satisfaction, as an earnest of the policy of the present administration towards India, the appointment of Sir C. Trevelyan to the Government of Madras. Nor would I for a moment deny the importance of any of those questions of domestic or foreign policy which are alleged; quite the contrary. But I say it is precisely the importance of those questions which makes our Indian policy, and the condition of our Indian empire, more important still. India disaffected is a palsy of England's right side; India in rebellion is a devouring ulcer in her flank. For months now our best troops and our ablest general have been thousands of miles away. Months must yet elapse before one European soldier—even of the tried 78th—reaches England from India. The 50,000 men whom 1857 sent thither,—the 30,000 or so who have followed them in 1858—have in great part melted away already. Recruiting for the Indian service must yet go on; the boys whom the recruiting sergeant is now picking up out of our vast courts and alleys will yet many of them perish like flies under the fierce Indian sun, in petty obscure partisan skirmishes with those who have been soldiers and will have to be hunted down as robbers, in the storming of small mudforts and fortified villages. Meanwhile, who at home is not conscious of feelings of vague distrust as to the future, latent in the minds even of the loudest declaimers for peace? The armed despotism of Louis Napoleon weighs upon Europe. His warlike preparations he no longer even takes the trouble to conceal. Even if we suppose his personal intentions towards us to be friendly, currents which he cannot control will always bring him round to a direction of opposition towards us. Freedom and despotism cannot stand long side by side. Freedom, however peaceable, is a standing warning against despotism; despotism, for very life, must be a perpetual threat against freedom. Few amongst us perhaps, during the Regina Coeli and Charles-Georges complications, could get rid of an uneasy suspicion that we were sacrificing the weak to the strong, pandering to a secret fear of a too-powerful ally, losing the opportunity of a mighty protest in favour of right. And the trial of M. de Montalembert, for the offence of having dared to speak well of England —even now that it has been sought to be wiped out by a hasty pardon—was an insult flung in the teeth not of England's Government, but of every individual Englishman. Our nation was lowered through his condemnation, by the police courts of a prince who yet called himself our ally. A score is thus being run up, which sooner or later, I fear, must be settled in blood. And M. de Montalambert himself has warned us as to the "common fund of animosity" existing against England on the Continent, as to the need of keeping up her military strength.

It is the condition of India that has made this state of things possible. With a happy, prosperous, and loyal India, England may safely bid defiance to the world. With Saxon thews and sinews in the West, and faithful Mussulman or Sikh sabres in the East, ready to be flung over the Indian Ocean, she would take European despotism in front and rear. And therefore I claim that nothing should tempt us to overlook the need of that large and distant empire, which is now, in reality, paralyzing our military strength, and must, sooner or later, tell weightily upon our financial resources. Therefore I say, that whilst any interval of rest and security is given to us at home, we should apply ourselves resolutely to the understanding of India's condition, to the setting it right as far as is humanly possible. Therefore I claim attention for fragments of contemporary history, relating to states in India of which many may never have heard before, or have heard with as little of vivid personal interest as they might have heard of the moon's mountains. In the problem, whether India, now and in future, is to be to us a hindrance or a help, a source of strength or a source of weakness, every English household is concerned, little as we may think it.

And the problem is one, be assured, which gathers interest as we enter more deeply into it. What more striking spectacle does this world afford than that of the oldest civilization in the world grappled by the newest?—of a heathenism, more ancient than that of which our school-books teach us, nay, apparently the fountain-head of that, placed face to face with Christianity? what stranger sight than that of the new everywhere permeating the old in resistless currents, driving away the false, and yet in the very process bringing out many a precious truth that is mixed up with it? To the seeing eye, the condition of India is as it were a synchronous picture of human development, all history, so to speak, made visible at once.

I need hardly say that I am no political partizan. I deemed Lord Palmerston prematurely hurled from power; I looked for a time to his re-instalment; I still deem his India bill to have been by far the preferable one of the three measures brought forward upon that subject, one of which has passed into law. And whilst heartily approving of the late Proclamation of the Queen's Government, and believing that every nerve should be strained by all well-wishers to India to carry it loyally and generously into effect,—that no punishment scarcely can be too great for those officials who should dare to disregard it or tamper with it,—I reserve to myself the fullest freedom of judgment as to the general policy of a Cabinet, for some members of which I have feelings of unfeigned respect,—but of thorough distrust towards one or two others.

I have, in this work, used proper names far more freely than I could have wished. But where I found them appended to state papers it seemed to me that it would have been affectation to avoid them. I have at least the satisfaction of thinking that I never have had the slightest communication with any of the gentlemen whose proceedings I have been led to criticize, and do not know one of them by sight; and therefore, that not a tinge of personal feeling can have influenced my judgments. There are those who may deem that the canvassing the past acts of the Indian government or of its officials can only have for its effect to embitter the minds of the natives against British rule, at a time when it seems most desirable that animosities should be allowed to subside. My answer is, that I believe the minds of the natives *are* embittered against many features of British rule; that animosities *have* been excited, which cannot subside by merely being overlooked. And all my experience hitherto has shewn me, that where a man does deem himself aggrieved, the two very worst things possible are, 1st.—to omit or refuse inquiring into his grievances, 2nd.—not to recognize them to the fullest extent where they are real. That such a grievance as the Inam Commission, for instance, is a real one, I cannot affect to doubt; and the longer it is left subsisting and unnoticed, I am convinced, the more harm will result. Of the folly in process of committal of forcing it upon the Madras Presidency it is difficult to speak in measured terms.

There remains for me but to add, that for the use of the greater part of the materials from which this book is written, I am indebted to the kindness of Mr. J. Dickinson, jun., Hon. Secretary to the India Reform Society.

Lincoln's Inn, January 31, 1859.

NOTE.—I find I have committed a grave error in my XIVth Letter, in speaking of the State of Dhar as restored. It is true that during the last session Lord Stanley, in answer to a question from Mr. J. B. Smith, stated that it was "the intention of the Government to disallow the policy of annexation as regards the territory of Dhar," and that the occupation of that territory was provisional only, "subject as to its duration to further explanation which we hope to receive;"* nor is there, I believe, any reason to doubt that instructions for restoration were sent out accordingly. But

* Hansard's Debates, vol. 15? (3rd Series), pp. 1919-20.

the territory remains unrestored to this hour, and the very despatch for its restoration, if rumour speaks true, unreplied to. Letter XIV. must therefore be read as written under the delusion of supposing that the directions of the Queen's Government were obeyed by the Indian authorities.

It is well known that under the Double Government many a benevolent despatch from the Court of Directors remained waste paper in India. It is more than suspected that the practice had grown up latterly of writing such despatches—as our Transatlantic cousins would say, for Bunkum—without any intention of their being carried out, but solely to make a show before Parliament and through the press.* There remains to be seen whether the Queen's Government will submit to either disgrace in future.

---

* The Moturfa abolition despatch for instance?

CONTENTS.

PART II.

THE PLEDGES OF THE PROCLAMATION TO THE PEOPLE OF INDIA.

THE PROCLAMATION

OF THE

QUEEN'S SOVEREIGNTY OVER INDIA.

Proclamation by the Queen in Council, to the Princes, Chiefs, and People of India.

VICTORIA, by the grace of God, of the United Kingdom of Great Britain and Ireland, and of the Colonies and Dependencies thereof in Europe, Asia, Africa, America, and Australasia, Queen, Defender of the Faith.

Whereas, for divers weighty reasons, we have resolved, by and with the advice and consent of the lords spiritual and temporal and commons in Parliament assembled, to take upon ourselves the government of the territories in India, heretofore administered in trust for us by the Honourable East India Company:

Now, therefore, we do by these presents notify and declare that, by the advice and consent aforesaid, we have taken upon ourselves the said government, and we hereby call upon all our subjects within the said territories to be faithful and to bear true allegiance to us, our heirs and successors, and to submit themselves to the authority of those whom we may hereafter from time to time see fit to appoint to administer the government of our said territories, in our name and on our behalf.

And we, reposing especial trust and confidence in the loyalty, ability, and judgment of our right trusty and well-beloved cousin and councillor, Charles John Viscount Canning, do hereby constitute and appoint him, the said Viscount Canning, to be our first Viceroy and Governor-General in and over our said territories, and to administer the government thereof in our name, and generally to act in our name and on our behalf, subject to such orders and regulations as he shall, from time to time, receive from us through one of our principal Secretaries of State.

And we do hereby confirm in their several offices, civil and military, all persons now employed in the service of the Honourable East India Company, subject to our future pleasure, and to such laws and regulations as may hereafter be enacted.

We hereby announce to the native princes of India that all treaties and engagements made with them, by or under the authority of the Honourable East India Company, are by us accepted, and will be scrupulously maintained; and we look for the like observance on their part.

We desire no extension of our present territorial possessions; and while we will permit no aggression upon our dominions or our rights to be attempted with impunity, we shall sanction no encroachment on those of others. We shall respect the rights, dignity, and honour of native princes as our own, and we desire that they, as well as our own subjects, should enjoy that prosperity and that social advancement which can only be secured by internal peace and good government.

We hold ourselves bound to the natives of our Indian territories by the same obligations of duty which bind us to all our other subjects; and those obligations, by the blessing of Almighty God, we shall faithfully and conscientiously fulfil.

Firmly relying ourselves on the truth of Christianity, and acknowledging with gratitude the solace of religion, we disclaim alike the right and the desire to impose our convictions on any of our subjects. We declare it to be our Royal will and pleasure that none be in anywise favoured, none molested or disquieted, by reason of their religious faith or observances, but that all shall alike enjoy the equal and impartial protection of the law; and we do strictly charge and enjoin all those who may be in authority under us, that they abstain from all interference with the religious belief or worship of any of our subjects, on pain of our highest displeasure.

And it is our further will that, so far as may be, our subjects, of whatever race or crëed, be freely and impartially admitted to offices in our service, the duties of which they may be qualified, by their education, ability, and integrity, duly to discharge.

We know and respect the feelings of attachment with which the natives of India regard the lands inherited by them from their ancestors, and we desire to protect them in all rights connected therewith, subject to the equitable demands of the State; and we will that, generally, in framing and administering the law, due regard be paid to the ancient rights, usages, and customs of India.

We deeply lament the evils and misery which have been brought upon India by the acts of ambitious men, who have deceived their countrymen by false reports, and led them into open rebellion. Our power has been shown by the suppression of that rebellion in the field; we desire to show our mercy by pardoning the offences of those who have been thus misled, but who desire to return to the path of duty.

Already in one province, with a view to stop the further effusion of blood, and to hasten the pacification of our Indian dominions, our viceroy and governor-general has held out the expectation of pardon, on certain terms, to the great majority of those who in the late unhappy disturbances have been guilty of offences against our Government, and has declared the punishment which will be inflicted on those whose crimes place them beyond the reach of forgiveness. We approve and confirm the said act of our viceroy and governor-general, and do further announce and proclaim as follows:—

"Our clemency will be extended to all offenders, save and except those who have been or shall be convicted of having directly taken part in the murder of British subjects.

"With regard to such the demands of justice forbid the exercise of mercy.

"To those who have willingly given asylum to murderers, knowing them to be such, or who may have acted as leaders or instigators in revolt, their lives alone can be guaranteed; but, in appointing the penalty due to such persons, full consideration will be given to the circumstances under which they have been induced to throw off their allegiance, and large indulgence will be shown to those whose crimes may appear to have originated in a too credulous acceptance of the false reports circulated by designing men.

"To all others in arms against the Government, we hereby promise unconditional pardon, amnesty, and oblivion of all offences against ourselves, our crown, and dignity, on their return to their homes and peaceful pursuits.

"It is our Royal pleasure that these terms of grace and amnesty should be extended to all those who comply with their conditions before the first day of January next.

"When, by the blessing of Providence, internal tranquillity shall be restored, it is our earnest desire to stimulate the peaceful ministry of India, to promote works of public utility and improvement, and to administer its government for the benefit of all our subjects resident therein. In their prosperity will be our strength, in their contentment our security, and in their gratitude our best reward. And may the God of all power grant unto us, and to those in authority under us, strength to carry out these our wishes for the good of our people."

LETTER I.

INTRODUCTORY.

THE QUEEN'S PROCLAMATION AND ITS PROMISES.

THE Queen's proclamation has gone forth throughout the length and breadth of India, telling its princes and its people that a new era has begun, that the age of middlemen has passed away, that the Sovereign has entered at last upon her inheritance. It is quite impossible to overrate the momentous nature of such a document. It is not only the first (if I mistake not) which has ever been directly addressed by the wearer of the English crown to the natives of India: It claims for itself a character of permanency, definitiveness, which no Governor-General's proclamation can lay claim to. So long as we have any national dignity at all, it must determine to all time the fundamental character of English dominion in India. It is, in truth, British India's Magna Charta; but one, not extorted from a cowardly tyrant, but freely granted by a gracious lady, ruler over willing subjects, lawful sovereign of free-born men.*

So deeply do I feel that the policy marked out by the proclamation, whatever minister's hand may have worded it, must be *the* abiding policy of England

* I am not overlooking the paramount authority of Parliament over India, asserted ere this by numberless statutes. But no Act of Parliament ever came home to the natives of India as the proclamation will have done.

towards India, that, had it gone against my own views, I should have bowed before it, convinced that fixity of purpose—not excluding, indeed, development and adaptation—is absolutely essential to the stability of empire. As it is, however, I place it gladly in the forefront of a work written in great measure before its promulgation, which it enables me to weed of many a train of reasoning useless henceforth, when, instead of having to establish my own footing, I have but to take up the standing-ground which is afforded to me.

The scrupulous observance of treaties—abstinence from extension of territory—the open avowal of Christianity, but respect to the native creeds—admission of natives to office—maintenance of native rights of property in land—form now the bases of England's Anglo-Indian policy. To show as a whole what should be built upon these foundations far transcends my powers, or, I take it, those of any single man. I wish only to sketch out some of the consequences which appear to me to be involved in that policy, dwelling upon one or two points which I deem of especial importance now. The work will be better done, I suspect, if the promises of the proclamation are taken up one or two at a time by single men, so as to show why it became necessary to put them forth,—how they can best be carried out,—what interferes with their fulfilment.

For let us be assured that something does interfere and will interfere with the fulfilment of every single gracious pledge which the proclamation contains. There never was a right thing done in the world (and never will be) but some wrong one has fought with it, and sought to strangle it from the first. In the present case, it is impossible to mistake the evil influences at work. At home, a Council containing some of the worst representatives of the old India House,—an East India Company still struggling to maintain a ghastly sort of existence after its political death,—a gloomy Leadenhall Street dungeon-palace (haunted, to the native's eye at least, with many a memory of injustice, and callousness, and despair), still shrouding the Government of India within its recesses, and cutting it asunder from the great shrines of our national greatness at Westminster, the Hall, and the Abbey, and the Palace, —in India, a whole generation of officials and their dependents, bred and trained up under another system, wedded to other traditions;—above all, perhaps, the feelings of imperious hatred to their darker fellow-subjects, which the rebellion seems to have called forth in the Anglo-Indian population at large,—offer of themselves obstacles the most serious to the loyal and thorough carrying out of the principles of the proclamation, even if there were no warfare going on, no armies on foot, no Tantia Topee to reduce, no native hatreds, treacheries, and discontents. Very ominous was it to notice, in the Times' Bombay Correspondent's account of the Proclamation festivities at that Presidency, that the quarter of the European residents was dark amidst native illuminations,—the Parsee residences in particular being all a-blaze with light.* Very dissonant with the Queen's proclamation

* At Madras—both governor and commander-in-chief being absent—there were no fireworks, no illuminations, no street pageants, so dear to the natives, no public entertainments, as there were even at minor stations throughout the country.

is that of the Governor-General which accompanies it, dated 1st November, 1858, which "summons" the faithful to co-operation, which will "*exact* a loyal obedience" from India's millions,—as if loyalty were capable of being exacted! I cannot wonder that earnest men, even now, dare hardly hope in the reality of the new policy. "There was not a single promise in the proclamation," writes one of such, "that has not been made in the most solemn way before, and as regularly broken; and after about six months' of the Queen's Government, I do not see a symptom in any department of measures to carry out the promises of the Proclamation; indeed, as far as symptoms go, I see indications of an adherence to the old Company's system." Such forebodings may be amply justified, yet for years to come, by events; in spite of amnesties and gracious promises, we may yet have other rebellions to subdue. And still, I believe that it would be most unwise not to accept the proclamation, in the very length and breadth of it, as *true*; as expressing that which ought to be, that which is, England's policy towards India; as supplying a definite standard by which to measure the future acts of Governors-General and of ministers. For though men's words often transcend their acts,—though the humiliating contrast between large promise and small performance meets us on all sides at every step,—yet it is no less true that words of grace and justice, once put forth, have a power as it were to draw up men's acts towards their own level. And it is characteristic of English history, that our national liberties have always developed themselves by taking men's words in earnest, at their full weight, from whatever lips they might proceed; by forcing those lips, however false, to keep them. How often was Magna Charta broken, how often confirmed, before it came to be what it is now, the very corner-stone of our social state, that for want of which continental fabrics of free government crumble away at a touch! Even so must it be with this our Sovereign's memorable proclamation, if the day should come again when ministers or governors-general,—or their subordinates, as powerful perhaps in smaller spheres,—shall play fast and loose with treaties, thrust of purpose forward the limits of empire, trample upon native rights and properties. By that proclamation must they be judged; to its standard must they be made to conform. They may violate every one of its promises,—but every promise will survive its own violation,—and avenge it.

PART I.

PROMISES OF THE PROCLAMATION

TO THE PRINCES OF INDIA.

LETTER II.

THE ANNEXATION POLICY HENCEFORTH GIVEN UP.

For the better consideration of the promises contained in the proclamation, let us divide them under two heads,—Promises to the princes of India; Promises to the people.

"We desire no extension of our present territorial possessions; and while we will permit no aggression upon our dominions or our rights to be attempted with impunity, we shall sanction no encroachments on those of others. We shall respect the rights, dignity, and honour of native princes as our own."

There is only one sense in which these words can be taken in India,—as the disavowal of an Annexation Policy. "Has there ever really been such a policy?" some of my readers may be tempted to ask. Fain, indeed, would I persuade myself that it has been but an evil dream. But, alas! its reality is written in blood. Nor can we appreciate the weight of the disavowal until we have examined into the need of it.

Let us observe, indeed, in the first instance, that in proclaiming that she desires no extension of territory, Her Majesty is putting forth no new doctrine in India, but that which has in its favour the authority of almost all our great Indian statesmen of old,—the authority of The Duke, and Lord Hastings, and Mountstuart Elphinstone, and Sir John Malcolm, and Sir Thomas Munro, and Lord Metcalfe, and St. George Tucker.

It would be tedious henceforth to reproduce at length their opinions; it will be quite enough, as a type of them all, to recall the weighty words of the Duke, that "wherever we spread ourselves," we make "additional enemies, at the same time that by the extension of our territory, our means of supporting our government, and of defending ourselves, are proportionably decreased."*

And there is one point about several of the above authorities which has not, I think, been adverted to enough. When we quote the names of the Duke of Wellington, Elphinstone, Malcolm, Munro, Metcalfe,— when we remember that they all bore witness against

* Those who wish to see the authorities above referred to collected, will find most of them in a pamphlet, published in 1850, by the late Mr. John Sullivan, formerly Member of Council at Madras, under the title of "A Letter to the Right Hon. Sir John Hobhouse, Bart., M.P., conveying the opinions of Sir Thomas Munro, Sir John Malcolm, and Mr. Elphinstone, on the impolicy of destroying the native states of India;" and in the fourth of the India Reform Tracts, published, if I recollect aright, in 1853, and intitled "The Native States of India;" see also the privately printed "Selections" from Mr. Tucker's papers, pp. 66, 89. Sir Wm. Sleeman (Journey through Oude, vol. ii. pp. 389—92); General Low, (Return to an Order of the House of Commons, dated July 27, 1854, for "Copies of the Treaty between the Honourable East India Company and his Highness Maharajah Raghojee Bhonsla, his heirs and successors, concluded in the year 1826; of all reports upon the failure of heirs of the late Rajah of Berar, and upon the annexation of the Berar territory to the East India Company's territories," &c.—to be hereafter quoted as the "Nagpore Annexation Papers,"—p. 39 and foll.); Major-General Briggs; and Colonel Alves, who must be named (India, its dangers considered in 1856, p. 9), are among the later maintainers of the anti-annexation policy. Lord Ellenborough has testified in favour of it, and acted to the contrary, as will be seen hereafter.

the policy of absorbing native states into our empire, we should also bear in mind that their testimony was founded, not upon preconceived theories, not even upon ordinary Indian experience, but upon Indian experience of a very peculiar kind. One and all of the deceased statesmen above named were formed in what may be called the great annexing school of Lord Wellesley, whose administration saw so many vast territories added to our rule. Three of them remained to take part in the annexations of Lord Wellesley's true successor, Lord Hastings. The Duke was Lord Wellesley's own brother. Sir John Malcolm had almost idolised the great Governor-General. One was the victor of Assaye; Mr. Elphinstone, though a civilian, in fact directed the battle of Kirkee, which first broke the power of the Peishwa; Sir John Malcolm bore the brunt of the battle of Mehidpore, which crushed that of Holkar; Sir Thomas Munro took part in the same war. Three, lastly, became in turn governors of presidencies: Mr. Elphinstone and Sir John Malcolm at Bombay, Sir Thomas Munro at Madras. These men, then, had shared in past annexations—had won renown in so doing—had watched their effects. They testified that those effects were evil.

The new policy of non-annexation is therefore the old policy of Anglo-Indian statesmanship. Indeed, as I look back, I can find but one great name among deceased statesmen which can be quoted against it,—that of Sir Charles Napier. I accept it therefore as a fact; and will not discuss its reasonableness. I will pass at once to the history of the contrary policy,—the policy of annexation.

It is between fifteen or twenty years, I believe, since "a party strong in intellect,"—to use the words of a recent pamphlet*—but mostly very young in experience; began advocating "British rule everywhere, and Anglo-Saxon improvements and ways in everything." The readiest pen at their command was that of "Brahminee Bull," *alias* that able but much-lauded and self-lauded man, Colonel Herbert Edwardes. Sir Henry Elliot, Sir Henry Lawrence, were leading members of the school; Mr. Thoby Prinsep helped it with a pamphlet in 1853; Mr. George Campbell with a big book; when its doctrines had been officially promulgated by a Governor-General in 1848, there was no lack of Members of Council to indorse them. Mr. Marshman and the "Friend of India" never tired of urging them; most of the Indian papers followed in his wake. Such a policy was therefore undoubtedly that of the bulk of the Anglo-Indian public, when Lord Dalhousie came to embody it in his minutes, his despatches, and his acts.

I wish, indeed, that I could have abstained from mentioning the name of the late Governor-General, considering the state of his health. But that name is too inextricably bound to the annexation policy to allow me to speak of the one without the other. For to him belongs the deliberate and complete adoption of that policy. Not, of course, that the practice began with him. We have undoubtedly been annexing and absorbing in India ever since we have been there. We took what we could, long before we ever thought that

* India: its Dangers considered in 1856, by a Retired Officer, (Jersey, 1858), p. 33.

there could be such a thing as a policy concerning the matter; sometimes, it might be, we took a little too much for our own strong stomachs, and then, perhaps, the House of Commons, or the next Governor-General, or the Court of Directors, stepped in to prevent our taking more, and succeeded for a little while in arresting or moderating the process. Lord Dalhousie was simply, so to speak, the philosopher of that process. He not only did the thing, but supplied a formula for the doing of it; or, perhaps, to speak with perfect precision, generalized one which had been incidentally sketched out by Lord Auckland. He had not been a year in India when he penned (30th August, 1848) that celebrated Sattara despatch, in which he took the occasion of recording his "strong and deliberate opinion, that in the exercise of a wise and sound policy, the British Government is bound not to put aside, or to neglect, such rightful opportunities of acquiring territory or revenue as may from time to time present themselves." There might, he admitted, "be conflict of opinion as to the advantage or the propriety of extending our already vast possessions beyond their present limits;" no man could more sincerely deprecate than himself "any extension of our territory which can be avoided;" but he could "not conceive it possible for any one to dispute the policy of taking advantage of any just opportunity which presents itself, for consolidating the territories that already belong to us, by taking possession of states which may lapse in the midst of them;" such was the "general principle" that in his opinion, "ought to guide the British Government in its disposal of independent states, where there has been total failure of all heirs whatsoever, or where permission is asked to continue by adoption a succession which fails in the natural line."*

It is very true that Lord Dalhousie afterwards attempted to qualify this exposition of his policy, in a minute on the Nagpore annexation (28th Jan. 1854); declaring that the opinion he gave "was restricted wholly to subordinate states—to those dependent principalities which, either as the virtual creation of the British Government, or from their former position, stood in such relation to that government as gave to it the recognized right of a paramount power in all questions of the adoption of an heir to the sovereignty of the state."† Considering that the Sattara despatch avowedly set forth the "general principle" that "ought to guide the British Government in its disposal of *independent* states," this restriction of it in terms to "*subordinate* states," and "*dependent* principalities" was curious in itself. But when we observe that Nagpore was one of the larger native states—a kingdom with a revenue treble that of Sattara—it would hardly appear that such restriction was of much practical weight. And we shall see ere long that the right of annexation was asserted against Nagpore, in the very minute from which the above is quoted, irrespectively of the question of the dependent or independent character of the state.

* Papers relating to the question of the disposal of the Sattara state, in consequence of the death of the late Raja; printed in conformity with a resolution of the General Court of Proprietors of East India Stock, of the 7th February, 1849, pp. 103-4. (I shall quote these hereafter as the "Sattara Annexation Papers.")

† Nagpore Annexation Papers, p. 35.

But the best comment on the annexation policy is surely afforded by Lord Dalhousie's final minute of the 28th February, 1856, "reviewing his administration in India, from January 1848, to March 1856,"* wherein he states that during the eight years of his rule, "four kingdoms have passed under the sceptre of the Queen of England, and various chiefships and separate tracts have been brought under her sway." The "kingdoms" are those of the Punjab, Pegu, Nagpore, and Oude; the chiefships, those of Sattara and Jhansee, with the territories ceded by the Nizam. The two first being stated to be "the fruits of conquest," the remainder may all be fairly deemed "the fruits of policy." By these various acquisitions, he further tells us, "a revenue of not less than 4,000,000 has been added to the annual income of the Indian empire." It is true that these figures have been most severely criticized; that Sir Erskine Perry in the House of Commons has asserted that they give only the gross revenue, without reference to the expenditure; that a writer in the "New Quarterly" has apparently shewn that actual deficiency stands in the place of several of the items of alleged increase.† But we have the fact before us, that the Governor-General who in 1848 recorded his strong and deliberate opinion that the

* Ordered by the House of Commons to be printed, 30th May, 1856.

† One thing is very clear, that if the revenues of the annexed states are all, as Lord Dalhousie represented them to be, bonâ fide additions to those of British India, native princes must be admirable financiers compared to ourselves, since their accounts would always exhibit a surplus, whilst British India always exhibits a deficiency.

British Government was "*bound* not to put aside or to neglect" rightful opportunities of acquiring territory or revenue, had, by his own shewing, in eight years, found seven such rightful opportunities of practising his doctrine on a large scale, to the total amount of £4,330,000 a year. Such then was the policy of annexation in its practice; such was the policy which is to be practised no longer, if the Queen's words are to be a truth: "We desire no extension of our present territorial possessions."

LETTER III.

THE ANNEXATION POLICY IN ITS BEARINGS UPON THE REBELLION.

Let us now endeavour to trace the effects of the Annexation policy, in its bearing upon the late rebellion. The time is past when it was necessary to prove that what England had to deal with in India was not a mere mutiny, but a rebellion. The proclamation settles this point. It deals frankly and manfully with the rebellion by that name. Ambitious men, it says, have led their countrymen into "open rebellion;" the Queen's power "has been shewn by the suppression of that rebellion in the field."

The history of the rebellion has yet to be written. It is not, indeed, over yet; but its leading features are by this time all before us. So far as we can disentangle it from the mutiny—so far as it can be recognized as something more abiding than the track of fire of a revolted regiment, — I think we may say that its chief centres have been Oude and Bundelcund in the North, the contagion spreading from the latter through the so-called Saugur and Nerbudda territories of Central India. In the Deckan, on the other hand, where its flames have hitherto been smothered in time, the chief seats of danger have been the South Mahratta country, and the Nizam's territory. And the influences which have bound almost all these different centres together, — the trains which have connected these several explosions, or attempted explosions, have been two — those of the Oude sepoys on the one hand, of the Mahratta race on the other; though the former influence belongs more properly to the mutiny, the latter to the rebellion. Oude soldiers filled our Bengal army; Oude soldiers the "contingents" of the native princes, which almost invariably turned upon their own masters; Oude soldiers, scattered through Bombay regiments, were the chief instigators of the partial outbreaks which have disturbed here and there the army of that Presidency. Oude itself has remained for now nearly a year and a half the great stronghold of the rebellion; the Oude Begum seems with Tantia Topee and Nana Sahib, our last remaining foe.

But the influence of the Mahrattas has gone far deeper. It was Nana Sahib the Mahratta, Maharaja of Bithoor, adopted son to the last Peshwa, claiming that title for himself, who first gave to a tumultuous outbreak against us the character of a semi-organized rebellion. He had prepared that outbreak, I do not doubt, long beforehand; when it came, he was the first chief of note who joined it, placing himself at the head of two mutinous regiments at Cawnpore; whilst by that butchery of the weak and the young, of which we seem at last to have obtained a correct history,—in which one rejoices to find that not one of our mutinous soldiers could be induced to share,—he did his best to forfeit England's pardon for the revolt. And though the early reports greatly exaggerated his capacity; though—if he have really remained for so many months quiescent in Northern Oude—he seems to be as much a coward as a fiend; still, his restless activity at one time rendered him really formidable. By his emissaries he stirred up, or endeavoured to stir up, Malwa, Bundelcund, the Deckan against us. In the second province we know how well he succeeded. The Bheels of Khandeish seem to have been commanded by his agents. For a time, as Mr. Russell told the "Times" in April, 1858, he had himself obtained a preponderating control over Rohilcund; had succeeded, in the Mahommedan city of Bareilly, in forbidding the killing of cows, and publicly celebrating Hindoo rites. His name, as Peshwa, commanded enormous prestige. The great rebel army of Bundelcund called itself "the army of the Peshwa." When Gwalior was wrested from its sovereign by the Calpee forces, it was a deputy of the Peshwa who was installed momentarily as successor to our faithful ally Scindia. Nay, the destinies of our Indian empire may be said to have hung for months upon the chances of the Nana's forcing his way into the Deckan, which, indeed, he was several times rumoured to have done. "This," wrote the Times' Calcutta correspondent on May 5th, 1858, "it is a great object to prevent, as he can thence reach our own Mahratta provinces, where his name will create an army. The mischief he might effect, in the present temper of the Mahrattas, is incalculable, and Bombay officers write with amazement of his folly in not making the attempt. Here he is merely an adventurer—on the Bombay side he would be the Peshwa, bringing before every Mahratta visions of principalities and plunder." So a gentleman then lately returned from India, wrote to me on June 13th, 1858: "The Deckan is in a very critical state at this moment, and a spark might fire the train any day. The villages in the Deckan and Mahratta country were everywhere looking for Nana Sahib, who is considered the legitimate successor of the Peshwa." So again, several months later, an officer in command of one of the cavalry regiments of the Nizam's Contingent, whose judgment and knowledge of the country may be relied on, wrote that should an outbreak occur (as he expected) in the Deckan, the struggle which had taken place in the north would be as nothing to it, and we should find ourselves only at the beginning of the war.*

* The following remarkable evidence shews that plots in the Deckan preceded the outbreak. It consists of extracts (transmitted to me from India) from the "18th Report of the German Evangelical Mission of the western coast of India," 1858. A writer from Guledagudda, in the South Mahratta country, says, "Long before the outbreak in the North-west, hints were received by silk mercers at Bagulcote from mercantile connexions in the north, to limit their engagements for the next year and call in their debts—gloomy rumours then gained ground from day to day, threatening Europeans and native Christians with ruin and death" (pp. 65-6). Again: "At this festival, which took place some time before the mutinies in the north broke out, Brother Kies' addresses were once and again met with the assertion, that the British rule would cease within the year."

Fortunately for us, Nana Sahib did not try this venture, whilst the rebellion was still at its height, before Sir Hugh Rose's brilliant victories, and Lord Clyde's patient but sure generalship, and the Queen's gracious amnesty—if faithfully used—had rendered its success hopeless, its extinction a mere question of time. That venture we know is now being tried, if not by himself, by that mysterious personage Tantia Topee, by some accounts an adoptive brother of the Nana's, by another account identified with him,—whose name (meaning a hat) is utterly unknown in Hindoo family nomenclature,*—the pattern of a Mahratta chief, always beaten and always on foot again after each defeat, and whose dash across the Nerbudda from Seronge, outwitting even the keen and wary Michel, breaking through the wall of fire which already closed in upon him by a feigned retreat to the north-east, and then dropping suddenly south, appears to me a most characteristic and brilliant feat. Nor must we forget that Ranee of Jhansee, widow herself of a Mahratta Brahmin, who made her late capital the centre of rebellion in Bundelcund, and by her personal example seems to have excited amongst our rebellious troops a bravery which they never exhibited elsewhere. For the first time, before Jhansee, they bore the fire of our artillery. For the first time they formed square, repelled two charges of our cavalry, advanced again after being broken by the third, were only driven headlong by the fourth. The struggle appears to have been the most

* If Tantia Topee be the Nana, or a man of straw used as a screen to conceal the latter's presence, the name "hat" would recall our own cant term "bonnet."

sanguinary of the whole war. No fewer than 8,000 Sepoys, the early accounts stated, were bayoneted within the town. But the Ranee and a large portion of her troops escaped, and made another stand at Koonch, where, however, Sir Hugh Rose again defeated them. Yet the indomitable Hindoo princess joined next the Calpee force, shared their single success in the taking of Gwalior, and was at last with her sister, dressed like herself in men's clothes, and like her a mere girl, killed at the re-capture of the place;—and though Sir Hugh Rose does not seem to have thought her death worthy of mention in his despatch, murderess though she were, do we suppose that her name will soon die out from native story and song?

Again, as I have said already, the South Mahratta country, of which Sattara is the heart, and which has been the chief recruiting field for the Bombay army (the cavalry excepted) has been for Western India a focus of disorder and discontent during the rebellion. When the 27th Bombay Native Infantry rose upon its officers at Kolapore, a relative of mine from Western India, then in England, wrote to me that he was "not surprised, as the men had been raised in the South Mahratta country." The 28th and 29th, both recently levied and formed of the same materials, both shewed signs of disaffection. At Sattara, sixteen men were blown from guns; others were executed at Belgaum. The widows and the adopted son of a deposed raja were arrested by the Collector of Sattara, and sent to Bombay, to be confined there.

But a more remarkable event has taken place than any partial outbreak. The claims of the Rajas of

Sattara, as titular sovereigns, and of the Peshwas, as encroaching ministers, are essentially rival ones; the former princes were expressly set up by Mr. Elphinstone, on the downfall of the latter. The deposed Raja of Sattara, in particular, was keenly alive to the danger of Brahmin usurpation, and it is alleged that Brahmin influence was the real cause of his downfall. Now, however, a "fusion" between the followers of both houses seems to have been effected. By intelligence from India, brought by the mail of the 24th April, 1858, and published in the *Standard*, but which the *Times* considered unworthy of reproduction, it appears that the Senaputtee, or former Commander-in-Chief of the Sattara state, and the ex-Commandant of the Raja's artillery, were found guilty of treasonable correspondence *with the Nana*, and were sentenced to be hung—a punishment involving loss of caste. The Senaputtee entreated to be blown from a gun instead; but finding his request refused, in an agony of terror revealed a plot, in which he was himself one of the principals, and which is said to have had for one of its objects, "the massacre of every European in the Deckan and South Mahratta country." In consideration of the importance of these disclosures, his sentence was commuted to transportation to the Andamans.

Of the spirit which might have animated a South Mahratta outbreak, had it not been checked in time, let the following sample suffice:—"Listen, all!" said one of the Sattara conspirators at the gallows' foot, on the 19th June, 1857, "*As the English people hurled the Raja from his throne*, in like manner do you drive them out of the country. I am illegally condemned. . . . This example is made to frighten you; but be not alarmed. Sons of Brahmins, Mahrattas, and Mussulmen, revolt! Sons of Christians, look to yourselves!"*

Now, if we recollect that the rancour of Nana Sahib is avowedly owing to the suppression of the Peshwa's pension,† the coincidence of sphere between the rebellion, or the dread of it, and the annexation policy, is most remarkable. For though the late Governor-General did not even advert in his final minute to the Peshwa's pension,—though he did not seem to have considered the withdrawal of £80,000 a year from a native family of the highest rank as worth mentioning to his Leadenhall-street masters,—it is obvious that that act belongs essentially to the policy which declared that the British Government was bound not to neglect any rightful opportunity of acquiring territory "or revenue." And with this addition, we see at once that the list of Lord Dalhousie's annexations by policy is that of our past dangers. He annexed the kingdom of Oude, the principality of Jhansee, and Oude and Jhansee have been strongholds of rebellion. He annexed Sattara, and Sattara has barely escaped becoming such a stronghold. He obtained a cession of territories from the Nizam, and Hyderabad has seen blood shed in its streets, and the Nizam's whole country has been as it were a powder-barrel, which a spark might explode. Nor should the name of Nagpore be absent from the list. There

* Mr. J. B. Norton's "Rebellion in India," p. 97.

† I shall say a few words more on this subject hereafter.

were fears for Nagpore as early as December, 1857, and a "pretty strong force of Madras troops" could not then "safely be spared out of it." By the mail of June, 1858, came news of an actual outbreak, of zemindars in open rebellion, who had murdered two telegraph employés; against whom troops had to be sent, —one of whom has just been executed. Mr. Norton, in his lately published "Topics for Indian Statesmen," speaks of "the discovery of the plot at Nagpore at the eleventh hour" as of a patent fact, though I am otherwise ignorant of the details.* And the same English traveller, to whom I have before referred, declared, from personal experience, that there was "much discontent in Berar,"—that the annexation of Nagpore was one of the causes which have "given rise to a very strong feeling against us."

I do not say that annexation was the sole cause of the rebellion. There is nothing more convenient, and nothing more fallacious, than to attribute great events to single causes. Where the scene of such an event is simply more than half of all India, this method becomes absolutely futile. I am quite persuaded that other causes concurred with annexation to produce the Indian rebellion; religious causes, economical causes, social causes, legal causes. I shall dwell upon one set at least of these causes hereafter. But I believe that the annexation policy, as such, supplied the rebellion—from Oude, with its disciplined soldiers—everywhere, with its leaders. Without Oude—without Nana Sahib and Tantia Topee of Bithoor—without Jhansee and its Ranee—with firm allies for us instead of a chafed ally

* P. 56.

and unquiet subjects at Hyderabad, at Sattara, at Nagpore, what remains of it? Khan Bahadoor Khan, the opium eater, at Bareilly; old Kooer Sing at Jugdespore; the Nawab of Banda in Bundelcund. Would these have convulsed an empire?

It is easy to treat such reasonings with contempt, as samples of the *post-hoc-ergo-propter-hoc* fallacy. Ex-financial Commissioners of Oude may establish to their hearts' content that a country, which it now requires five armies to quell after more than a twelvemonth's warfare, was rendered happy by annexation. I have not the least doubt that as plausible a case may be made out for Jhansee, and for Sattara, and for Nagpore, by any official from those countries. But plain men, when they see the annexation policy of the last ten years followed by a trail of blood throughout the length and breadth of India, will be little influenced by such pleadings. And if, which God forbid! the lust of power should prompt a political party in this country once more to justify that policy, to find fault with the present Ministry for disclaiming it in future, let us remember Lucknow, and Cawnpore, and Jhansee, and say: "By the blood spilt and the treasure spent during the last two years, these men have, so far, done well."

LETTER IV.

INVIDIOUSNESS OF LATE ANNEXATIONS; EXPEDIENCY OF RESTORATION.

Is it enough, however, to give up the annexation policy for the future, as unwise? If we recognize how weightily it has told upon the rebellion, will not a further question arise: Must it not have left stings behind which need extracting? wounds which will fester if they be not healed? To answer this question, it will be necessary to go somewhat deeper into the consideration of past annexations, tedious as this may seem to many.

Now, if we put aside wholly for the present all questions of right, we shall find that there was, about all the annexations of the last ten years which have been enumerated, an element of broad, human pathos, which was of a nature to stir the hearts of all who might look upon them otherwise than in the light of a policy, which yet calls for something more direct, more individual than the mere reversal of that policy for the future.

For, in the first place,—excepting in the instances of Pegu and the Punjab (and of the latter I shall have more to say hereafter) all those various annexations were perpetrated in a time of profound peace, on purely technical grounds, at the expense of *friends*. The last ruler of Sattara, besides numerous internal reforms effected, had assisted the British Government during an insurrection in Kolapore, had offered to place all his military means at its disposal during the Affghanistan war.* The rulers of Jhansee claimed to be the first in Bundelcund who had tendered their allegiance to the British Government.† No breath of suspicion attached to the faithfulness of the last Nagpore Raja. Of the Nizam, Lord Dalhousie wrote that "for more than half a century, relations of amity and intimate connexion have existed between the British Government and the Nizam."‡ The rulers of Oude had "ever been faithful and true to their friendship with the British nation." The Raja of Tanjore, the Nawab of the Carnatic,—our earliest allies of any,—had expressly given up their territorial sovereignty on the faith of the maintenance of their dignities and pensions. We did not scruple to absorb the fort, a few estates and other relics of kingship retained by the former. We did not scruple to suppress the dignity of the latter.

Now, consider the obloquy which a landlord incurs—and most justly—among ourselves, when he resumes the land of a faithful tenant of his family, of

* Sattara Annexation Papers, p. 51.

† Return to an order of the House of Commons, dated 17th July 1855, for copies of a treaty, &c. and of all reports and correspondence relating to the annexation of Jhansi to the British territories (to be hereafter quoted as the "Jhansee Annexation Papers"), p. 24.

‡ Return to an order of the House of Commons, dated 6th April 1854, for copies of all papers relative to territory ceded by his Highness the Nizam, in liquidation of debts alleged to have been due by his Highness to the British Government, ordered to be printed 26th July 1854, (to be hereafter quoted as the "Nizam's Cessions Papers"), p. 36.

an enterprizing farmer, simply because he fancies he can do better with it himself. Think of the bitterness of feeling engendered by such evictions, when, as in Ireland, the landlord is of one faith, the tenant of another; the tenant perhaps a descendant of a former dispossessed Celt, the landlord a new man, a Saxon. Then conceive the sort of feelings which are aroused in India, when faithful Hindoo and Mussulman allies or dependents are absorbed by the alien infidel, whether their territories be prosperous or the reverse; even though, as at Sattara, the two last rulers may "have done more for the improvement of the country than our own government can pretend to have done in any part of its territory." *

Again:—The majority of annexations being grounded on the alleged right of escheat by lapse, place necessarily the British Government in that most justly invidious of all positions, where absolute strength is opposed to absolute weakness,—the strong man to the widow, to the child. The elder widow of the Sattara Raja came forward with her husband's will, which he was dictating on the morning of his death, placing his adopted son under her charge, bidding her "preserve the friendship of the British Government, and obtain the Resident's advice in every affair; even should his advice be occasionally such as to occasion loss, still you should not deviate from it; even should you be advised by a brother or father, yet you should make no difference in your friendship for the British Government, but act by the advice of the Resident;" † or

* Tucker's Selections, p. 90. † Sattara Annexation Papers, p. 48.

again, with a memorandum, detailing "How the Maharaja cherished the friendship of the British Government, and how all that he did was intended to meet the approval of the British Government, and how the affairs of the state were conducted, and what were the charitable acts done by him for the good of his subjects."* The widow of the Jhansee Raja came forward in like manner, praying that her late husband's adoption might be sanctioned,† detailing—without, the Political Agent tells us, "in the slightest degree" over-estimating them,—the instances of fidelity and loyalty shewn by him and his predecessors to the British Government.‡ Nagpore was annexed, over the heads of the Raja's widows, within a few weeks after the right of adopting had accrued to them. The senior Ranee of Tanjore had to come as a suitor to the Madras Supreme Court, praying for the restoration of the private property of the late Raja, which had been taken possession of by the British Government—even to "two pennyworth of buttons, an eye-squirt, some marbles,"—on pretence that it was so mixed up with state property that it could not be distinguished from the latter, and which was afterwards retained on the ground that all the widows were alleged to be entitled.§ Such were the claimants against whom a technical, and, as we shall find, a disputed, a denied right paramount of succession by escheat was asserted on grounds of policy, and carried out by overwhelming force. Surely the natives of

* Ibid. pp. 53-4. † Jhansee Annexation Papers, p. 14.

‡ Ibid. pp. 24-6.

§ Mr. J. B. Norton, Case of the Tanjore Ranee, passim.

India must be less than men, if their feelings could fail to be moved under such circumstances in favour of the victims of annexation, and against the annexer. Surely there was not a woman whom such annexations did not tend to make our enemy, not a child whom they did not tend to train up in hatred to the Feringhee rule. Surely Lukshmee Baee of Jhansee, vainly urging in 1854 her husband's fidelity to England, murdering Englishwomen in 1857, dying in the field before Gwalior in 1858, is but a type of feelings that must have been shared, more or less acutely, by thousands of Hindoo wives and widows.

If we consider then, on the one hand, the evident invidiousness of these acts of the annexation policy in themselves at the time,—on the other the fearful consequences which they have evidently since helped to bring forth,—I think there is the strongest ground for saying that, as a mere matter of policy, apart from all grounds of justice, it would be most wise dispassionately to examine how far they can yet be safely undone. Victors on all sides, none can say henceforth that we should yield to fear in so acting; on the contrary, as a sovereign act of grace, the restoration of territory would naturally rank beside the generous amnesty which has been granted by the proclamation. There would be limits, of course, to the one as to the other. No clemency, as the proclamation most rightly declares, can be shewn to those who may be convicted of having "directly taken part in the murder of British subjects;" —"to those who have willingly given asylum to murderers, knowing them to be such, or who may have acted as leaders or instigators in revolt, their lives alone can be guaranteed." The Peshwa's pension as such was no doubt wiped out for ever in the slaughter-field of Cawnpore; the Jhansee massacre cannot be soon forgotten; the Sattara plots impose the duty of rigid scrutiny into the conduct of Sattara pretenders, as the Oude rebellion into that of its captive king. And yet surely it would be worthy of England's dignity—of the clemency of her Queen—it would tend on all future occasions to sow disunion in the camp of rebellion, to neutralize the ties of family or clanship, if we were, so to speak, astute in finding out any innocent members of the families, dispossessed or impoverished by the annexation policy, which have shewn themselves most our enemies, in order to confer benefits upon them. I would not even except that of Bajee Rao, in spite of all Nana Sahib's atrocities.* Tippoo Sultan had been

* The terms of the late Peshwa, Bajee Rao's, surrender at Asseerghur were, that upon fulfilling, as he did, certain conditions, he should "receive a liberal pension from the Company's government for the support of himself *and his family*," not less than £80,000 a-year. This sum, although deemed excessive by Lord Hastings, was only £10,000 larger than the figure of one granted in 1803 by the Duke of Wellington to a competitor of Bajee Rao (Amrut Rao), whom we then treated as a usurper, for the lives of himself and his son. Bajee Rao gave us no further trouble,—obtained from us a petty sovereignty in Bithoor,—contributed divers lakhs of rupees to Indian loans,—and died, having adopted Dhoondoo Punt Nana. Lord Dalhousie suppressed the pension, as only given for life. I believe there is not an English lawyer who would have ventured to treat the words "*and his family*" as surplusage; Mr. Rolt, Q. C., at all events gave an opinion that even upon strict construction the words meant, "for his life and the life of his children, whether natural or adoptive." In remembering Nana Sahib's atrocities, let us not forget that he did not resort to murder till he had exhausted years in the effort to obtain, what he at least deemed to be, justice, nor yet for himself only, but for all the household of the late Peshwa, who remained at his charge.

privy at least to a massacre of English prisoners, yet Tippoo Sultan's descendants are to this day, I believe, our pensioners—nay, our servants—and who can doubt that their existence as such is a source of strength to us, and not of weakness?

I shall be able to shew hereafter that this view of the expediency of restoration, in connexion with the establishing of the Queen's government, was put forth before the proclamation repudiating the annexation policy was published, by an experienced Indian officer. But he puts it upon another ground, that of justice. Let us follow him upon it.

LETTER V.

THE PLEDGE OF RESPECT TO TREATIES IN ITS BEARING UPON LATE ACTS OF ANNEXATION.

SECTION I.

ANNEXATIONS BY ALLEGED RIGHT OF ESCHEAT.

"We hereby announce to the native princes of India that all treaties and engagements made with them, by or under the authority of the Honourable East India Company, are by us accepted, and will be scrupulously maintained; and we look for the like observance on their part."

So runs the Queen's Proclamation. Let us consider late annexations by policy from the point of view which it supplies. It applies to all of them without exception.

We had treaties with Oude, with Sattara, with Jhansee, with Nagpore, with Tanjore, with the Carnatic; we have treaties with the Nizam. But there is this difference between the cases: Oude was annexed on the ground of breach of treaty, though not towards ourselves. The Nizam's cessions were obtained on a somewhat similar ground. All the other instances, as will be seen from Lord Dalhousie's final minute, group themselves under the single head of lapse for want of heirs. Let us view this group first of all; in other words, let us consider the claim of the British government to the escheat of native states; and let us take the three instances of Sattara, Jhansee, and Nagpore, for our leading examples.

The treaties with these three states are very different in their wording; the first with Sattara standing out however among them, and among the general slip-slop of our Indian treaties, by the superior clearness, terseness, and appropriateness of its language; bearing, if I mistake not, the stamp of the master-mind of Mountstuart Elphinstone. What impression do they convey?

No doubt they are in no instance dealings between equals. The British government is everywhere visibly the preponderating power. It has "invested" the Raja of Sattara with his sovereignty; it agrees to "cede" to him his territory, which he is to hold "in subordinate co-operation to the British government."* It "constitutes" the soobadars of Jhansee hereditary

* See "Return to an order of the House of Lords, dated 16th June, 1853, for copies of the treaties and engagements between the East India Company and the Native Princes of Asia" (to be hereafter quoted as "House of Lords' Return of Treaties)," p. 280, and foll.

rulers.* The Raja of Nagpore has "succeeded" to the musnud by its "favour."† Still, these instruments are no letters-patent granted by a sovereign to a subject of his "special grace, certain knowledge and mere motion;"‡ they are not "*sunnuds*" (or grants), like those under which the chiefs of the Hill States on the Sutledge hold their possessions.§ They are, as the diplomatists say, synallagmatic in form. They are contracts between two parties, visibly treated as equally capable of contracting together. There is a valuable consideration on both sides, in the mutual obligations which are entered into. There is no hint of any further claims by the preponderating power, which may lie behind the treaty. If any such claims had existed, as, for instance, those "rights" of the Peshwa

* Jhansee Annexation Papers, p. 1, and foll.

† House of Lords' Return of Treaties, p. 398, and foll.

‡ The formula of a Royal Charter. Observe that the natives understand well the difference between a "grant" and a "treaty." Thus Mr., now Sir R. Hamilton, writing from Indore, 21st November, 1844, says: "The term 'sunnud' [grant] conveys neither rank nor importance in Malwa, while there is great honour, of which the chiefs and sirdars are very tenacious and sensitive, in being connected by treaty with the paramount power." Return to an order of the House of Commons, dated 17th July, 1849, for copies of any despatches from the Governor-General of India in Council to the Court of Directors of the East India Company, reporting the circumstances attending the succession by adoption of any sovereign Princes in India in alliance with the British Government, from the year 1820 downwards; also copies of any despatches referring to the States of Colaba and Mandavie, in which the sanction of the British Government to adoptions by the chiefs of those states was refused; ordered to be printed, 15th February, 1850 (to be hereafter quoted as the "House of Commons' Return on adoptions"), p. 103.

§ See p. 478, and foll. of the House of Lords' Return of Treaties.

over the principality of Jhansee, spoken of in the preamble of the Jhansee instrument as having been "transferred to the British Government," the obvious bearing of the treaty is to substitute its definite obligations for any such indefinite claims. The legal maxim, *expressio unius est exclusio alterius*, shews that the minuteness of the treaty stipulations rendered an express reservation of any claims beyond those stipulations necessary, if they were to be kept on foot. Where the right of cutting timber on the western slopes of a hill range was reserved in treating with Sattara,—where the furnishing of supplies was provided for with Jhansee, and the collecting of brinjarries with Nagpore,—is it credible that a right of succession by escheat could have been tacitly reserved? But what claims could be reserved which, apart from treaty obligations, could derogate from the "perpetual sovereignty of Sattara,"—could be paramount to the "perpetual defensive alliance" with Nagpore?

Indeed an expression runs throughout the treaties, which to a person ever so moderately acquainted with English law, is conclusive on the point. The terms used in reference to the native prince are the technical ones consecrated to our own sovereigns. In every instance his "heirs and successors" are referred to. The Sattara territory is ceded "in perpetual sovereignty to the Raja of Sattara, his heirs and successors." The soobadar of Jhansee, "his heirs and successors," are constituted hereditary chiefs. The "dominions of the Nagpore state" are guaranteed "to Maharaja Ragojee Bhoslah, his heirs and successors." Those words, I repeat it, are words of sovereignty. No peer, though he wear the strawberry leaf, is entitled to them. A private corporation sole, such as a bishop or parson, has "successors." A private corporation aggregate, such as a public company, has "assigns." The King has "heirs and successors." "Heirs,"—that is, persons who according to the laws of inheritance can fill his throne. "Successors,"—that is, persons who can be called to fill it by some other title, not flowing necessarily from himself, but from the perpetual individuality of the state which he governs. Thus our William the 3rd could succeed to all the dominions and prerogatives of James the 2nd, without being his heir. From the moment we speak of a prince, "his heirs and successors," we deal no more with the descent of an estate, but with the transmission of the functions of government over a country.

Do you wish for an instance of this use of the words? Listen to the 3rd paragraph of the Queen's proclamation:—

"Now, therefore, we do by these presents notify and declare, that . . we have taken upon ourselves the said government, and we hereby call upon all our subjects within the said territories to be faithful and to bear true allegiance to us, our *heirs and successors.*" . .

Can we doubt that such words are meant to denote the permanence of the royal power of England, whatever hands may wield the sceptre?

Now the careful repetition of these words is most remarkable throughout the first Sattara treaty. It seems as if its far-sighted framer, fearful of a change of policy on the part of the power which he represented, had sought to place his work under the guarantee of one of the leading formulas of English law.* But the looser wording of the other treaties bears witness no less strongly to the existence of the same views. The Jhansee instrument for instance sounds in a great measure entirely personal. "Ram Rao Chund hereby binds himself," "Ram Rao Chund hereby agrees," "Ram Rao Chund engages," such are its formulas of obligation on the part of the native chief. Yet the name of the ruler is clearly used as the mere personification of the state. It is synonymous with "the principality of Jhansee," with the "Jhansee Government," and the two terms, "the Jhansee Government" and "the British Government," are treated as exact correlatives. When "the Jhansee Government" apprehends aggression, it is to report the circumstances to the "British Government;" the "Jhansee Govern-

* Perhaps I shall be told that it is by native law that these treaties should be construed. It would be, I should say, a contemptible plea to seek shelter under, if it were available. The British Government should surely allow its own obligations to be measured against it by the Queen's English and by English law. But whilst protesting against any attempt to carry the question into the domain of Hindoo conveyancing, by way of burking it altogether, I believe the attempt would be simply futile. The disregard of the rights of succession to native states appears to have been as great with respect to the Hindoo law, as with respect to English. Thus in the Jhansee case, the agent, Major Malcolm, points out that the native word used in the treaty means "successors in general, *as opposed* to ... heirs of the body or collateral heirs." (Jhansee annexation papers, p. 24.) So at Sattara the largeness of the Mahratta version was so unquestionable, that the advocates of annexation, as I shall have occasion to shew, all fled to the English, either unaware that it was quite as conclusive against them, or presuming upon the ignorance of their adversaries.

ment" agrees to abide by the award of the "British Government." The Jhansee forces are to co-operate with the British on all occasions where the interests "of the two governments may be mutually concerned." It is carefully provided that British commanding officers, in their passage through or occupation of the the Jhansee territories "*shall not in any manner interfere in the internal concerns of the Jhansee Government.*"* Of the Nagpore treaties—the last of which has for primary alleged object "the welfare, dignity, *and independence* of the Raja of Nagpore,"—it is suffi-

* The distinction made by writers on international law, between real and personal treaties, is one which has been as glibly used for the extinction of native states as it has been little considered. Grotius, for instance, in a passage quoted by Mr. J. B. Norton (Rebellion in India, p. 105), expressly cautions us that "if a contract is made with a king, it is not therefore presently to be reputed personal ... if it be added to the treaty, that it shall stand for ever, or that it is made for the good of the kingdom, *or with him and his successors* ... it will from hence fully appear that the treaty is real." So Mr. Wheaton, the latest authority, says, that "the obligation of treaties, by whatever denomination they may be called, is founded not merely upon the contract itself, but upon those mutual relations between the two states which may have induced them to enter into certain arrangements. Whether the treaty be termed real or personal it will continue so long as these relations exist." (International Law, p. 41.)

The most modern form of treaty among civilized powers uses the expression the "high contracting parties," and is clearly meant to include the successors of the contracting sovereign. But with ruder powers the form of the treaty is still usually personal; as in our slave-trade suppression treaties with African or Arabian chiefs. Take for instance that with the Imaum of Muscat (2nd October 1845; confirmed by Act of Parliament, 11 & 12 Vic., cap. 128), where all the engagements are simply taken by "His Highness the Sultan of Muscat," without the slightest mention of successors.

cient to say that the provision which gives the greatest power to the British Government is precisely the one which negatives the idea of any tacitly reserved rights on its behalf. Where the British Government, in the event of "gross and systematic oppression, anarchy and misrule," reserved to itself the right of re-appointing its officers "to the management of such district or districts of the Nagpore territory . . . for so long a period as it might deem necessary," it is simply incredible that, without saying a word about it, it should also have reserved the right of absorbing the whole territory in absolute sovereignty by right of escheat.

When the British Government wished to provide for itself a right to take absolute possession of all or part of a native state under given conditions, it knew very well how to do so. When it treated with Raja Poorunder Sing of Assam in 1833, it could stipulate that if the Raja "should in any way depart from a faithful adherence to the same," then "the right is reserved to the government of the Honourable Company, either to transfer the said country to another ruler, or to take it into its own immediate occupation."* When it treated with the Raja of Cachar in 1824, it could make him stipulate his "allegiance to the Honourable Company," and could provide that if he failed to pay his tribute, "the Honourable Company will be at liberty to occupy and attach in perpetuity, to their other possessions, a sufficient tract of the Cachar country."† It could make Toola Ram Seenaputtee, in 1834, agree that "in case of failing to

* House of Lords' Return of Treaties, pp. 182-3.

† Ibid. p. 184.

abide by" certain conditions, "the British Government shall be at liberty to take possession of my country."* Or the case of failure of issue might be provided for, as when, in 1826, in the engagement entered into on dividing Alwur and Tijara, to which the British Government was a guarantee, it was provided that if the Raja of Tijara "or any of his descendants die childless, and no heirs of his body remain, then the territory settled shall revert to the principality of Alwur," †—*i. e.* to the state, part of the territory of which was ceded to form the other one. Why these express clauses, if the rights they created were implied already in the relation between the parties?

On the other hand, it is observable that the wording of the first Sattara treaty of 1819 is similar to that of a whole group of other treaties with subordinate states; ‡ as the Nagpore treaty of 1816 was already similar to one of 1817 with Scindia, to one of 1805 with the Guicowar. The resumption, therefore, in either instance, of the one territory on a technical ground of right was, so to speak, a threat to all the others.

The case of Tanjore, and that of the Carnatic, were such again as to alarm all that class of princes who, by a somewhat strained application of a term of German

* House of Lords' Return of Treaties, p. 185. † Ibid. p. 470.

‡ Sawunt Warree, 1819, House of Lords' Return, p. 336; Bhopal, 1818, *ibid.* p. 419; Odeypore, 1818, *ibid.* p. 425; Jeypore, 1818, *ibid.* 429; Jodhpore, 1818, *ibid.* 435; Jessulmere, 1818, *ibid.* 437; Bickaneer, 1818, *ibid.* 439; Kota, 1817, *ibid.* 441; Jhullawur, 1838, *ibid.* 447; Kishengur, 1818, *ibid.* 452; Doongerpore, 1818, *ibid.* 459; Banswarra, 1818, *ibid.* 461.

public law, have been termed "mediatized;"—that class, namely, who, originally British allies, then debtors to the British, have eventually consented to transfer the whole management and revenues of their country to the British Government, in consideration of being allowed to retain the externals of royalty, of a yearly stipend, and of some small reserved territory exempt from British jurisdiction; and who, impotent individually, may yet become dangerous centres of disaffection if once alienated as a body by British policy.

In both these instances the leading treaties * contain the expression "heirs and successors." In both, the last treaties,—those vesting the management of the country in the East India Company,—although that expression may not occur, contain a formal confirmation of "such parts of all former treaties as are intended to establish the friendship and alliance between" the two parties, or, "as are calculated to strengthen the alliance, to cement the friendship and to identify the interests of the contracting parties." In both the last treaties the intention of permanence is plainly expressed. The treaty of 1799 with Tanjore is full of such expressions,—a "regular and *permanent* system for the administration of the revenues,"—a "*permanent* system," —a "fixed and *permanent* revenue." The treaty of 1801 with the Nawab of the Carnatic is concluded for the purpose of "establishing the connection between the

* Concluded with both in 1787 and 1792. See "A Collection of Treaties and engagements with the native princes and states of Asia, concluded on behalf of the East India Company by the British Government in India" (E. Cox & Son, 1812), pp. 405, 409, 424, 434.

said contracting parties on a *permanent* basis of security, *for all time to come*;" the administration is to be "*for ever* vested in the said English Company." By separate explanatory articles, certain sums are to be "considered as *permanent* deductions, *in all times to come*, from the revenue of the Carnatic."* It is thus evident that whether we consider the last treaties as incorporated with the preceding ones, or upon their own special footing, they equally come within Grotius's description of treaties which are not personal, though only made with individual sovereigns.

Yet the late Governor-General, as we have seen, annexed Tanjore, and disposed as follows of the Nawabship of the Carnatic:

> "As the treaty by which the Musnud of the Carnatic was conferred on the Highness's predecessor was exclusively a personal one; as the Nawab had left no male heir; and as both he and his family had disreputably abused the dignity of their position, and the large share of public revenue which had been allotted to them; the Court of Directors has been advised to place the title of Nawab in abeyance, granting fitting pensions to the several members of the Carnatic family."†

Now Mr. Norton shews that every one of the pleas thus assigned was false. The treaty could not be considered personal, for the reasons before assigned. Its permanent character had already been acknowledged, as several heirs had already succeeded under it to the Musnud, and had been recognized by the Company, without any fresh treaty. The statement that there was no male heir was so baseless, that the late Nawab's

* A Collection of Treaties, &c. pp. 460, 466. The Carnatic treaties are also to be found in a pamphlet published by Madden, 1856.

† Minute of 28th February, 1856, p. 13.

paternal uncle, Azeem Jah, was not only "beyond all question," by Mahommedan law, his heir and successor, but had been on several occasions officially recognized *in writing* by the Court of Directors as the next heir; lastly, Mr. Norton declares, after 15 years' residence in Madras, that "foolish and improvident as the young man was, his conduct had never been of a quality approximating to what would justify such a punishment,"—inflicted, be it observed, not on himself, but upon his innocent heirs. By parity of reason, as he says, William IV. might have been forbidden to succeed George IV., and any peerage with the family estates might be confiscated for the sins of the last holder.†

It seems moreover to have escaped his Lordship that if the treaty of 1801 was "exclusively a personal one," it must have been equally so as respects the engagements of the Nawab towards us, and our own towards him; and consequently, that the transfer of the administration and revenues to the British Government must have gone with the nawabship,—reverting, I presume, to the Nizam, as the original suzerain.

Now can we hope that the announcement to the native princes of India, that "all treaties and engagements" made with them, "will be scrupulously maintained," will convey entire assurance for the future,

* Rebellion in India, pp. 103-107; Topics for Indian Statesmen, pp. 159-162. It is remarkable that the House of Lords' Return of Treaties contains none with Tanjore, or with the Nawabs of the Carnatic; why, it would be difficult to say, as the Return includes the most obsolete engagements with the soobadars of Bengal, or with Cheyte Sing of Benares.

whilst the past interpretation of such treaties as I have quoted by the late Governor-General is held to stand good? Why are the same words to be used in one sense for the Queen of England, in another for her native allies? What "true allegiance" can be borne to her "heirs and successors," when the most solemn guarantees to the "heirs and successors" of native princes have been set at nought?

But we have only seen a portion yet of the mischief wrought by the past policy in this respect.

SECTION II.

THE CESSIONS FROM THE NIZAM.

THE territories of the so-called Nizam form, since the extinction of the Oude sovereignty, the last great fragment of the Mogul empire—the remains of its greatest vice-royalty, that of the Deckan. With the Carnatic and Tanjore pensioners, the Nizam represents the last of our earliest Indian allies. The history of the wars of Clive and his contemporaries is full of our support of one Nizam of the Deckan, and Nawab of the Carnatic, against their respective rivals, supported by the French. With this "old ally," as Lord Dalhousie himself termed him, we have had no cause of political complaint for more than half a century. The "sole source"* (according to the same authority) of all discord between him and the British Government, has been the payment of a certain force termed the Nizam's Contingent, which grew up out of a treaty of offensive

* The Nizam's Cessions Papers, p. 98.

and defensive alliance between the two powers, and of which it is enough to say that (always according to Lord Dalhousie, 30th March, 1853) there was no treaty obligation on the Nizam to maintain it. "The plain intention of the treaty," to quote his Lordship literally, "was, that whenever war arose, the Nizam should reinforce the British army by a body of 15,000 of his own troops. *It never contemplated that the Nizam should be made to raise and pay a large body of troops, distinct from his own, to be placed at all times, in peace and war alike, under the sole control of the Government of India.*"* The treaty further declares, says his Lordship, "in the most emphatic terms, that the Government of India *binds itself in no way to interfere with his Highness's subjects, servants, or concerns.*"†

The Nizam nevertheless kept up the Contingent, in peace and war, for upwards of 50 years. He having suffered, however, its pay to fall into arrear, "the Government of India"—I quote always from his Lordship, (3rd June, 1853)—

"Justly considering that its good faith was pledged to a body of troops which was commanded by British officers, and subject to its control, advanced the money which was necessary to make good the shortcomings of the Nizam. These advances amounted in 1851 to upwards of seventy lacs of rupees. During this course of neglect, and while the debt was accumulating, the warnings and remonstrances of the Government of India were incessant, but they were unavailing. Every effort to check the reckless conduct of the Nizam having failed, the Government of India intimated to his Highness that no further debt could be allowed to accrue; that the pay of the contingent must thenceforth be regularly supplied; that the principal sum of debt must be liquidated; and that, if his Highness

* Ibid. p. 100. † Ibid. p. 99.

failed to meet that demand by payment within a year, territory must be made over in satisfaction of it."*

(Lord Broadacres and Squire Claypole being intimate friends, for divers good considerations, agree, among other things, that whenever his Lordship shall be shooting in the neighbourhood of Claypole Park, the squire shall provide him with a keeper and a certain number of beaters; but nothing in the agreement is to authorize Lord Broadacres to interfere with Claypole's servants or concerns. Claypole straightway engages at high salaries the whole stipulated staff, over and above his other sporting household, and keeps them up for many years, during which time his Lordship scarcely once comes down to shoot. Eventually the squire's money concerns go wrong, and the pay of what we may call the contingent keeper and beaters falls into arrears. Lord Broadacres takes his friend roundly to task for so doing, and, after a while, sooner than let the men go unpaid, pays them out of his own purse. When the payments so made amount to a good round sum, he claims of Claypole repayment of the whole within a year, or an adequate slice of the Claypole estate in satisfaction. In what material point does this case differ from the story of our claims upon the Nizam?)

The Nizam did not pay within a year, within eighteen months. Hereupon the British Resident was instructed "to demand the *temporary* assignment of

* Ibid. p. 5. This minute, it will be observed, is more than two months' posterior to the one last quoted, though according to those mysterious arrangements which distinguish Parliamentary papers, it occurs 92 pages before it.

territory for the liquidation of the debt." So wrote Lord Dalhousie to his Leadenhall-street masters; but in a minute of 1st January, 1851, he observes already, that "probably we shall find ourselves compelled to retain *permanently*, for the regular payment of the contingent, those districts which we may now occupy temporarily for the liquidation of the debt." * And the Resident is accordingly instructed, in forming his opinion regarding the territories to be made over, to "bear in mind the probable necessity of retaining them permanently." †

This was on the 4th January, 1851. Six months more elapsed in deciding upon the territories to be demanded, and upon the exact nature of the demand. On the 6th June, 1851, a letter was addressed by the Governor-General to the Nizam, to the effect agreed upon. "The efficient maintenance" of the contingent is treated in it as "a duty imposed on the Government of Hyderabad by the stipulations of existing treaties." The Nizam is apprized that the demand now made "is peremptory," and "will neither be withdrawn nor postponed;" that "it will be necessary" that he "should in due form convey to the Resident the districts named, and should vest him with full authority for their administration and control." ‡

The Nizam, strange as it may seem, was astounded at such a simple demand (I omit others with which it was coupled). He observed that "it was not customary with the Honourable Company to transfer territory in payment to its creditors." §

The British Resident and Government, however,

* Ibid. p. 10. † Ibid. p. 12.

‡ Ibid. pp. 40-43. § Ibid. p. 48.

were perhaps more astounded still when he proposed to pay off the whole debt in about three months, and to give security for the regular payment of the contingent in future. The demand for cession was suspended; half the sum, or rather more (£340,000), was actually paid down in bills, leaving a balance of £320,000 to be paid by the 31st October, 1851, the cost to the Nizam being indeed much greater than the amount realized. Of the second instalment, however, by the 5th December, only about £87,000 had been paid. A further delay of a month was granted, and yet prolonged—a reference being made home for approval. The debt was again increased by new payments on account of the contingent. It amounted to somewhat over £460,000 when Lord Dalhousie penned his leading minute of the 30th March, 1853, in which, as I have before observed, he expressly admitted (in direct opposition to his own letter of the 6th June, 1851), that the Nizam was under no treaty obligation to maintain the contingent. He admitted as expressly that "the aggregate expense of the Nizam's contingent is unusually and unnecessarily heavy," whilst its quality is not better than that of bodies less highly paid. He declared that "the Government of India owes much consideration to the Nizam in regard to his contingent force." And he concluded—to the demanding a cession of land in discharge of the debt and the standing expenses of the contingent; the cession to be demanded, even if the contingent should be disbanded, to meet the expenses of the force during such disbandment, which must be gradual. The Resident was "instructed to contend for the cession to the utmost." *

* Ibid. pp. 97—116.

The form of a new treaty was forwarded to him, which the Nizam was to enter into.

I know nothing more instructive, as to the procedure of the Indian government of late years towards native princes, than the negociations with the Nizam, as they are set forth in the Parliamentary paper relating to the subject; though the very despatches, I am told, are garbled, and English eyes have read in the originals passages of haughty contempt towards the native sovereign, which would not bear translation.* He was very averse to the new treaty; he did not want any, said he to the Resident, "however much soever you or any other person or persons may fancy it to be advantageous to my interests." He consents, however, to read the proposed new treaty, and compare it with the old one; sits up nearly all night conversing about it; meets the Resident the next morning (30th of April, 1853); Colonel (afterwards General) Low never knew him "more acute in argument or more fluent in conversation" than on this occasion. "Did I," he asks, "ever make war upon the British government, or intrigue against it, or do anything but co-operate with it, and be obedient to its wishes, that I should be so treated? . . . . . Two acts on the part of a sovereign prince are always reckoned disgraceful; one is, to give away unnecessarily any portion of his hereditary ter-

* This is what Mr. Bright is understood to have referred to in his great speech of June 24, 1858, when he said:

"Only think of a Governor-General of India writing to an Indian prince, the ruler over many millions of men in the heart of India, 'Remember, you are but as the dust under my feet.' Passages like these are left out of despatches when laid on the table of the House of Commons."

ritories, and the other is, to disband troops who have been brave and faithful in his service." He promises that the contingent shall be paid in future on the 1st of every month, like the Company's own troops; he offers the guarantee of others for his word. He suddenly orders every one to retire, entreats the Resident, "as a personal favour, to give up the scheme of a new treaty, and to advise his Lordship to trust to his highness's word that all future payments, in which the British government are in any way concerned, will be paid with the utmost regularity."

"Gentlemen like you," he bursts out, "who are sometimes in Europe, and at other times in India; sometimes employed in Government business, at other times soldiers; sometimes sailors, and at other times even engaged in commerce—at least I have heard that some great men of your tribe have been merchants—you cannot understand my feelings in this matter. I am a sovereign prince, born to live and die in this kingdom, which has belonged to my family for seven generations; you think I could be happy if I were to give up a portion of my kingdom to your government in perpetuity; it is totally impossible that I could be happy; I should feel that I was disgraced. I have heard that one gentleman of your tribe considered that I ought to be quite contented and happy if I were put upon the same footing as Mahomed Ghouse Khan;* to have a pension paid to me like an old servant, and have nothing to do but to eat and sleep and say my prayers. . . . . You, too, don't comprehend the nature of my feelings as a sovereign prince; for instance, you talked of my saving at least eight lacs of rupees [£80,000] per annum by making this treaty, as something that I ought to like. Now I tell you, that if it were quite certain that I could save four times eight lacs of rupees, I should not be satisfied, because I should lose my honour by parting with my territory."†

---

* *i.e.* The Nawab of Arcot, or of the Carnatic—whose title was *extinguished* two years later on his death. See ante, p. 48.

† Nizam's Cessions Papers, p. 116 and foll.

In another interview of the 10th of May, 1853, the prince again offered the guarantee of some of the principal noblemen of his court for the regular payment of the contingent every month, and again engaged to pay off the debt in four months. He was answered that "the Governor-General will not consider any personal guarantee as sufficient security for the pay of the contingent,"—nothing would do except to have "British officers in exclusive charge of districts that will yield net revenue to the amount required." The case of the contingent being dispensed with was put, and disposed of as prescribed by Lord Dalhousie, by the answer that it could only be disbanded gradually, and in the mean time "we must still have command temporarily of districts" for the regular payment of the force. The Nizam now sent for six or seven of his chief officers and nobles; explained to them, says Colonel Low, "in a very distinct and even lucid manner, the chief propositions of the British government;" in fact, stated the case "very fairly," and concluded by asking their advice. One only replied: "If it is the Governor-General's determination to have districts for the pay of the contingent, what advice need we give? Your Highness does not require our advice or any further consultation on the subject." Colonel Low pressed him to give his answer about signing the treaty. "I could answer in a moment, but what is the use of answering? If you are determined to take districts, you can take them without my either making a new treaty, or giving an answer at all."* Further negociations take place; modifications of the proposed

* Nizam's Cessions Paper, pp. 123—8.

arrangement are consented to; and so eventually a treaty is obtained (21st of May, 1853), by which the contingent, somewhat reduced in number, was placed upon a permanent footing. It was to be "commanded by British officers," "controlled by the British government through its representative, the Resident at Hyderabad," and might be employed out of the Nizam's dominions if disturbances broke out in any districts belonging to the Company. For payment of its expenses, interest upon debt, &c., districts in Berar were handed over "to the exclusive management" of the British authorities, the surplus revenue, however, to go into the Nizam's treasury;* and though these terms had been expressly agreed upon "in consequence of the repugnance of the Nizam to cede any territory 'in perpetuity' to the British government,"† Lord Dalhousie, with equal disregard of the words of the treaty and of the feelings of his ally, chose to record, in his final minute, as the last in order (not in date) of the territorial acquisitions of Great Britain in India during his sway, that "His Highness the Nizam" had "assigned in *perpetual* Government to the Honourable East India Company the province of Berar and other districts of his states."

Curiously enough, the key to these transactions is to be found less in the Parliamentary papers specially affected to them, than in those relating to Nagpore; and it is clear from these that the Nizam's cessions in 1853 led to the annexation of Nagpore in 1854. For, as Lord Dalhousie phrased it, the "essential interest

* Nizam's Cessions Papers, pp. 135-7. † Ibid. p. 134.

of England" required that the territory of Nagpore should pass under British government. "The great field of supply of the best and cheapest cotton grown in India lies in the valley of Berar" (ceded by the Nizam) "and in the districts adjacent to it." Those "districts adjacent" were in Nagpore. "During the past year," the Government had obtained, "by treaty with the Nizam, not the sovereignty indeed, but the perpetual possession and administration of the valley of Berar." This cotton-field, however, was "inaccessible for want of railroads;" the possession of Nagpore would enable us to make them. We took both, as has been seen.*

The Nizam, to use Lord Dalhousie's words respecting him (30th March, 1853), was "neither cruel, nor ambitious, nor tyrannical." But the Parliamentary papers shew clearly that he had felt himself deeply aggrieved by the demand made upon him. Fortunately for us, as Mr. Norton observes in his late valuable work, "Topics for Indian Statesmen," the old Nizam died just before the mutinies, and his successor has hitherto been faithful to us, owing, it is supposed, to the influence and ability of his Minister, Salar Jung; and although insurrection has been attempted in Hyderabad, it has been choked with grapeshot. But officers who know the Nizam well, aver he is sure to go against us if a promising opportunity offers. As to the feelings of his subjects, an old Indian officer, who knew the Nizam's country intimately many years ago, told me a short time back, that from the accounts he now received, the bearing of the people towards us there must have wholly changed. Formerly intimate

* Nagpore Annexation Papers, pp. 33-4.

relations existed between Englishmen and natives of rank, and even without intimacy, the natives would go out of their way to oblige us. Now, friendly intercourse between the two races has almost wholly ceased, and any Englishman is an object of scarcely concealed aversion to the native. Meanwhile, Wahabism—one of the forms of Mussulman religious reform—is spreading largely in the Deckan; and the intolerance of Mussulman fanaticism at Hyderabad is notorious. With less of fanaticism, there is probably equal Mussulman discontent on the western coast of the Deckan. There the once rival elements of Mussulman and Mahratta have palpably coalesced against us. The plot which caused the arrest of the ex-qeeens and boy-prince of Sattara had been got up by the Mussulman Moulvies (or priests) of Poona and Belgaum.*

I have myself seen a letter from Salar Jung to an English gentleman (the officer before referred to), in which he expresses his master's extreme anxiety to recover the possession of the ceded districts. By all

* "Hyderabad has been a constant subject of uneasy apprehension. . . . Had Hyderabad gone, it is impossible to say what might have been the consequences. The discovery of the plot at Nagpore at the eleventh hour, shows how ripe the neighbouring state was for revolt. It is well known that the Mussulmen of Triplicane were only waiting the signal of a rising at Hyderabad to put their hands to the harvest; and there is not a military man with whom I have conversed on the subject, who has not expressed a decided opinion, that if Hyderabad had risen, we could not have escaped insurrection at Kurnoul, Nagpore, Bellary, Cuddapah, Bangalore, Madras, Trichinopoly, and other cities; while it is scarcely possible that the Bombay Presidency, so much more uneasy as it has proved itself than Madras, could have resisted the spread of such contagion."—*Topics for Indian Statesmen*, p. 56.

accounts, the present Sovereign is even more tenacious of his rights than his predecessor. Is it then to be credited, that, as stated in a late number of the "Homeward Mail," he should have been actually pressed of late for the absolute relinquishment of the districts? Say rather, is it consistent with the dignity of the British Crown that a sharp bargain, founded avowedly on a claim which could not be based upon treaty, enforced with such disregard of the very courtesies of alliance, so galling to a faithful friend, should not at once be generously and graciously rescinded?

SECTION III.

THE ANNEXATION OF OUDE.

I have treated ere this of the Oude annexation in a special publication.* But Sir William Sleeman's Journal of his Tour in Oude, and other documents, as well as the facts of the past year, have thrown a flood of new light upon the story; whilst our consideration here of previous acts of annexation by Lord Dalhousie will serve, perhaps, to set the subject of the annexation of Oude in new and contrasted lights.

Oude and Hyderabad were the two great Mussulman States of India. Oude, like Hyderabad, was the remains of one of the great Mogul vice-royalties which we had detached from the parent empire by treating with it as independent, sometimes against that parent

* The War in Oude (Macmillan, 1858.)

empire. Oude, like Hyderabad, was an old ally. The treaties under which we operated in both instances for enlarging our territories belong to the same period—to the same rule—that of Lord Wellesley. We obtained the Berar cessions on the plea of a treaty with the Nizam in 1800; we annexed Oude on the ground of a treaty with its Sovereign in 1801. Both allies had been equally faithful. Of the Nizam, Lord Dalhousie recorded that "the treaty which makes the friends and enemies of the one (contracting power) the friends and enemies of the other, is in full force and operation." His proclamation annexing Oude declared of its Sovereigns that they had "ever been faithful and true to their friendship to the British nation." And, on the other hand, both States were held up as cardinal instances of native misgovernment, of the internal mischief of the maintenance of native sovereignties. The Resident at Nagpore contrasted the state of things there "with the condition of Hyderabad or Oude," to give a measure of Nagpore prosperity.

Here, indeed, the parallel ceases, and a series of singular contrasts begins. The treaty of 1808 with the Nizam, as we have seen, expressly declared, as Lord Dalhousie states, "in the most emphatic terms, that the Government of India binds itself in no way to interfere with his Highness's subjects, servants, or concerns." By the treaty of 1801 with Oude, on the contrary, the ruler bound himself to act always in conformity with the counsel of the Company's Government. And by a further treaty of 1837, in the event of gross misgovernment, the British Government was invested with "the right of appointing its own officers to the management" of any portions of the Oude territory in which such misrule should have occurred, for so long as it might deem necessary. In the case of the Nizam, we find the British Government exercising its pledge not to interfere by insisting on the appointment of a Minister, on the ground that "it is a delusion for his Highness to suppose that he, the Sovereign, alone can properly direct the difficult and complicated business of a great kingdom"* (Jan. 1st, 1851); by paying the Nizam's own troops, and then claiming territory in satisfaction for such payments. In the proclamation annexing Oude (Feb. 1856), it was made a ground of complaint that "it is notorious throughout the land that the King, like most of his predecessors, takes no real share in the direction of public affairs;" whilst the treaty of 1837, giving the express right of interference, was treated as null and void, and deliberately overlooked for the purposes of the annexation. In the case of the Nizam, Lord Dalhousie (27th May, 1851) expressly refused to occupy the country on the plea of internal misgovernment, absolutely repudiating, on the part of the British Government, any "right of deciding authoritatively on the existence of native independent sovereignties, and of arbitrarily setting them aside, whenever their administration may not accord with its own views, and although their acts in no way affect the interests or security of itself or its allies." Oude was annexed, when "fifty years of sad experience" had "conclusively shewn that no effectual security can be had for the release of the people of that country

* Nizam's Cessions Papers, p. 10.

from the grievous oppression they have long endured, unless the exclusive administration of the territories of Oude shall be permanently transferred to the British Government." Lastly, the Nizam was compelled to cede the valley of Berar, as owing to us some £460,000. We annexed Oude, owing ourselves to it nearly £2,000,000.

It cannot be too clearly understood that internal misgovernment, in breach of the treaty of 1801, was the sole plea alleged by Lord Dalhousie for the annexation of Oude. It cannot be too clearly understood that the treaty of 1837 gave the British Government an unlimited right of interference for the correction of misgovernment. It cannot be too clearly understood that although a portion of that treaty which imposed a pecuniary burden on the King of Oude, was disallowed by the Court of Directors, the rest of it

* Perhaps the most painful thing connected with this treaty is, that its disallowance,—so far as it went—was owing to the feeling that it was *too great an encroachment* on the authority of the King. Mr. St. George Tucker, for instance, called for its abrogation as an act of justice, as likely to be "highly grateful to the King," to "tend to compose those feelings which have been so painfully and so unnecessarily excited," and to "have some effect in removing those impressions of our cupidity which, I fear, are but too prevalent throughout India." (Selections, pp. 101-2.)

Measure by Mr. Tucker's words, written in 1838, and by Lord Dalhousie's acts in 1855, the depths to which the policy of our Indian Government has fallen, as measured by a moral standard. The sovereign of whom Mr. Tucker wrote: "Our government can assume no right to dethrone the King of Oude, or any other independent prince, and it is essential that all doubt upon a question of such vital importance should be removed from the minds of the local authorities,"—was dethroned by Lord Dalhousie. The same treaty was treated as subsisting by the British Government for some fifteen years after; that Lord Auckland (July, 1839) only informed the ruler of Oude that he had been authorised to relieve him from "part" of a clause in the treaty; that Lord Hardinge, twice in the year 1847, insisted upon the obligations of the treaty; that in November of that year, in a conference with the King, he caused a memorandum which he had drawn up to be read, in which he referred to the treaty of 1837 "as confirming the original treaty of 1801, and not only giving the British Government the right to interfere, but declaring it to be the intention of the Government to interfere if necessary for the purpose of securing good government in Oude" (Sleeman's Oude, vol. ii. p. 202); that in 1845 the treaty of 1837 was included in a published official collection; that in 1853, it was again included in a "return to an order of the House of Lords, dated 16th June, 1853, for copies of the treaties and engagements between the East India Company and the native powers in Asia" (see p. 92); that so late as 1844 it was always dealt with as subsisting by the British Residents at Lucknow (see, for instance, Sir W. Sleeman's Oude, vol. ii. p. 419). It cannot be too clearly understood that in the face of all these facts, Lord Dalhousie treated it as void in 1859, and found a Council, consisting of Mr. Dorin, Mr. J. P. Grant, General Low, and Mr. Peacock, to support him in so doing, and a Court of Directors and a Board of Control to sanction the act.

of which Mr. Tucker recommended the immediate abrogation, in order to remove the prevalent impressions of our cupidity, became for Lord Dalhousie a mere "difficulty" and embarrassment in the way of annexation!

Be it observed, moreover, that Sir Wm. Sleeman, on whose report the annexation was decided on, who filled the post of Resident at Lucknow for six years—1848-54—and personally travelled all through the country, not only insisted upon the treaty of 1837 as binding, but as affording the only means of stopping Oude misgovernment without danger. As early as November 24, 1851, he wrote that "Lucknow affairs are now in a state to require the assumption of the entire management of the country," adding the significant qualification, "provided we leave the revenues for the maintenance of the royal family in suitable dignity, and for the benefit of the people." In October, 1852, he wrote to Sir James Hogg:—

"The treaty of 1837 gives our Government ample authority to take the whole administration on ourselves. . . . . but if we do this we must, in order to stand well with the rest of India, honestly and distinctly disclaim all interested motives, and appropriate the whole of the revenues for the benefit of the people and royal family of Oude. . . Were we to take advantage of the occasion to *annex* or *confiscate* Oude, or any part of it, our good name in India would inevitably suffer, and that good name is more valuable to us than a dozen Oudes. . . Annexation or confiscation are not compatible with our relations with this little dependent state."*

In January, 1853, he says, of the idea of annexation, which was fast gaining ground:—"It would be most profitable for us in a pecuniary point of view, but most injurious, I think, in a political one. It must tend to accelerate that crisis which the doctrines of that school must, sooner or later, bring upon us."† On

* Sleeman's Journey through the Kingdom of Oude, vol. ii. pp. 377, 378.

† Ibid. p. 393.

the 5th March, 1854, writing to Colonel Low, he referred again to the treaty of 1837:—"Our Government would be fully authorised at any time to enforce the penalty prescribed in your treaty of 1837, and it incurs great odium and obloquy for not enforcing it."*

But there is this point further to be considered. No claim of allegiance could possibly be put forth against the Oude sovereigns,—no rights of escheat could possibly be set up in derogation of their sovereignty. The annexation of the country, as I have said, took place by virtue, it was alleged, of Lord Wellesley's treaty of the 10th November, 1801. By that treaty, Saadut Ali Khan gave up half his territory "in perpetual sovereignty" to the Company, in discharge of a yearly subsidy which he was bound to pay. The famous 6th article of that treaty then runs as follows:—

"The territories ceded to the Honourable Company by the first article of this treaty shall be subject to the exclusive management and control of the said Company and their officers, *and the Honourable the East India Company do hereby guarantee to his Excellency the Vizier*† *and to his heirs and successors, the possession of the territories which will remain to His Excellency* after the territorial cession, *together with the exercise of his and their authority within the said dominions; His Excellency engages that he will establish in his reserved dominions such a system of administration*, to be carried into effect by his own officers, *as shall be conducive to the prosperity of his subjects, and to be calculated to secure the lives and property of the inhabitants;* and his Excellency will always advise with and act in conformity to the counsel of the officers of the said Honourable Company."‡

---

* Sleeman's Journey through the Kingdom of Oude, vol. ii. pp. 419.

† The "Viziers" of Oude took the title of Kings in 1819.

‡ House of Lords' Return of Treaties, pp. 76-7.

It was argued from this,—1st. That the Sovereign of Oude was bound by treaty to well-govern his subjects; 2nd. That his omission to do so was a distinct breach of treaty, giving a right to the other party to enforce due performance of the neglected engagement, ultimately by confiscating the whole territory of the defaulting party.

Does the article in question express or imply anything of the kind? Is it not plain that the guarantee and the engagement to well-govern are synallagmatic, reciprocal; that the breach of the latter engagement only releases the other contracting party from the former? If you guarantee my territories, says the prince, I will undertake for their well-being. If you undertake for the good government of your territories, say the English, we will guarantee them. If they fall short of their guarantee, what then? He is free to govern his country according to his own notions, subject to his own risks. If he misgoverns his country, what then? they are dispensed from the guarantee; he may be deprived of his authority by internal revolution, without their interference. Surely it is a mere mockery to say that the whole treaty is annulled by any breach of either stipulation; that the perpetual "peace, friendship, and union so long subsisting between the two states," as pledged by the treaty of 1798, confirmed by that of 1801, is put an end to.

The fatal fallacy upon which the annexation of Oude turned seems to have arisen from assimilating the position of the Oude sovereigns to that of a mere leaseholder, bound by a series of covenants to his reversioner, who, on breach of any, acquires a right of reentry. But it is impossible to conceive of a more monstrous perversion of the relations between the two states. Oude was not ours to lease: we could have no reversion in it. The treaty of 1801 may be likened to an arrangement between the owners of two neighbouring estates, the one of which is charged with a rent in favour of the other. To be released from his rent-charge, the owner of the estate subject to it gives up the fee-simple of half his property; and in consideration, we will say, of his neighbour's undertaking all the expense of preserving his game, and of any law proceedings arising thereon, he engages to cultivate the reserved half in a certain manner, to plant so many acres of buckwheat, &c. &c. Suppose he fails to do so, what then? he must bear his own expenses of preserving and his own law costs. Is there a Welsh attorney who would dare to advise his neighbour, on breach of the cultivation clause, to walk into the property, and turn out the owner altogether?

Let it be observed that I say nothing here as to the suppressed treaty of 1837 with Oude, though I look upon it as perfectly binding on the British Crown to this hour. Nor do I enter upon the question by which of the two contending parties art. 6 of the treaty of 1801 was first broken. But I will say here, that I do not think any one can read Sir Wm. Sleeman's Diary attentively, without seeing that the sovereigns of Oude had quite as much right to complain of the mode in which we fulfilled our undertaking to guarantee the exercise of their authority within their dominions, as we had to complain of their misgovernment; and that that misgovernment is, to say the least, in great measure to be traced to the want of adequate support from us in enforcing the regal authority.*

I say, therefore, that the plea of escheat, upon which Sattara, Jhansee, Nagpore were annexed, the Tanjore Raj and Nawabship of the Carnatic suppressed; the plea of breach of treaty upon which Oude was confiscated, were such as to alarm every native prince of India, Hindoo or Mussulman. Nor let it be supposed that treaties have no existence but for the princes alone. An officer in command of a cavalry regiment in the Nizam's Contingent, whose men belong to the gentry of India (several nawabs among them), so that he can associate with them upon terms of comparative familiarity—whilst many of them are natives of Oude—was asked, one evening, soon after the annexation, by several of his troopers: "Is it true that the Honourable Company has taken possession of our king's territories?"—"It would seem so."—"And . . . on what grounds have the Honourable Company done it?"—"They say the king governed his country very badly, although he had promised over and over again to do otherwise."—"*But are there not treaties?*" . . .

And now let me quote the words upon this question of a distinguished officer, who has had ample opportunities of observing the native character, as Agent to the Governor-General in Rajpootana. In a supplement to his pamphlet entitled "India and its Dangers,

* See, for instance, vol. ii. p. 200, where Sleeman shews that the auxiliary British force in Oude was "assuredly less than it should be with a due regard to our engagements and the Oude requirements." See also vol. i. p. 186, where he enumerates the forces which we should have kept up "to do our duty honestly by Oude."

as considered in 1856," the "Retired officer" writes as follows:

"Next to reassuring our native allies, comes the more delicate question of what should be done in the way of restitution. . . . Having everywhere successfully met the most appalling difficulties, we cannot be misunderstood in rendering justice to the injured. Let it never be said that, at the moment *of introducing the Queen's name into the government of India, we were wanting in the moral courage to do what was just*, because some persons might misrepresent or be unable to comprehend the high character of our motives. The natives of India are no fools; and all classes of them possess a clear perception of right and wrong, and a strong feeling against every act of injustice of whatever kind; and *we have now the opportunity, almost thrust upon us, of regaining a host of moral strength to our rule; let it not be lost.* The most prominent objects that present themselves are the families of Sattara and Nagpore:* these might be restored to their capitals, even if with reduced territory, on condition of paying a handsome nuzzerana on succession. Here would be a favourable opportunity of introducing the principle. Hereafter some unoffending member of the Jhansi family might be similarly treated; and many minor cases would follow as a matter of course. It deserves consideration also, whether the family of the King of Oude might not be restored to his splendid capital, with a small territory around it, to be managed, if necessary, under the superintendence of an agent to be placed with him, leaving the future disposition of the whole of that province to the solution of time and circumstances. Very plausible objections may be offered to this course; but can they weigh in the balance against the claims of justice, and the effect that will be produced on every Mahomedan mind by witnessing royal palaces and gardens degraded by being used as stables and barracks, or cleared away as ruins; and those palaces and gardens the property of a family ever loyal to the hand that pulled it

---

* "Deprived of territory and power, successions and adoptions will continue to be made in the household, and perpetuated by the Bhats (bards) of the tribe, in the hope of one day succeeding to a reality. We can but ill afford to have such smouldering embers of rancour existing against us."

down! As surveillèd residents in any other portion of India, the members of that family would for generations prove a blight and a sore to our Government."*

That restoration should be treated rather as a matter of policy, than of judicial investigation, as respects past annexations, I fully admit. All the cases I have referred to are really so gross, that if substantial justice can be done in them, the less said about them in future, the better for our country's honour. I quite agree also, of course, that where the claimants to the suppressed throne have openly acted against us, it would be necessary to select other condidates. But I cannot admit that, if innocent claimants can be discovered, the sovereignties themselves should be restored, otherwise than by the freest agreement, with diminished territories, except so far as our own safety or the honour of our country may imperatively demand it. The case of Oude would no doubt require exceptional treatment, as the real sovereignty at the date of annexation was in fact fast passing from the hands of the king into those of the talookdars. Here, the "Retired officer's" suggestion of restoring to the prince merely his capital and a small territory would probably meet the needs of the case as towards the deposed family; the great talookdars being the real authorities to be dealt with as respects the remainder of the country. If, with certain guarantees, they are now ready to become faithful subjects to Her Majesty, by all means let them be welcomed as such. Ten months ago,† ere Lucknow was

* Is it much safer to know them residing at the capital of our "august ally," Napoleon III.?

† In my "War in Oude."

re-occupied, I urged the treating with the Oude chiefs as to the terms on which their country should be restored. The idea seemed wild to many, it is probably now out of date; but would a second campaign have been necessary, such as that which is now being carried on, if Oude had been restored to its gallant people? What would have become ere this of Tantia Topee, if the main army could have borne down upon him?

LETTER VI.

THE PLEDGE OF RESPECT TO THE RIGHTS OF NATIVE PRINCES, IN ITS BEARING UPON ADOPTION.

"We shall respect the rights, dignity and honour of native princes as our own," says the Queen's proclamation. That the assertion of the British claim to the escheat of native sovereignties must be felt as derogatory to the dignity of the native princes, has perhaps been shewn already. That the enforcement of territorial cessions, in discharge of a very questionable debt, and in contempt of repeated pledges of early repayment, was deemed by the Nizam an infringement of his honour, has clearly appeared. But there is a momentous right, shared by the Hindoo princes with the whole Hindoo people, which they assert to have been invaded. It is that of adoption,—on the disallowance of which the British claim by escheat has mostly been founded. Let us now look into it.

The principle of adoption is one familiar to perhaps every system of jurisprudence but our own. Under the French Civil Code, for instance,* the adopted son has the same rights to the property of his adopted father at his death as a child born in wedlock, even though there should be such children born after the adoption. And though our jurisprudence repels the idea, our theology admits it, as in the Christmas-day collect of the Church of England, "being regenerate and made Thy children by adoption and grace," and in the practice of baptism, which is, to say the least, easily understood when looked upon as the ceremony of a Divine adoption. But whilst with all other nations adoption is simply a right, the Hindoo faith goes further, and erects it into a religious duty; the welfare of the man in the after-world being made to depend in great measure upon the fact of the ceremonies of his funeral having been performed by a *son*. I need not quote the original texts of the sacred books for this purpose; it will be sufficient for me to extract the following passage from the preface, by Mr. J. C. Sutherland, to his translation of two Sanscrit treatises on the Hindoo law of adoption, published in 1821. "The religious ordinances of the Hindoos," he says, in language much stronger than I have used myself, "inculcate the indispensable necessity that a man should be survived by male offspring for performing his exequial rites and other purposes. In consequence, on defect

* Code Civil, art. 359.

of real legitimate issue, the affiliation under prescribed rules of a kinsman or other person is enjoined; and an individual thus regularly adopted acquires the filial rights which attach to the real son."*

But this duty, though enjoined, would certainly not always be performed. Accident might interfere with the fulfilment; the natural reluctance of a man to give up the hope of direct issue, to place a collateral or a stranger on the same footing with such direct issue, whilst still possible, would tend to delay that fulfilment till the latest moment, when perhaps the dying man would be no longer capable of carrying out its prescribed ceremonies. Hence no doubt grew up the practice, which seems at first sight so strange to a European, but which, with slight variations in its conditions, is found to prevail nearly throughout all India, of allowing widows to adopt sons to their deceased husbands. Thus Mr. Sutherland, in his synopsis of the law of Hindoo adoption which follows the translations before referred to, after referring to one Hindoo writer who denies generally the authority of a widow to adopt, goes on to say: "But it is reasonable to admit, consistent with practice, and the opinion of other authors, the validity of an adoption made by a widow under the sanction of her husband written or formally expressed during his lifetime, and perhaps in some places, under that of kinsmen."† So Sir Thomas Strange in his "Hindoo law" (1830) expressly states

* The Dattaka Mimansá and Dattaka Chandrika, two original treatises on the Hindoo law of adoption, translated from the Sanscrit by J. C. C. Sutherland, Esq. (Calcutta, 1821), Preface.

† The Dattaka Mimansá, synopsis, p. 43.

that the right of the widow to adopt with the assent of her kinsmen, according to the principles of the Benares and the Mahratta schools, prevails in the peninsula, although denied in Bengal; and that under the Benares' principles adoption even by a mother is thought good, if duly authorised.*

It should be clearly understood that the right of adoption, however made paramount over the claims of blood, by no means sets them at naught. In default of adoption, the Hindoo law regulates the right of succession with the utmost nicety, extending it to kinsmen within twenty-one generations. The best idea perhaps which we can form to ourselves of the right of adoption is to consider it with the late Mr. St. George Tucker, for instance—or with Mr. Frere, the able Commissioner in Scinde†—as analogous to a modified right of testa-

* Strange's Hindu law, p. 29. Sir Francis Macnaghten, in his "Considerations on the Hindoo Law, as it is current in Bengal (Serampore, 1824)," p. 155, says, that "adoption by a widow without the consent of her husband is a mere nullity,"—following evidently the doctrines of the Bengal school, to which Sir T. Strange refers. On the other hand, he says nothing about the notice to the king, to be presently referred to. The right of the widow to adopt under a power from her husband may be considered as finally decided by the case of *Huradhun Mookurjia* v. *Muthoraneth Mookurjia*, 4 Moore's Indian Appeal Cases, 414—on appeal from Bengal.

† "The right of adoption is somewhat analogous to that under which, by means of a testamentary deed or will, we give a destination to our property in this country, after the demise of the testator." (Selections from the written opinions of Henry St. George Tucker, pp. 98-9). "The motives which seem to have influenced Mahrattas in their selection of adopted children can be likened to nothing that I know of, in our country, so exactly parallel as those which guide childless persons of property in England in disposing of their estates by will." (Mr. Frere, in Sattara Annexation Papers, p. 137.)

mentary disposition. The Hindoo cannot, I believe, dispose of his property by will; but he may, under certain conditions, introduce collaterals, or even strangers into his family, and so give them a share, or if he has no issue, the whole of his property. And the right of adoption is thus really a means of keeping the family efficient, infusing new blood into it when worn out. How this right can have been made a ground of confiscation by the state remains now to be seen.

The Indian formula of adoption requires that "the party proceeding to adopt should previously give notice to the ruling power," should invite his kinsmen, and should "venerate" the King and righteous Brahmins by the offering of certain prepared food; if the King be at a distance, he is in like manner to "venerate" the "chief of the village." The commentators, however, says Mr. Sutherland, seem agreed "that the notice enjoined and the invitation of kinsmen are no legal essentials to the validity of the adoption, being merely intended to give greater publicity to the act, and to obviate difficulty and doubt regarding the right of succession."*

But as, according to invariable Oriental practice, the inferior can only approach the superior with a gift in his hand, it is easy to see how the prince would become interested in insisting upon a previous notice, how prone he would be to treat it as a necessary condition of the validity of the act, to turn the notice given into a sanction requested. Public opinion too might favour

* Dattaka Mimansá, pp. 167, 218; see also Strange's Hindu Law, p. 94.

the change; for, the right of adoption being confined by law within well-defined limits, which the will of man would be always wishing to overleap, the condition of a previous sanction by a superior would offer a safeguard against an illegal or sometimes even a wayward or capricious exercise of it. Two kinds of practice might thus grow up. According to the one, the prince, acting as guardian of the law, might claim the right of inquiring into the circumstances of the adoption, to see if it be lawful and formal; according to the other, he would treat it as a mere source of revenue.

The latter, I am inclined to think, is the shape which the sovereign's customary sanction to the exercise of the right of adoption by a feudatory has taken in the native states generally. I believe it has the same weight with them as the Royal license to assume a certain name and arms with us. Just as, by virtue of the Queen's prerogative and payment of fees, John Smith becomes John Thompson, member henceforth of the Thompson family, so under his sovereign's sanction, and by payment of a certain gift or "nuzzur," may one Hindoo pass into another Hindoo's family. If John Smith takes the name of Thompson without obtaining the Royal license, he remains simply in the eyes of the law, "John Smith *alias* Thompson," or "commonly called Thompson." No Commissioner of her Majesty's Treasury would ever dream of seizing Thompson Park into her Majesty's hands because no license had been applied for. If the estate were forfeited by the omission to do so, it could only be as between private individuals,—from the un-Thompsonised Smith to some other claimant from a deceased Thompson. A Crown claim to Thompson Park, under such circumstances, would startle any judge on the bench into fits. Yet this monstrous piece of false logic,—of concluding from the Government sanction to a Government confiscation for want of it,—is what we Englishmen have been acting on for years in India, and latterly on the strength of it absorbing kingdoms as if they were cottages.

I shall be told, perhaps, by some, "Why insist on fixing the attention of Englishmen on such technicalities as the Hindoo law of succession by adoption? What can they understand of it? What can they care for it? Leave such matters to Indian officials, or at best to barristers in the Supreme Court."

It might be sufficient to say, that if the question of succession by adoption has any bearing whatever on the late rebellion, no Englishman worthy of the name should deem himself entitled to care nothing for it. But apart from any such connexion, the law and custom of succession among a people is surely one always worthy of interest, as an expression of the feelings and modes of action of that people. In this custom itself, we may see at once the hold which religious motives must have on the Hindoo mind, when the succession to the throne may be bound up with a religious ceremony, and that one relating to the welfare of a dead person. But if we take the right of succession by adoption in the form which it has assumed in those Hindoo states which are considered to take the lead among all others, to give the tone to all others, I must say that I hardly know of any law of succession which is more likely to be consonant to the national will, which takes more pains to be so consonant, and which should therefore commend itself more to us Englishmen. The Rajpoot prince in adopting a son to succeed him in default of male issue, is required to do so with the consent of the chiefs of the state. If he dies without having done so, those chiefs, foremost among whom are his widows, elect his successor from among his relations, the senior widow performing the religious ceremony of adoption, and if the successor be a minor, acting as regent, with the assistance of the chiefs, forming the council known by the (to us) queer name of "Raj Punch." All here, it will be seen, is free, deliberate, and if I may venture the term in speaking of these feudal polities of the Rajpoots, constitutional. I repeat, I cannot imagine any system better adapted to the manners of the people, any which is more likely to keep alive among them all feelings of national,—or, if you choose it, *tribe* unity,—as well as of individual manliness and self-respect; any which is more worthy of being maintained, encouraged, developed at our hands, extended if possible to other Hindoo states, as a genuine indigenous counterpoise to that slavishness of Oriental despotism, as we are pleased to call it, which ought to be, to us freemen, one of the main obstacles in our way wherever we met with it.

Still, it will be said, as a matter of fact, adoption has often not worked well, especially during long minorities, under a female regent. Suddenly emancipated—to a great extent at least—from the thraldom of the zenana, to be entrusted with the burthen of state affairs, the widow, if young, is generally found to give herself up to the unbridled gratification of her passions. Perhaps she completely neglects the child-prince, who has often no blood whatever in common with herself; perhaps she systematically steeps him in sensual pleasures, in order to prolong her own power. Her paramours reign under his name and hers; the resources of the state are squandered. So the ill-success of an adoption in Jaloun could be quoted by Lord Dalhousie as a ground for annexing Jhansee.

I do not deny the cogency of these arguments. They are one-sided, indeed, in their choice of facts, for some female reigns or regencies are celebrated in Indian history; thus the rule of Alya Baee formed the golden age of the Holkar state. It is almost impossible that the same excesses can take place in states like Rajpootana, where the chiefs exercise a voice in the government; and at any rate, if they were *normally* characteristic of the system of adoption, it appears incredible that it should ever have perpetuated itself as it has done, seeing that the excesses complained of are essentially those of the *weak*, and not of the strong. For whilst it is easy to conceive how nations may habitually endure a large amount of misgovernment at the hands of a king, it is almost impossible that they should do the same at the hands of a queen-regent and a child. If therefore the evils complained of were now characteristic of female regencies in the name of adoptive sons (and observe that they may equally be characteristic of such regencies, though the minority should be that of a successor by blood) it must be in great measure because of some alteration in the condition of things under which they take place. That alteration it is easy to discover in *the British guarantee*, which, by taking away the check of a national rising, assures impunity to misconduct which would not otherwise have been tolerated. It is one of the instances, unfortunately in India not a few, in which we have first made the evil, and then sought to eradicate it by tearing away the whole side of social life which it grew out of.

But in this instance especially, the cure lay side by side with the evil. The event of a female regency, if it gives power to the inexperienced denizen of the zenana, gives power also to the British representative. Then is the very time for the British Government to step forth in its truly conservative character, to insist upon guarantees for the proper training of the infant sovereign,* for the due maintenance of the public weal; if *absolutely* necessary, for the temporary management of affairs by selected persons, or even by its own Resident. Some of the brightest pages in the history of British influence in India belong to periods such as these,—witness the stock instance of Sir R. Jenkins in Nagpore. I do not hesitate to say, that with judicious English Residents, the much talked-of mischiefs of the adoption system, and of the female regencies which it brings with it, can never gain head; and consequently, that if they ever do, it is only through bad Residents, or the removal of good ones.

Observe, moreover, that if the British power in India is to be worthy of the name, a rule of opinion, a rule resting upon the golden fame of the good government

* "The improvement of the native prince is within our own power," says Mr. Mansel, Commissioner at Nagpore, in a passage to which I shall hereafter refer.

of its own dominions, of its moderation and equity towards other states, and not one of mere hard power, always grasping after more land and more revenue, the adoption system is one most entirely favourable to its stability. The British sanction which is asked for each adoption, even if given as a matter of form, accustoms native eyes to look to the British Government as paramount, whilst succession by lineal descent turns them away from it. The opportunities which adoptive succession affords during minorities of making British influence felt in matters of internal improvement, in the training of the infant prince, are such as do not offer themselves on the succession of an heir of full age, and may be more grudgingly granted on that of an infant heir by birth.

The value of adoption, towards pouring new blood into a decaying dynasty, is unmistakeable. The very idea of adoption implies a selection, though the choice may be circumscribed by usage. A favourable horoscope may perhaps turn the scale in favour of a particular candidate; but it is clear that considerations of physical, intellectual vigour, as well as of moral disposition, have also their weight,—and may have it more and more, according to the Resident's advice. Mr. Frere, Resident at Sattara, after examining a vast number of instances taken indifferently from all ranks of society, and at all periods of Mahratta history, declares that, "according to Mahratta usage, propinquity of blood has nothing whatever to do with necessary preference in the selection of an adopted son;" that "the age of the adopted, the number of his brothers, his personal qualities, and the prognostics of his horoscope, seem to have been much more attended to than nearness of blood."* Even where, as with the Mahrattas of Gwalior, nearness of blood seems to form a leading qualification, adoption may have for effect to bring to the throne—as at the latter capital in 1842—the son of a soldier whose only subsistence is 15 rupees —30*s*—a month.† Nay, the most favourable horoscope—as at the same capital in 1817, or at Indore in 1844—will in practice generally be, I take it, that of the boy who, out of several candidates, has the advantage in point of personal appearance, intelligence, and health.‡ Thus the successor by adoption is, *cæteris paribus*, likely to be more energetic, able, manly, than the lineal heir. And, as a matter of fact, it is most remarkable that the preservation of our sway in North-western India during the rebellion, has been in great measure owing to two princes whom adoption has seated on the throne;—Scindia, the spirited young ruler of Gwalior (the trooper's son before mentioned), and Holkar, the noble-minded chief of Indore, whose faithfulness has stood proof, amidst every temptation, against all the supercilious insolence of a Resident, all the supercilious neglect of a Calcutta Council.§

So utterly, therefore, has the lust of territory—the "land-hunger," as the natives call it—obscured true policy in the eyes of our Indian officials, that the practice of succession by adoption, which they have

* Sattara Annexation Papers, p. 137.

† See p. 37 of the House of Commons' Return on Adoptions.

‡ House of Commons' Return on Adoptions, pp. 24, 93.

§ Compare these two princes, for instance, with the last products of succession by blood in Oude.

sought to put down, when closely considered, is seen to coincide with the interests both of the dominant and of the protected race. As respects the one, it tends to keep up national feeling, to check despotism, to promote efficiency of rule, by substituting the healthy offspring of the trooper or the cultivator for the weakly outcome of the luxurious zenana, or at least by giving weight to personal qualities against the dry claims of birth. As respects the other, it tends to keep up the sense of subordination to a paramount power, to open avenues to the English superior of healthy, useful, truly conservative influence, sometimes in the choice of the candidate, at all times with reference to his education, and the training him to the duties of sovereignty. No boy-ruler enthroned by adoption need be anything but what the Resident makes him; and when the Resident has any kindliness and right feeling about him, he may make of him what Sir Robert Hamilton has made of Holkar,—a perfect gentleman, a firm friend in the hour of need. If we Englishmen did our duty in India, we should find then this native custom of adoption a help; it is only because we do not do our duty, but follow our self-will, that it meets us as a hindrance, and we blindly seek to crush it.

I will go further, and say, that the endeavour to confine Hindoo successions to lineal heirs, so far as it grows from the selfish wish to cut short Hindoo sovereignties, appears to me to be founded on the most short-sighted calculations. We hear sometimes of the danger of supposititious adoptions. But which is easier —to suppose a birth in the depths of the zenana, or to suppose an adoption? The one event is in its nature more or less public; nothing is easier than to require it to be more so. The other is essentially private; the common decencies of human nature, still more the jealousies of oriental usage, forbid its being dragged to the light of day. Are you prepared to force new treaties on every native sovereign to provide for this delicate point? Is the Resident to be head of a Commission *de ventre inspiciendo?* Is the Residency surgeon to attend *ex-officio* all parturient princesses? You know very well that you cannot, dare not, take any step whatsoever of the kind.* If not, then there is absolutely no guarantee against the most fraudulent successions, pretended to be lineal. And thus the earnest pleadings of the native princes for the privilege of adopting a successor become

* I fear I spoke too soon. Even since this book was begun I meet with the following passage in one of Mr. Russell's letters, written from the Himalayas, Sept. 14, 1858:

"In the hills amid which I am now writing, our policy has been so diverse and fantastic as to have endangered our reputation for honesty and justice. Some years ago it was our policy to avoid the hills, and to shun any accession of territory among them. We therefore scrupulously respected the Hindoo rights of adoption, and in defect of heirs we sought out distant relatives, and placed them on the 'guddees' of these little principalities. Now our policy is altered. We desire the acquisition of territory in the hills. There is a day-dream of colonization and tea-planting in the minds of some of our people, and we wish to define our frontier; therefore the right of adoption is denied. *We rigidly scrutinize the claims and the legitimacy of heirs, and inquire into the purity of pregnant ranees*, and the natives, whose memories are long, look on and wonder."—*Times*, Nov. 9, 1858.

Mr. Russell's testimony is especially valuable, as applying to a quarter of India to which I shall not otherwise refer, and shewing the same policy working there by the same means, which I am tracing elsewhere.

a signal proof of their own sincerity and upright feelings, which we are so ready to put in doubt. The instant these chiefs make up their minds to be dishonest, the game is pretty nearly in their hands. They need never want for a successor, so long as the zenana and its mysteries are their own.

And lastly, as Christians, as promoters of sound morality and social advancement, we must not shut our eyes to the fact that the disallowance of the right of adoption tends essentially to promote polygamy, to perpetuate the pernicious seclusion of women, both of which the mere contact with European civilization would otherwise tend to check. For if the maintenance of native sovereignties is to depend solely or mainly upon the existence of lineal heirs, who will find fault with the heathen prince for seeking to multiply his chances of offspring? who will be surprised if a new bar be thereby raised to his reception of Christ's Gospel?

Surely, the Hindoo prince's right of adopting a successor is one of those which must be covered by our Queen's solemn pledge. There remains to be shewn that in respecting it she will be simply reverting to a practice which the henceforth condemned annexation policy has interrupted.

LETTER VII.

HOW SUCCESSIONS BY ADOPTION WERE RESPECTED TILL 1841.

It is only of late years that the very idea of hindering or disallowing native successions by adoption seems to have been entertained by our Government. And yet there was in issue, half a century ago, a question closely akin to this, but relating to Mussulman princes only, as that of adoption relates only to Hindoo. Lord Hastings thus speaks of it, in that most valuable "Private Journal" of his—poohpoohed by the "Times,"—which has been lately published:

"In nothing do we violate the feelings of the native princes so much as in the decisions which we claim the privilege of pronouncing with regard to the succession to the musnud. We constantly oppose our construction of Mahomedan law to the right which the Moslem princes claim from usage, to choose among their sons the individual to be declared the heir apparent."*

What Lord Hastings would have thought of the far deeper violation of native feeling by the forbiddance or disallowance of adoption may be inferred from the above passage. Let us examine the various steps by which this violation has eventually been carried out. They are very instructively set forth in a "Return" to an order of the House of Commons, ordered to the printed on the 15th February, 1850, and beginning with Lord Hastings's own days.

* Private Journal of the Marquess of Hastings, vol. i. p. 48.

Starting from the year 1819-20 (the Bhopal case), we find that, at this time, the idea of a right of the British Government by lapse had apparently occurred to no one; the adoption, even by a Mahomedan princess, of a son and successor to her husband dying without male issue was sanctioned as a matter of course.* Nearly ten years elapse, and in the Kotah case (1825-29), the Supreme Government say that the ruler "must be considered to possess the right, in common with all other Hindoos, of making an adoption in conformity with the rules of the Shaster." † In the first Gwalior succession case (1826-7), we see an adoption not only sanctioned, but pressed upon the prince during his life in vain; we find the British Government announcing beforehand, that in the event of his death without having performed the ceremony, and without having authorized his widow to perform it, they "will *of course* be satisfied . . . with the selection made by the general voice, or by a majority of the chiefs and principal persons of the country, according to usage, whether the letter of the written law be closely adhered to or not;" we find the adoption made finally by the widow, though unauthorized by her husband, with the full acquiescence of the Government. ‡ In the first Indore succession case (1833-4) we find equally an adoption by the widow of Holkar deemed unobjectionable by the British Government, though eventually a collateral heir of full age made good his pretensions against the infant heir by adop-

* House of Commons' Return on Adoptions, p. 103 and foll.

† Ibid. p. 153 and foll.

‡ Ibid. p. 1 and foll.

tion, and was recognized by all parties.* In the Dutteeah case (1833), the right of the Rajas of Bundelcund to adopt whom they please was admitted in the person of a foundling, or pretended foundling, adopted by the last Raja, who succeeded and was recognized, as against the claims of a collateral.† In the second Gwalior succession case (1836-43), we find a series of circumstances singularly resembling those of the first; the prince urged to adopt by the British Government, but dying without having done so; the adoption performed by the widow, and recognized by the British Government.‡ So in the case of Dhar, near Indore (1834), adoption by the widow was sanctioned;§ so in that of Oorcha in Bundelcund, the Raja's claim to adopt was admitted as a matter of right, against the promptings of the British agent for Bundelcund, and notwithstanding the existence of grounds of serious complaint against the prince and the father of his adoptive son.‖ In the case of Banswarra (1838, 1844) we see first the election of a collateral heir as successor to a prince dead without male issue, with the consent of his widow and of the principal chiefs, and next the immediate adoption by him of a son with the like consent, whose succession in later years was duly recognized by the British Government.¶

The instance of Colaba, to which I shall refer in my next, forms as it were the watershed between two policies on the part of the Supreme Government. The

* House of Commons' Return on Adoptions, p. 43 and foll.

† Ibid. p. 114 and foll.

‡ Ibid. p. 28 and foll.

§ Ibid. p. 110 and foll.

‖ Ibid. p. 118 and foll.

¶ Ibid. p. 168 and foll.

coming spirit of annexation has nevertheless been looming already through the dispatches of subordinates since 1833. "It is a question," wrote Mr. Ainslie, the agent for Bundelcund, in the Dutteeah succession case, "whether in failure of legitimate offspring, of appointing a successor by adoption, or of the existence of any near relation, *the Raj would become lapsed to the paramount state*, or be left in abeyance *ad infinitum*,"—though it is evident that he considers the native right of adoption as altogether precedent to any question of a right in the British Government by escheat. The following passage, however, is more ominous, and foreshadows already Lord Dalhousie's Sattara proceedings: "I avail myself of the present opportunity to point out another feature in the engagements entered into by the British Government with the chiefs of Bundelcund. The treaties with the chiefs of Bundelcund were made with individuals in possession, *and their successors. Does that term necessarily include that person's relatives through his father?* His uncles and brothers, and their children, might, strictly speaking, be considered in no respect parties to the engagement."* Mr. Simon Fraser, a subsequent agent for Bundelcund—the same who was murdered at Delhi in 1857—wrote in the same strain, after the accession of the adopted foundling: "Acting upon the principles laid down by the Honourable Court, to recognize him as the heir *de facto* appears to be the most regular course, but it implies a total renunciation of all *reversionary right of succession to the Raj on the part of the British Government* under any contingency, for it renders necessary

* House of Commons' Return on Adoptions, p. 116.

that we should allow whoever can support his authority in the principality to assume the exercise of authority, and seize the Raj, and this without reference to his being the rightful heir to the guddee, or in any way connected with the original party to the treaty; but this again alters materially the character of our engagements, which are with a specified chief, and his heirs and successors in perpetuity."*

It is evidently Mr. Fraser's notion that, where there is a treaty with a prince, his heirs and successors, the "character" of the engagement is altered, if, by usurpation or otherwise, any other than the "rightful heir" succeeds. The very slightest amount of reflection would have shewn him that, were this the case, the whole system of English laws and treaties would have to be constantly renewed. For if there be one principle of our municipal law which is fixed, and which, instead of being narrowed, has always gone on widening in its international application, it is that the king *de facto* is the one to be acknowledged—the one upon whom the burthen of previous engagements descends—with whom new engagements are to be contracted. Thus our law-books are clear upon the point, that treason to the king *de facto* may be punished by the king *de jure*, when he succeeds to the throne.† And, to take the case of France for instance, we all know that, in wise deference to the lessons of the revolutionary wars, government after government is now recognized, not only by England, but by all Europe—some

* House of Commons' Return on Adoptions, p. 125.

† See, for instance, Blackstone, iv. 77: "The king here intended" (in the Statute of treasons) "is the king in possession, without any respect to his title."

petty prince of Italy perhaps alone excepted—without reference to the canon of legitimate succession, and that every previously existing treaty is held binding upon and towards every such government in succession. *Upon* and *towards*, I say, for it is generally overlooked by the annexationists, that if their logic held good in our favour, it must also hold good against us. In many instances, we allege supremacy over a native state, and enforce annexation on lapse, as having succeeded by conquest to the rights of the Peshwa, or some other native sovereign. Did it ever occur to an annexationist who might doubt, like Mr. Ainslie, whether "successor" might "necessarily" include "a man's relatives through his father," whether it might also necessarily include one who turned a man out of his house, and put him in prison? It has not seemed to the annexationists that, "strictly speaking," a man's "uncles and brothers and their children" were "parties" to his engagements; did it seem to them that the conqueror was, "strictly speaking," a party to the engagements of the conquered? If they held that the character of *our* engagements was "materially altered," if any one who could support his authority might seize the Raj, without reference to his being in any way connected with the original party to the treaty, was not the "character of a native prince's engagements materially altered," when the Raj of his superior was actually seized by foreign invaders? Arnold spoke once of "those one-eyed men, the political economists." Might we not say also, "those one-eyed men, the Indian annexationists?"

Upon every principle, therefore, of municipal and

international law which is recognized by England, which is enforced by it in India, which is essential to the stability of the Queen's throne, to the maintenance of her Indian empire, it was impossible that the succession to the throne of Dutteeah, of any person whomsoever, should of itself in anywise alter the character of our engagements with the chief of that principality, his heirs and successors. It is but just to say, however, that in the despatches from the Supreme Government in this case there appears no trace of the agent's misapprehensions.*

Mr. Fraser however did not stop here. He was left as agent in Bundelcund, and a few years later (1837) in the Oorcha case, we find him, in an elaborate report (7th Oct. 1837),† exhibiting genealogical trees of the various Bundelcund states and chiefships, the successions to which had been sanctioned; the existing revenues of territories held by rulers who had no lineal descendants, of territories which, according to the writer, had "already passed into the hands of persons who had originally a doubtful claim to it," and of territories to which lineal heirs were actually in existence. "The right," said he, "of the British Government, as paramount power, to resume hereditary territory which lapses for want of heirs, has, I believe, been asserted and acted upon in other parts of India, and I am not aware of any peculiarity in the case of Bundelcund which should exempt it from the

* House of Commons' Return on Successions by Adoption, pp. 115-128. The carelessness with which this part of the Return is compiled (seemingly by the India House) is almost incredible. Six several documents are printed twice, and two others misplaced.

† House of Commons' Return on Adoptions, p. 132.

operation of the general rule." He spoke repeatedly of Government's "waiving" its claim. In guarded language, indeed, he respectfully "submitted" what appears to be, under the name of "suitable arrangements," a mere scheme of annexation. Fortunately for India, the Lieutenant-Governor of the North-West was then Sir Charles Metcalfe. In a celebrated minute of his, of the 28th October, 1837,* he pointed out a trifling flaw in Mr. Fraser's reasoning,—he had forgotten the difference between princes and subjects!

2. "The question is," wrote Sir Charles, "whether chiefs and princes, not having heirs of the body, have a right to adopt a successor, to the exclusion of collateral heirs, or of *the supposed reversionary rights of the paramount power;* and whether the British Government is bound to acknowledge the adoption?

3. In the disposal of this question there is a wide difference, to which Mr. S. Fraser has not adverted, between sovereign princes and jageerdars; between those in possession of hereditary sovereignties in their own right, and those who hold grants of land or public revenue by gift from a sovereign or paramount power.

4. *Those who are sovereign princes in their own right and of the Hindoo religion have by Hindoo law a right to adopt, to the exclusion of collateral heirs, or of the supposed reversionary right of the paramount power; the latter in fact in such cases having* NO REAL EXISTENCE, *except in the case of absolute want of heirs, and even then the right is only assumed in virtue of power; for* IT WOULD BE MORE CONSISTENT WITH RIGHT THAT THE PEOPLE OF THE STATE SO SITUATED SHOULD ELECT A SOVEREIGN FOR THEMSELVES.

5. *In the case, therefore, of Hindoo sovereign princes, I should say that in failure of heirs male of the body, they have a right to adopt,* to the exclusion of collateral heirs, *and that the British Government is bound to acknowledge the adoption, provided that it be regular, and not in violation of Hindoo law.* . . .

6. *In the case of Mahomedan sovereigns there seems to be greater*

* House of Commons' Return on Adoptions, p. 141.

doubt. I do not know that they have by law a right to adopt to the exclusion of collateral heirs. Mahomedan sovereigns have, however, more than once claimed a right to nominate a successor from among their sons; but the Mahomedan law appears to be loose with regard to succession to sovereignties, and the safest way, where we are paramount, or have any right to interfere, is to acknowledge the legitimate successor according to Mahomedan law.

7. With respect to chiefs who merely hold lands or enjoy public revenue under grants such as are issued by a sovereign to a subject,* the power which made the grant, or that which by conquest or otherwise has succeeded to its rights, is certainly entitled to limit succession *according to the limitations of the grant, which in general confines it to heirs male of the body, and consequently precludes adoption. In such cases, therefore, the power which granted, or the power standing in its place, would have a right to resume on failure of heirs male of the body.*"

The agent in Bundelcund was therefore requested to classify the princes and chiefs within his superintendence with reference to the above data, and to report to which class the Raja of Oorcha belonged. The impression on the Lieutenant-Governor's mind was that he was a "sovereign prince, and being a Hindoo, fully entitled to adopt a son and successor in the event of his having no heirs of his body;" but the recognition of the adoption would depend on the decision of the Governor-General. Mr. Fraser having moreover commented on "the apparent incoherence of the past deci-

* Observe the careful wording of Sir Charles: "Grants *such as are issued by a sovereign to a subject.*" The definition was afterwards stretched so as to include all cases in which territory was in any way granted, confirmed or restored, though under circumstances entirely negativing the idea of a grant as "to a subject." It must however at once be stated that Mr. Elphinstone, in a passage to be hereafter quoted, treats by implication jagheers even as inheritable by right of adoption, though under heavy fines.

sions of our Government in acknowledging successors among the Bundelcund chiefs," as not being "based on any fixed principle," Sir Charles Metcalfe quietly pointed out that "the principle which has generally operated on such occasions has been that *of recognizing the succession apparently agreeable to the prince and the people, or to the latter on the demise of the former; that is,* the principle of non-interference in the internal affairs of other states."

If the spirit which prevades this remarkable minute had continued to animate the rulers of India, I believe we should never have heard of an Indian rebellion. It is the assertion of a broad, human, common-sense policy, against a narrow, selfish technicality, masked, it may be, in regard—feigned or real—for the Indian masses. Sir Charles disdains to enter into any consideration of the money-revenue which we may have foregone, which we may yet forego, by not asserting the "supposed reversionary rights of the paramount power." He shews clearly that there can be no such rights as against any sovereign state, only against mere grantees from the crown, holding in general their lands in fee-tail. He shews that to abstain from meddling,—to defer to the will of the prince and the people,—is a rule above all rules, a uniformity above all canons.

Yet even in this noble paper there is an imperfection,—hardly to be called an error,—which in after-times allowed it to be wrested from its true purpose to far other ends,—which gave a very fulcrum to the annexation lever. The classification of the chiefs of Bundelcund which it directed might lead, and did lead in effect, to the substitution of official generalizations for specific treaty obligations. The minute did not sufficiently point out that, as against ourselves, the actual engagements entered into with the several chiefs were what they had a right in the first place to appeal to; that no theory of agents, or lieutenant-governors, or governors-general, as to whether a chief came or not within the category of sovereign princes could stand against the words of a definite treaty. The time came when Lord Dalhousie wielded Sir Charles Metcalfe's definitions with terrible effect to overthrow those native principalities, which it was Sir Charles's especial object to preserve.*

The next time the point is mooted, in the Oorcha case (1841), it is easy to see that the annexation doctrines are gaining head. Mr. (now Sir Robert) Hamilton, officiating secretary to the then lieutenant-governor of the North-West, speaks of a recognition by the British Government of the adoption as "that which, under any circumstances, must be a relaxation of its own strict right of resumption on failure of direct heirs." Mr. (now Sir T. H.) Maddock—who, I trust, has since seen the error of his ways,—being then secretary to the Supreme Government, endeavours in a long note to confute Sir Charles Metcalfe's opinion as to the Raja of Oorcha being a sovereign prince,—talks of the princes of Bundelcund in general as having become, "in effect,

* I do not speak of Lord Metcalfe only as of a statesman. I speak of him as of my father's friend,—as one in whose honest face, when I looked upon it in after-days, seared already with the disease which laid him in the grave, I could not but see that I had before me "an Israelite indeed, in whom there was no guile."

feudatories and dependent jageerdars, whose estates, in default of heirs, would lapse to the British Government,"—and (to use a vulgarism) muddles up after the manner of later Indian officials the right of the paramount power to sanction adoption with that of seizure on pretence of lapse. Lord Auckland, however, in a most creditable minute (2nd January, 1842) disposed of the whole string of fallacies.

3. "I cannot," he wrote, "for a moment admit the doctrine that, because the view of the policy upon which we may have formed engagements with native princes may have been by circumstances materially altered, we are not to act scrupulously up to the terms and spirit of those engagements.

4. I have referred to our treaty with the Raja of Oorcha, concluded on the 23rd December, 1812, and I find that its preamble commences in these words: 'The Raja of Oorcha is one of the chiefs of Bundelcund by whom and his ancestors his present possessions have been held in successive generations during a long course of years, without paying tribute or acknowledging vassalage to any other power.' And the treaty formed with the Raja is designated as one of 'friendship and alliance;' the territory which from ancient times has descended 'to the Raja by inheritance, and is now in his possession, being guaranteed to the said Raja and to his heirs and successors.' Upon words so distinct and positive as this, I hold it to be impossible to raise a question, and I am of opinion, therefore, that the Raja of Oorcha must be regarded as one of those sovereign rulers who, according to the very proper rule laid down in the letter of Sir Charles Metcalfe, of 28th October, 1837, is entitled to make an adoption, in his own discretion, which the British Government is bound to acknowledge, 'provided that such adoption be regular and not in violation of Hindoo law.' "*

This is putting the matter upon its truest ground,—that of express treaty obligation.

* House of Commons' Return on Adoptions, pp. 128-152.

LETTER VIII.

HOW THE RIGHT OF ADOPTION WAS INVADED, 1841-8.

THREE principles have regulated the policy of the supreme government of India towards allied native states up to the period at which we have arrived. First, that of respecting native laws and usages, as administered by native sovereigns. Second, that of respecting the will of the native peoples, when manifestly exhibited in the selection of a sovereign. Third, that of respecting the letter of treaties, as against ourselves. Perhaps the spirit of our rule, at its noblest epoch, is nowhere better expressed than by these words of Lord Hastings to the Nawab of the Carnatic, a mere pageant sovereign, in 1813:

"I answered, that a treaty plighted the public faith of the nation, so that it must be my duty to maintain its terms according to their true spirit, *which ought always to be construed most favourably for the party whose sole dependence was on the honour of the other.*"

We enter upon a new era, in which the words of treaties are tortured to reduce sovereigns to the status of dependent vassals,—in order that their dependency in turn may be made a ground for extinguishing the states over which they rule; in which the desires of the native peoples are only regarded, so far as they may make annexation dangerous; in which the transfer of

* Private Journal, vol. i. p. 11.

masses of men from kindred rule to foreign, is deemed a purely technical matter; in which the British Government acts as the supreme interpreter of native law and custom, and even when it bends to them, almost disdains to do so otherwise than as "an act of grace."

The rule of the weak and vacillating Lord Auckland,—than whom no man perhaps ever did more harm, meaning less—fitly inaugurates such a period. We have seen him, with simple English straightforwardness, maintaining the rights of the Raja of Oorcha at the close of the last. We have to see him now sacrificing those of the widows of the chief of Colaba.

With the Colaba case (1841-4) begins indeed the era of annexation. There had been a treaty with the chief, guaranteeing to him, his "heirs and successors," on certain conditions, "the integrity of his dominions," but reserving to the British "entire supremacy," and "the right of conferring investiture on any vacancy." British Courts of justice were not to be introduced against the will of the chief, "his heirs and successors." In the absence of legitimate descendants of the founder of the state, the Supreme Government refused to allow the widows of a deceased chief to adopt illegitimate ones. The Home Government sanctioned the measure, although contrary to the views of the majority of the Bombay Council, including the Governor—the parties nearest at hand and most interested. Lord Auckland and his Calcutta Council were unanimously of opinion that our policy should be "to persevere in the one clear and just course of abandoning no just and honourable accession of territory or revenue, while all existing claims of right are, at the same time, scrupulously respected."* The privilege of adoption, it was now declared, "rests entirely in the discretion of the paramount government. To permit the adoption would therefore be to give up, by an act of mere grace, a territory which has undoubtedly lapsed to the British Government, as the paramount power." (25th May, 1841.)†

This is one of those cases which shew the dangers of the system of generalization formulized in Lord Metcalfe's famous minute. Try the character of the Colaba state by the test of absolute sovereignty, and it becomes impossible to contend that a chief who acknowledges the "entire supremacy" of the British Government over his state, can be considered as sovereign in the full force of the term. But try the actual case, as any English judge would, by the evidence, and it becomes no less clear that in treating with the chief, his "heirs and successors," the British Government acknowledged the individuality of the Colaba state, apart from the mere family of the chief. This is fully shewn by the clause that "the British Courts of justice, laws and regulations," are not to be "introduced into the principality, against the will of Raghojee Angria, his heirs and successors,"—a clause which becomes almost nugatory, if the British Government is to have the right of determining that there shall be no successors at all.‡

* I quote these words from a minute by Mr. Willoughby in the Sattara Annexation Papers, p. 85.

† House of Commons' Return on Adoptions, p. 214.

‡ The existence of "semi-sovereign states" is fully admitted by writers on international law. Mr. Wheaton expressly says, that "Tributary states, and states having a feudal relation to each other, are still considered as sovereign, so far as their sovereignty is not affected by this relation." International Law, pp. 45-51.

The fatal step was not taken without the fullest warning as to its consequences. In the "Selections from the written opinions of Henry St. George Tucker" will be found an elaborate paper by that eminent member of the Court of Directors against it.

"The principality of Colaba," he wrote, "has been held by the family of Angria for nearly two centuries, in a state of independence. It has never been in our possession. Our connection with it rests upon the foundations of a formal treaty, freely contracted; and while a vestige of the Angria family remains, it belongs of right to them, and cannot be seized and appropriated by us otherwise than by an act of violence, perpetrated by our superior power. . . . It is assumed that the principality has lapsed to the paramount state, by reason of the failure of heirs. . . . But the ground I rest upon is, that the widow of Raghojee Angria possessed, under the authority of that prince, which is not disputed, *the right to adopt, and still possesses that right unimpaired.** Adoption, with a Hindoo, is both a *right* and a *duty;* for the tenets of his religion require that, failing a natural heir, a substitute should be raised up to perform certain ceremonial rites enjoined by that religion; and even if we admit that the principality of Colaba was a mere dependency of our Government, and that the paramount éstate, in certain cases, can refuse to sanction an adoption, this power is not to be exercised lightly and capriciously upon insufficient grounds. It is a reservation intended to guard against irregular and illegal adoptions.

The right of adoption is somewhat analogous to that under which, by means of a testamentary deed or will, we give a destination to our property, in this country, after the demise of the testator; but with the Hindoo a religious motive is superadded, to render the act of adoption necessary; and it would not be more unjust to prohibit a British subject from executing a will than it would be to prevent a Hindoo from raising up an heir by means of an adoption.

Whether the case before us be considered to involve a question of international law, assuming Colaba to be an independent state; or a

---

* The italics are here the writer's.

question of inheritance, viewing it as a mere dependency; it is clear there are no grounds for the forcible interference of the British Government. The principality is, at the least, a territorial domain or estate, held under the protection of the law, and should the proprietor or claimant be compelled to resort to a Court of justice, in order to establish his rights, I cannot for one moment doubt that the august tribunal in the last resort in this country would extend to him its protection, and grant redress for any wrongs which he may have suffered at our hands.

I never can satisfy myself that true policy can comport with injustice and oppression. The native princes and chiefs of India will see, in the fate of Colaba, their own future destiny; their fidelity and attachment cannot be relied upon while they have such cause for distrust and alarm, and although they may be overawed and kept down by our irresistible military power, the occasion may arise when their hostility might become dangerous. The feelings of our Indian subjects are not to be trifled with; and it is not wise nor safe to depart from that conciliatory conduct, nor to efface from their minds those impressions of our justice, wisdom and good faith, which have hitherto constituted our bond of union with the people, and the true basis of our power in India."*

The Colaba case was followed in the next year, 1842, by that of Mandavie, where lapse was enforced by the British Government, "as the Peishwa's representative," against the claim of adoption by widows, and those of collaterals. So technical was the question of annexation already becoming, so utterly regardless had the British Government grown by this time, as to

* Selections, pp. 97—100. At a later period Mr. Tucker wrote: "I remonstrated against the annexation (I am disposed to call it *confiscation*) of Colaba, the ancient seat of the Angria family, . . . and far from having seen reason to recall, or to modify the opinion recorded by me on that proceeding, I have availed myself of every suitable occasion to enforce my conviction, that a more mischievous policy could not be pursued than that which would engross the whole territory of India." . . . Ibid. p. 89.

the feelings of those with whom it dealt,—that the enforcement of the escheat turned upon the point of whether the succession to a very ancient Hindoo principality was to be reckoned from its foundation, or from its restoration after twenty years of subjection, nearly a century before the date of the discussion.* The same plea, it is obvious, might be raised for suppressing—as a continental power at least—the kingdom of Sardinia, or any other state which was restored after the great Napoleon's conquests, in case of failure of issue of the princes actually restored.

From henceforth, though adoptions may still be sanctioned, though Governor's-General may shrink yet awhile from enforcing escheat in the case of the larger states, the whole aspect of affairs is changed. Instead of Residents and Agents suggesting annexation, it is from head-quarters that the suggestion comes; it is only not carried into effect, when the subordinate officer happens to be a man of sufficient character to resist the temptation to please his superiors, of sufficient weight to make his superiors shrink from overruling his views. Such a man was the late Colonel Sutherland, agent for Rajpootana; a man of very wide Indian experience, thoroughly familiar with native usages, and at the same time one whose chivalrous straightforwardness was itself a rebuke to the covetous longings of others. To the consistent course which he pursued is owing the still maintained integrity of the Rajpoot states, held by the flower of the Hindoo race, and thereby, as I firmly believe, their fidelity

* House of Commons' Return on Adoptions, pp. 216-17.

during the present revolt, with the exception of the still doubtful case of Kotah.

The Kishengurh (1841), Oodeypore (1841-2), Doongerpore (1846) successions shew clearly the influence of Colonel Sutherland. In the former there had been an adoption by a widow, under protest from the next of kin. The Calcutta Council doubted whether the widow could adopt without express authority, and directed inquiries. Colonel Sutherland had them made, and, without taking the hint thrown out, reported that "there is no question that an adoption by a widow from among the nearest, although not the next of kin to her deceased husband, when that adoption has been made in conformity with the voice of the chiefs of the state, is in the estimation of the Rajpoot world, valid."* In the second case Colonel Sutherland actually committed his superiors to the sanctioning an adoption made by the ruling prince without previous formal intimation to the British authorities, by a letter in which he spoke of its being "the wish of the British Government that all sovereign princes of this country who had no issue, should name their successors during their life-time," and stated that it was "desirable" that the prince "should adopt an heir in conformity with Hindoo law and with the usages of his principality." Although this step passed unquestioned, the recognition of the adoption was withheld at head-quarters during the adoptive father's life-time; and it is observable that in the despatch of the Supreme Government to the Home authorities, instead of treating the Maharana of Oodeypore as a sovereign prince, as

* House of Commons' Return on Adoptions, p. 173 and foll.

Colonel Sutherland had done, an expression is borrowed from his subordinate, the Agent for Meywar, and the mode of the adoption is spoken of as "altogether inconsistent with the deference due from a *dependent ally* of the British Government."* In the Doongerpore case, again, before sanctioning a proposed adoption, made under very peculiar circumstances by the chief, the Governor-General wished to know what arrangement Colonel Sutherland would suggest in the event of the chief's death while yet a minor. "Is the state of Doongerpore to revert to Dulput Singh in such case, and he to have the power of a second time adopting an heir to the principality; or is *the state to become an escheat to the British Government, in the manner of other states to which no heir exists?*"

The case put, it will be presently observed, was precisely the one on the occurrence of which the sovereignty of Indore had been cut down to a succession by lineal descent only. The idea of escheat had already in the present case been thrown out by the Meywar agent, Colonel Robinson. The Supreme Government would only have been too glad to obtain the sanction of a man of Colonel Sutherland's authority to the policy which they were striking out.

Colonel Sutherland's reply was decisive:

"I do not see the least reason why a second adoption should not be had recourse to, if the first child should die either before or after attaining his maturity; *and I do not understand by what process a Rajpoot principality, with which we are only connected by treaty, can ever escheat to the British Government; for there must, in all*

---

* Ibid. p. 184 and foll.

Rajpoot principalities, be numerous collateral heirs; and even if we had the right of succession, I should consider it very undesirable that we should burthen ourselves with such a state as Doongerpore, if it could be otherwise disposed of; *for under our system of administration, it could never, in all probability, be made to pay its own expense.*"*

There was no driving on the annexation policy with such an agent. In all these instances the adoption was confirmed, with some display of ill temper in the last, on the part of the Supreme Government; and the precedent thus established by Colonel Sutherland appears to have been followed after his death in the case of Kerowlee, 1848-9.†

If the maintenance of the Rajpootana states is due to Colonel Sutherland, the existence of a native ruler of Indore, our faithful ally, is apparently due to Sir Claude Wade; though we may fail to trace in the latter, the insight and decision which characterized the former. In the second Indore succession case, indeed,

* House of Commons' Return on Adoptions, p. 193 and foll. On grounds of law, however, I am bound to say, that there does appear to me considerable doubt as to a widow's right to adopt a second time, when the first adopted son has been able to perform the due funeral rites. The Privy Council have decided, though with considerable hesitation, that the second adoption by a man, the first adopted son being alive, is void; *Rungama* v. *Atchama*, 4 Moore's Indian Appeal Cases, p. 1; and if we take the religious duty as our guide in adoption cases, it would seem that whenever that has been fulfilled, adoption becomes impossible.

† House of Commons' Return on Adoptions, p. 209 and foll. I am told by an Indian officer that there are some further papers relating to Kerowlee, which have not been called for; that "Lord Dalhousie was ordered to restore that petty Rajpoot state to its rightful successor, and he did so."

(1841-3), the precedent of Colaba was probably deemed too recent to follow up; the ruler was encouraged to adopt a son, who was recognized after his death.* But the child died in less than six months, and a very different course was followed (1844).

Without apparently the slightest inquiry, it was assumed on all sides by the British authorities, that there was no person having a claim to succeed, or to exercise the right of adoption, and this in the face of a genealogical table forwarded by the Resident, from which it was evident that there were relatives in existence, far within the twenty-one degrees of relationship allowed by the Hindoo law,—in the face of customs, at least local, allowing kinsmen to adopt in default of the widow;† and more than all, in the face of the fact, that there was then living a lad (Martund Rao) whose adoption by a widow, had been sanctioned by the British Government eleven years before, and who had only been set aside on the popular voice declaring itself in favour of a collateral of full age. And the first step taken by Lord Ellenborough—for I am

* House of Commons' Return on Adoptions, p. 56 and foll.

† Among the Rajpoots, there is even a right in the Council of the State to select a successor. Thus the Maharana of Oodeypore, (who must be deemed a high authority in such matters), writing to Colonel Sutherland in 1841, says, "If the adoption is not made during the life, then the Raj Punch may, from the nearest of kin, select and place on the guddee the person who is best qualified to rule." (House of Commons' Return on Adoptions, p. 188.) An instance of this occurs in the Banswarra case of 1838, where the Supreme Government speak of a prince having been "elected, with the consent and approbation of the leading chiefs of the principality, to fill the vacant guddee." (Ibid. p. 168.)

sorry to say, he was the sinner on this occasion,—was to endeavour, if possible, to effect an annexation of the whole country. "Where," said he, (5th February, 1844), "there is no person having the shadow of hereditary claim to succeed to the guddee of a native state, and no person possessing a legitimate right to adopt a successor thereto, and where moreover that state itself is of comparatively modern origin, owing its existence to a conquest made by predatory troops, it must always become a question how far it may be expedient to maintain the separate existence of that state, for the benefit of none but the immediate followers of the Court."*

The Resident was therefore directed to "endeavour to ascertain whether there is any feeling which can be deemed to partake of a national character, for the maintenance of the state itself." But he was sincere enough to report as follows, (17th February, 1844):

"The measure of assuming the government of the country ourselves, would, in my humble opinion, be unpopular, and attended with considerable risk to the existence of tranquillity. *There is nothing which has tended more to confirm the attachment of the retainers of the state, as well as its subjects, to the authority of our government, during the late events which have happened here, and the disturbances at Gwalior,*† *than the impression arising from the disinterested conduct we have manifested in the desire to preserve the integrity of the chiefship* in the family to which it has heretofore belonged; and although the feelings of the people may not par-

---

* House of Commons' Return on Adoptions, February, 1850, p. 87. Of course the assertion that a native state is maintained solely for the benefit of courtiers, is the merest petitio principii.

† *i.e.* The Gwalior campaign of 1843.

take of that decidedly national character, by which we are accustomed to view them in other countries, yet where there is no actual oppression or misrule urging them on to wish for a change of government, they have a respect for existing institutions, and a pride in their continuance in the family which they have long been in the habit of acknowledging as their head, that would induce them to view any such design on the part of our government with a strong aversion."*

So Lord Ellenborough's views of aggrandisement were foiled for the moment. By way, probably, of shewing the weight of British protection, he left the question of succession in abeyance for two months and more,—a princess, the widow of a previous sovereign, considered the head of the family, and termed the Mah Sahibeh, acting as regent; the Resident, moreover, being directed to make known "distinctly to the sirdars and to all the subjects of the state, that we shall regard with severe displeasure any attempt to put forward in any manner the pretensions of Martund Rao, or of any one else to the guddee."† In other words, native claims, even should they be rights, must depend on the good pleasure of his Lordship. Sir Claude Wade meanwhile left India, and was replaced by Mr. (now Sir Robert) Hamilton; and now the Governor-General was pleased to take up again the succession question. The Resident reported, that the Mah Sahibeh had expressed her anxïety to have it settled; that, whilst perfectly willing to acquiesce in the Governor-General's decision, she could not "in the face of her religion" disguise her wish to see Martund Rao raised to the throne; that he had been duly adopted, ejected when

* House of Commons' Return on Adoptions, p. 88.

† Ibid. p. 89.

a minor; "that she was convinced such a step would give universal satisfaction, and be grateful to the people;" that, if not approved of, his youngest brother was the most eligible. The Resident added, that "the troops were devoted to the Mah Sahibeh, for whom they entertained the greatest respect;" and that she had "ever maintained a high character for her kindness of disposition and benevolence of her rule." He further forwarded an extract of a letter from the magistrate of Poona, giving a favourable account of Martund Rao himself.*

Now let us weigh these circumstances. Martund Rao had been adopted in 1843, with the sanction of the British Government; he had been set aside, an infant, to make way for a collateral claimant of full age, designated by the voice of the people. That collateral claimant had now died, and his adoptive son after him. What could be more natural than that the former adoptive candidate should now be reinstated in his rights, the people of the state being willing to receive him? He had renounced them, it is true, but this very renunciation, given for the sake of public tranquillity, should have constituted a title in his favour, at a time when there was no danger to be incurred by recognizing these rights. He was still moreover an infant, and such a renunciation would have been held invalid on his behalf, by any English Court of justice. Will it be believed, that precisely *because* Martund Rao had the best claim, therefore the Calcutta Council would not allow him to succeed? "Martund Rao," wrote Mr.

* House of Commons' Return on Adoptions, pp. 90, 91.

(now Sir F.) Currie, as secretary to the Supreme Government, "having been once already upon the guddee, by real or pretended* adoption, *her restoration now would have, to a certain degree, the appearance of a succession by legitimate right*; whereas, inasmuch as he has really no legal claim, and the guddee is really vacant, and no one of the Holkar family now possesses the right of adopting a successor thereto, *it seems desirable that the selection of a successor should be manifestly the sole act of the British Government as the paramount protecting state*." So Martund Rao, as well as his brother,—*i.e.* the two persons whom the Regent pointed out as having the best claim,—were set aside, and the Resident was directed to inform her, that the Governor-General in Council had come to the conclusion, that it was expedient that the candidate named third by her should succeed.†

* Why "pretended"? Not a shadow of doubt had been cast upon the reality of his adoption.

† House of Commons' Return on Adoptions, p. 92. Even this was accompanied with an insult to the Princess. She had recommended the candidate in question, being a younger son, probably on some ground of personal promise in the boy. "Perhaps," observes the despatch, "her Highness may see some convenience to herself in a more protracted minority." The high character given to this aged lady by the Resident might have saved her from this insinuation. But it was visibly gratuitous, for Martund Rao, the candidate whom she especially recommended, was, as appears from the Blue-book, between fourteen and fifteen, (having been between three and four in 1833, while Mr. Currie writes in 1844), whilst the candidate who was actually selected by the British Government, being third on her list, was ten. Yet this piece of insolence was deemed so clever, that it was retailed to the Home authorities. See p. 83 of the Return.

Mr. Hamilton, who had transmitted the expression of the Mah Sahibeh's wishes that the matter might be speedily decided, "as the want of a head to the state was embarrassing to public business, led to intrigues, and moreover, the wishes of the people were strong that the guddee should not remain vacant," made no secret of the news, but communicated it to the durbar, and fixed a day for the installation of the new prince (27th July; the chiefship having been in abeyance since the 17th February). For this he was severely blamed by the Calcutta Council. One specimen of their handywork will suffice: "The Governor-General in Council would fain hope that you left upon the minds of all the impression that the younger son of Bhao Holkar *was placed upon the guddee by the mere will of the British Government.*" And the intention was intimated of transmitting a *sunnud*, or grant, nominating the young prince,—in other words, of transforming Indore from a sovereign state into a mere fief, according to the fatal classification system of Sir Charles Metcalfe's minute. This notion was, however, withdrawn, after Lord Hardinge's succession to the Governor-Generalship, and the actual installation of the young chief; but it was intimated to the Resident that "the opportunity of marking an important line of policy had been lost to the Government" by his proceedings.*

* House of Commons' Return on Adoptions, p. 99. The consequences of insisting on the "sunnud" were thus indicated by Mr. Hamilton. "Had a proposal, that the successor to the vacant guddee should owe his position solely to a *sunnud* from the British Government, been made whilst this question of succession was unsettled and conflicting parties ripe for action, I am confi-

It is difficult for subordinates to preserve their independence before such expressions of opinion from the supreme authority. Mr. Hamilton now suggested that, in the first letter from the Governor-General to the young chief, being in fact the confirmation of his authority, "*the future succession should be distinctly limited to the heirs male of the Mahàraja's body lawfully begotten*," so as effectually to "*put an end to the objectionable system of adoption.*" This was caught at, of course, and the khureeta, or letter, contained the following paragraph: "*It is the intention of the British Government, in thus bestowing upon your Highness the principality of the Holkar State, that the chiefship should descend to the heirs male of your Highness's body lawfully begotten, in due succession, from generation to generation.*"* In giving account of the transaction to the Secret Committee, Lord Hardinge and his Council trusted (23d December, 1844) that "enough had been done to stamp the measure as *an act of free grace on the part of the paramount power*, and to *strip the accession of the young chief of all pretension to succession by either hereditary right, or by that of adoption.*" † And thus

dent the troops would have resisted, and the chiefs and sirdars have been distrustful and passive. . . And, confidence in the integrity of our purpose once shaken, recourse to an armed force would have become necessary to carry out our views. The unsettled state of the adjoining territory of Scindia, the wild character of the Bheels, hordes of persons thrown on the world by the recent changes at Gwalior, all afforded elements of commotion, which delay and procrastination on our part would have fermented."

* House of Commons' Return on Adoptions, p. 101.

† Ibid. p. 85.

Indore has become, or rather, been sought to be transmuted into an entailed state, with an alleged reversion in the British Government.

Let us measure the enormous strides which have been taken towards systematic annexation since the beginning of this survey.

On the 26th November, 1819, Major Henley, on a mission at Bhopal, says of the British Government, that, in the position which it now occupied, "it must often inevitably assume the office of umpire in disputed or doubtful successions." * On the 8th June, 1844, Mr. (now Sir F.) Currie, writing as secretary to the Supreme Government, deems it "desirable that the selection of a successor" to the important state of Indore "should be manifestly the sole act of the British Government as the paramount protecting state." †

On the 3rd July, 1828, the Supreme Government, writing home, say that "the ruler of Kotah must be considered to possess the right, in common with all other Hindoos, of making an adoption in conformity with the rules of the Shaster."‡ On the 30th September, 1844, the Resident of Indore advises the limiting the succession of that state to heirs male of the body, as "this will effectually put an end to the objectionable system of adoption;" the suggestion is followed, and the Supreme Government in writing home (23d December, 1844) speak of the step taken as "precluding the possibility of adoption." §

* House of Commons' Return on Adoptions, p. 106.

† Ibid. p. 92. ‡ Ibid. p. 153. § Ibid. pp. 99, 85.

On the 31st July, 1834, speaking of an Indore succession, the Supreme Government write home: "Our duty .... would be to maintain whatever arrangement might appear to be unequivocally consonant to the general wish." * On the 23rd December, 1844, speaking of another Indore succession, they report that they have rejected a candidate to whom the Resident "believed the people generally were favourable, and would be gratified by his being nominated Maharaja," because his enthronement "would have, to a certain degree, the appearance of a succession by legitimate right."†

It remained for Lord Dalhousie to systematize the new policy thus tentatively struck out by his three last predecessors, Lords Auckland, Ellenborough, and Hardinge.

LETTER IX.

HOW THE ANNEXATION POLICY DEALT WITH THE RIGHT OF ADOPTION.

It will not be a waste of time, after the survey which we have taken, to cast another glance at the circumstances attending the different claims of lapse by disallowance of adoption which were enforced by Lord Dalhousie.

The Colaba and Mandavie cases had gone no further than a refusal to allow adoptions by widows in what

* House of Commons' Return on Adoptions, p. 44.

† Ibid. p. 83.

were termed dependent principalities. The last Indore case had been confined in effect to the refusal to allow of a particular adoption by one, who, though not the widow of the last prince, was the admitted head of the family. Between this and the enforcement of the paramount's alleged right of escheat, in the face of an actual adoption, the gulf was enormous. The Supreme Government had shrunk from spanning it in the Oodeypore case, and had contented itself with withholding recognition of the act during the life-time of the offender. Nor was this in anywise inconsistent, even with the now strengthening policy. *Fieri non debet, factum valet,* is a rule often available in our law. Hindoo jurists, as we have seen, are agreed that notice to the ruling power is no legal essential to the validity of adoption.

Over this gulf, in the Sattara case, the late Governor-General leapt, so to speak, at a bound. There were two claimants by adoption, one through the dethroned, one through the late reigning Raja. Not a shadow of doubt could be cast on the formality of either adoption in itself. The Governor-General treated it as clear that the boy adopted by the late Raja, "in justice, and as his right, ought to succeed as heir to the personal and private property of the prince who adopted him." If such provision should not be sufficient, he recommended that a stipend should be allowed to the boy out of the revenues of the state. He recommended equally that "some provision should be made" for the maintenance of the boy adopted by the dethroned Raja. But he treated it as a general rule, established "beyond cavil or doubt," that adoption by a prince "is of no power or effect whatever in constituting him heir to the principality or to sovereign rights until the adoption so made has received the sanction of the sovereign power, with whom it rests to give or refuse it." And, without saying, in fact, one single word as to the rights of collaterals, beyond referring to the "near relationship" of the adoptive son of the dethroned Raja "to the late and ex-Raja,"—he jumped to the conclusion, that Sattara ought to be annexed.*

I have shewn elsewhere† the enormous fallacy of concluding from the power of consent to the power of confiscation; how it would authorize the appropriation of partnership interests by copartners, of shares in a public company by Boards of Directors, of the fortunes of wards by their guardians, of the fee-simple by a tenant for life. I might multiply such instances to a perfectly wearisome extent. It is the leading one of the two fallacies on which Lord Dalhousie's minute is founded. The other is the equally monstrous one as to the words "heirs and successors."

"The words 'heirs and successors' must be read *in their ordinary sense, in the sense in which they are employed in other treaties between states;* and in the absence of all evidence or reasonable presumption, founded on known facts, or on some special wording of the English instrument, in favour of a wider interpretation, these words cannot be construed to secure to the Raja of Sattara *any other than the succession of heirs natural,* or to grant them the right of adopting successors to the Raj without that sanction of the sovereign state, which may be given or may be withheld, and which by ordinary

---

* Sattara Annexation Papers, pp. 100-105.

† British India, its races and its history, vol. ii. p. 259.

and invariable practice, is necessary to the validity of such an act of adoption by the prince."

Words absolutely fail an English lawyer to express his sense of the ignorance of English constitutional law and history which such a passage exhibits. In plain language it is something very closely approaching—of course quite unintentionally—to high treason; and in old times men have been hanged, drawn, and quartered for less. It is plain that by "heirs *natural*," the Governor-General meant "*lineal* heirs," (though the blunder is already one that most well educated men would be ashamed of committing), since, as before observed, he did not allude to the claims of collaterals. Thus, "heirs and successors," according to his Lordship, in their "ordinary sense," and as "employed in other treaties," mean lineal heirs,—heirs of the body. *Argal,* since Queen Victoria was not lineal heir to William IV. every enactment in an act of Parliament, every clause in a treaty, dated previously to her accession, which speaks of an obligation to be fulfilled within the realm by or towards any deceased monarch, his heirs and successors,—which speaks of the relation of a foreign monarch and his subjects with such a deceased English monarch his heirs and successors and their subjects, is at an end. In other words, all internal government, all international security, is swept away by the accident of a death. By such fallacies has India been governed.

Of course, when a Governor-General thus expresses himself, one need not wonder at any language whatsoever from the lips of a subordinate official. Mr. Les-

* Sattara Annexation Papers, p. 102.

tock R. Reid, for instance, (now a Director of the East India Company) may go unscathed for the nonce, who with delicious *aplomb* says, "In the present instance we need consider only the first term used, that of 'heirs.' *We can have no concern with a successor who is not an heir,*"*—or again: "Our treaty of 1819, was with Pertaub Sing, his heirs and successors. *All his ancestry, and those springing from them, are passed by,*"†—as if the world had ever seen such a thing as a treaty with a man "his heirs and ancestors!" The most lamentable fact connected with the matter, as shewing the sort of training which Indian officials must have received, is—as I have before observed—that the persons who insist on the escheat, from the Governor-General downwards, all rely upon the English version, while those who contend against the escheat—Sir George Clerk, Mr. St. George Tucker, Captain Shepherd, Major Oliphant, Mr. Leslie Melville,—all suffer themselves to be entangled in the question of the native versions, apparently ignorant that the English one was conclusive in their favour.‡

* Sattara Annexation Papers, p. 82. † Ibid. p. 83.

‡ I have spoken of the ignorance manifested by Indian officials with respect to English constitutional law and history. What shall we say to Mr. Willoughby, who grounds England's relation as lord paramount to the Sattara state, amongst other things, upon her position "as successor to the Peishwas, the *de facto* rulers of the Mahrattas," (Sattara Annexation Papers, p. 90)—it being notorious that the Peishwas ruled as ministers to the Rajas of Sattara, and to use Lord Hastings' words, kept up "the farce of asking once a year the orders of the Raja." If this is the relation of "lord paramount" in any sense in which an honest man has a right to call it so, then may I lock up my next door neighbour (being a bachelor) in his house,

There is indeed one strong contrast between the Governor-General and the other apologists for the annexation, which we must not overlook. Their arguments generally turn more or less confusedly upon the qnestion whether the Sattara state was to be considered or not as sovereign. Mr. Mangles alone seems to have seen the question clearly; and in an elaborate paper endeavoured to prove that it could not. "I have taken pains," he writes, "to establish this position of the dependency of Sattara upon the British Government, by what appear to me conclusive proofs, because upon that point absolutely hinges the question whether that Government possess the right to be consulted in respect to the adoption of a son by the late Raja, and to give or to withhold, at its discretion, its consent to that measure." He had said before that "if the Raja were created a sovereign in the ordinary acceptation of the term, he was unquestionably competent to adopt a successor to his royal rights, as well as an heir of his personal property." It will be seen that, although Sir Charles Metcalfe's minute is not referred to, the distinction here taken is precisely the one which is established; and here, even more strongly than in the case of Colaba, we see the mischiefs to which it leads,—the special pleading with respect to facts which it begets, in order to escape from the plain words of a treaty.* The Governor-General, whilst adopting

and on his death without issue, (by starvation or otherwise) lawfully succeed to his property by right of escheat as "lord paramount" over him. Lord Dalhousie endorsed the fallacy. (Sattara Annexation Papers, p. 102.)

* I do not choose to discuss the question so elaborately treated by Mr. Mangles, of the *degree* of independence of the Satara Raja. The treaty forms a written contract, far too plain to admit of any

Mr. Willoughby's reasonings as to the need of the sanction of the British Government to the adoption, as the "lord paramount of the state of Sattara," went far beyond in the principles which he laid down. In his despatch of the 30th August, 1848, setting forth the general policy of annexation, he pronounced himself openly against sanctioning any adoption, otherwise than exceptionally:

"While I would not seek to lay down any inflexible rule with respect to adoption, I hold that *on all occasions where heirs natural,*

---

importation of extrinsic evidence into its construction. But it is instructive to look back at Lord Hastings's views, at the time of the restoration of the Sattara state, as they come out, in their most genuine form, in his newly published "Private Journal."

"February 28th, (1818.) . . The capture of Sattarah is useful, from the position of the fort; but it is further so *from the habitual contemplation of that place by the Mahrattas as the heart of their empire. The Raja of Sattarah is the hereditary sovereign of the Mahrattas;* and though held a prisoner by the Peishwa, who (like the French maires du Palais) usurped the powers of government, he is still nominally the chief. . . . Aware of the probability that we should endeavour to give the Raja *an independent sovereignty,* the Peishwa on his flight from Poonah took the unfortunate prince, who is only fourteen years of age, out of the fort, and has been dragging the young man about with him." (Private Journal, vol. ii. pp. 281, 282.)

"March 9th. . . What was still more important, the Raja of Sattarah and his family fell into our hands. If their exultation upon finding themselves transferred from the Peishwa (by whom they feared to be murdered) to us, with whom they believed their lives to be safe, was great, their astonishment was not less, when they were informed that we meant *to raise the Raja to an independent sovereignty.* The Peishwa was aware that such was likely to be our policy." (Ibid. pp. 290-2.)

Poor Lord Hastings! how little he knew his own intentions, as compared with Mr. Mangles.

shall fail, the territory should be made to lapse, and adoption should not be permitted, excepting in those cases in which some strong political reason may render it expedient to depart from this general rule."*

And he openly declared, in words already quoted, that "such is the general principle which ought to guide the conduct of the British Government in its disposal"—not of dependent, but—"of *independent states.*" The majority of the Court of Directors, however, having preferred to subscribe to Mr. Mangles's system of special-pleading away the independence of the native states one by one, it would seem that his Lordship himself saw the advantage of falling back upon it, as will be seen in other annexation cases. But it would be folly to blind oneself as to the breadth of the foregone conclusion which will from henceforth form the starting-point of his reasonings in such cases, or to overlook the fact, that the Sattara annexation had established a precedent, capable of sustaining any possible superstructure of annexation by escheat. In the Jhansee case, it was found convenient to recur to Mr. Mangles's reasonings, and to Sir Charles Metcalfe's distinction between "dependent" and "independent" states. The words "heirs and successors," as I have shewn ere this, occur in the Jhansee treaty, as in the Sattara one. The Raja of Jhansee, like him of Sattara, had adopted a cousin. The Governor-General this time expended a considerable amount of argument upon the proof that Jhansee was "a dependent principality, in like manner as, and even more distinctly than Sattara;" that "it was held by a chief under a very recent

* Sattara Annexation Papers, p. 103.

grant from the British Government as sovereign;"—that "it was therefore liable to lapse to the Government that gave it on the failure of heirs male."* I need not, I trust, myself dwell upon these arguments, seeing that they simply reproduce the Sattara ones. On one point, however, they are even more fallacious. The Raja of Sattara was only a nominal sovereign when we made him a real one. The chief of Jhansee on the contrary was, at the time we entered into the treaty referred to, by right or wrong, the actual ruler of his territories; we had ourselves treated with his predecessor thirteen years before; he was already hereditary,† at the time when we so "acknowledged" and "constituted" him. To speak of this as a "grant"

* Jhansee Annexation Papers, p. 20. Sir Charles Metcalfe is here quoted, but as if his minute of the 28th October, 1837, applied only to Bundelcund: "In reference to the chiefs of Bundelcund, Sir Charles Metcalfe wrote thus,"—"the particular rules laid down for successions in Bundelcund by Sir C. Metcalfe." Any one who chooses to look back at the despatch, will see that it is as general as possible. But however convenient its generalization as to dependent sovereignties might have proved, its generalization as to independent ones was extremely inconvenient to all annexationists. So it was quietly restricted to Bundelcund.—The orange is sucked; fling it aside.

† "November 9th. I remained in the same camp, and received the young subahdar of Jhansee. As the title implies, the chiefs of that territory were only officers entrusted by the Peishwa with the temporary command of the district; but one of them, who was a man of head as well as of courage, *succeeded in making the subahdarship hereditary in his family*, maintaining in other respects towards the Peishwa relations of fealty with some pecuniary payments. The subahdar is now our feudatory."—Lord Hastings's Private Journal, vol. ii. p. 235.

from the British Government of the principality, of the liability of that principality to lapse "to the government that *gave* it," is surely a gross abuse of terms.

The Nagpore case was in one sense less extreme than the two former ones. There was no adoption by the sovereign; only widows possessing the right to adopt. In other respects it was far more so, for the claims of Nagpore to be deemed an independent state, with unlimited rights of adoption in its sovereigns, were far greater than any yet considered. General (then Colonel) Low, member of council, in two minutes which will constitute his best claim to be remembered,* expressly states his full belief, that Lord Hastings "considered the Raja whom he placed on the throne of Nagpore in 1818, to be in possession of precisely the same rights, both present and future, respecting heirs and successors," as if his predecessor had never offended. He shews that Mr. Cavendish, when Resident in 1837, was the first person who ever started the idea that the late Raja could be precluded from adopting.† He quotes the careful expression of opinion, in 1840, of the next Resident, Major Wilkinson, to the contrary. Major Wilkinson, "after the most mature deliberation," could not come to any conclusion as re-

* Nagpore Annexation Papers, p. 39—51.

† Mr. Cavendish was perhaps the real originator of the Sattara annexation. His words, as quoted by General Low, are, "The territories of *Nagpore*, Mysore, and *Sattara*, were granted by the Honourable Company, and no one but a descendant of the grantee ought to succeed, or can by the laws of the land advance any just claim to the succession." All the Reid-Willoughby-Dalhousie-Mangles' sophistry in the Sattara case is here prefigured in brief.

spects the treaty, than that the late Raja "was placed in the exact position Appa Sahib was removed from, which was that of an independent prince, possessing the same power and authority as any other independent prince in India;" that "as such he entered into a treaty of alliance with the British Government, on the 1st December, 1826, which treaty was subsequently modified by the treaty of the 26th December, 1829;" that, "by neither of these treaties did he relinquish any right, in failure of sons legitimate, to adopt. If therefore other independent princes or their widows have the power to adopt," he continued, "it seems to me that he or his widow has the same,"—"for, if we had intended to restrict the succession to the lineal male descendants of his Highness the Rajah, such would have been expressed in one or other of the treaties referred to." General Low himself expresses his full concurrence with Major Wilkinson on all these points. Nay, the Governor-General in Council, in 1844, had admitted by implication the right of adoption (at least in the Raja himself), by instructing the then Resident, Colonel Speirs, "in the event of the death of the present Raja without leaving children *or an adopted son*," to make arrangements for conducting the government, pending the orders of the government of India, which orders would be "based on the circumstances that may present themselves at the time, *and the right to make the adoption which might be considered to attach to any surviving member of the Raja's family*,"* whilst

* Lord Dalhousie says of this passage, "Thus, no recognition of the right of adoption was made, but the question was left entirely open!"

Mr. Jenkins, in his Report submitted to the government of India iu 1826, had laid down as a "maxim generally acknowledged" in Nagpore, that "on the death of a Raja, leaving no male heir, it is the privilege of his principal widow to adopt a child from the relations of her husband, to succeed him."

The difficulty of treating Nagpore as a dependent state was very great. The difficulty of absolutely denying the right of adoption, in respect to it, was very great also. Both were passed by in the boldest manner.

"The case of Nagpore," the Governor-General declared, "stands wholly without precedent...We have not now to decide any question which turns upon the right of a paramount power to refuse confirmation to an adoption by an inferior. We have before us no question of an inchoate, or incomplete, or irregular adoption. The question of the right of Hindoo princes to adopt is not raised at all by recent events at Nagpore, for the Rajah has died, and has deliberately abstained from adopting an heir. His widow has adopted no successor. The state of Nagpore, conferred by the British Government in 1818, on the Rajah and his heirs, has reverted to the British Government on the death of the Rajah without any heir. The simple question for determination is, whether the sovereignty of Nagpore, which was bestowed as a gift upon a Goojur by the British Government in 1818, shall now be conferred upon somebody else, as a gift a second time.

Justice, and custom, and precedent leave the Government wholly unfettered to decide as it thinks best. Policy alone must decide the question."†

Perhaps all my readers do not at once perceive the fallacy of this argumentation. A little reflection will shew, that while professing to consider the question of

* Nagpore Annexation Papers, p. 23. † Ibid. p. 30.

the independent character of the Nagpore state as immaterial, it is in fact entirely devised to meet the case of its independence.

For if Nagpore were a dependent state, then, according to the (supposed) established rule, since actual adoption was void as against the paramount power, the right to adopt must have been so equally, and there was no need of a minute 16 pages long. But if it were independent, then a precedent for annexation had to be created, and Lord Dalhousie's precedent implies the new sophism, that a power is null until it is exercised. For if the state was independent, and the widow had a right to adopt—as, I think, by this time, it will at least be admitted that there is fair ground for contending—then such right, if exercised, must prevail against the British Government. But, said his Lordship, on the 28th January 1854—the Raja having died on the 11th December 1853, only a few weeks previously—the widow "has adopted no successor." Therefore "policy alone must decide the question."

(Property is devised to a man, with remainder to such persons as he shall appoint, or in default of his appointment, to such persons as his widow surviving him shall appoint. He dies and makes no appointment. For seven weeks after his death his widow makes none. Imagine the original testator's heir at law resuming the property,—not temporarily until any appointment by the widow, but absolutely,—on the ground that as she has not appointed, "justice" leaves him "wholly unfettered to decide as he thinks best," and that "policy [illegible]ne must decide the question," whether he shall [illegible] her to do so or not! Is not this the Nagpore case, if the widow—and the British Government—had really any right?)

Nor can I pass under silence a passage in the minute of Mr. Halliday, then member of Council, since Lieutenant-Governor of Bengal, whom one is sorry to find in such bad company. We have seen the strenuous and successful efforts of Colonel Sutherland, while agent in Rajpootana, to preserve the right of adoption to Hindoo sovereigns and their widows. We are now quietly told that this is quite exceptional. Colonel Low, says Mr. Halliday, "announces a doctrine regarding succession to a Hindoo principality, which, *except as regards Rajpoot states*, I never heard of before, which I am satisfied no Hindoo lawyer ever heard of, and which would make it impossible that any Hindoo succession should ever fail." And again, "No Rajpoot prince could suffer any apprehension from this precedent, because *a different rule is avowedly allowed and followed in cases of Rajpoot succession*."* The announcement by Mr. Halliday, that he never heard before of a widow's right to adopt, except as regards Rajpoot states, (for this is what, I presume, he refers to) when compared with the authorities quoted above, will probably seem a strange one. But what should be noticed, is the skilful way in which annexationists dispose of adverse precedents. Sir Charles Metcalfe sketches out, in the broadest way, principles of succession as to jagheers on the one hand, and independent states on the other. They are treated—as soon as they become inconvenient—as "particular rules laid down for successions in Bundelcund." Colonel

* Nagpore Annexation Papers, pp. 51-3.

Sutherland succeeds in enforcing the application of Hindoo law and custom within the limits of his functions. This is treated equally as a rule "allowed and followed in cases of Rajpoot succession." Everything, in a word, is stretched or shrunk to the convenience of the annexationist.

There is another instance of invasion upon the right of adoption, very similar to that of Nagpore, that of Tanjore.

This also, as we have seen, was the case of a treaty with a prince, his "heirs and successors," and one involving the question of the right of adoption by widows. Bnt the Raja's dominions, instead of comprising an extensive territory like that of Nagpore, were confined to a fort and some villages. It was of course far less difficult to set aside the alleged right in such a case. But its consideration must not be omitted, as it extended the application of the anti-adoption policy to the far south of India—to another branch of the great Mahratta family, already struck at by that policy at Sattara, Jhansee, Nagpore, Bithoor. And it is moreover remarkable, as an instance of the manner in which the East India Company was wont to use opposite pleas in the same case, according to the object to be attained. The Court of Directors, in their despatch approving of the extinction of the principality, three times speak of the Rajaship of Tanjore as "titular." Lord Dalhousie's despatch of the 22nd January 1856, has reported the death of the "titular Raja." The Resident has proposed to recognize a daughter as successor to the "titular dignity." It is out of the question that they should perpetuate "a titular principality." Two years have not elapsed, and we find the Company in the Supreme Court defending the confiscation of all the Raja's private property, on the ground that he was "an absolute sovereign."* I shall have to revert to these proceedings.

If we now look back to the bearing upon the question of succession by adoption of Lord Dalhousie's eight years of rule, we find the following results:

The class of states which are assimilated to jagheers for the purpose of excluding adoption, was widened to include every state endowed, reconstituted or confirmed by the British Government;

The right of widows to adopt was treated as non-existent while yet unexercised, without reference to the character of the state itself;

Adoptions formally made were set aside for the purpose of enforcing escheats;

A course of policy was laid down, according to which "on all occasions where heirs natural shall fail," native states should be "made to lapse."

The British Government was declared to be "bound not to put aside or to neglect such rightful opportunities of acquiring territory or revenue as may from time to time present themselves."

Adverse precedents, such as those of Metcalfe or Sutherland, were treated as restricted to particular provinces of India.

What further invasions of the Hindoo law of succession were practised, I shall have to shew in my next.

* See Mr. Norton's Rebellion in India, pp. 111, 112, and his "Case of the Tanjore Ranee, pp. 5, 12, &c.

LETTER X.

HOW THE ANNEXATION POLICY DEALT WITH RIGHTS OF SUCCESSION BY BLOOD OR MARRIAGE.

WE cannot confine our views of the invasions upon the Hindoo law of succession practised by the annexation policy to the right of adoption only. That right is one so important in the eyes of the Hindoo, from its religious bearings, that it tends entirely to overshadow those of a purely civil character. Hence the frequency of adoptions of the nearest male collateral; the occurrence of cases in which the successor by birth goes through the form of passing through the arms of the widow of a deceased prince, in order to rank as his adopted son. We must therefore realize the fact, that in default of successions by lineal descent, successions by adoption among the Hindoos have been *the rule*, successions by collateral descent or other title altogether the exception; that therefore, while the tie of kinship has been carefully kept up, for the purpose of matrimonial connexion, eligibility to adoption where the field is restricted by custom, &c., the precise right of every individual kinsman has been hitherto a matter of far lesser importance in the eyes of a Hindoo as compared with our European notions.

It is entirely owing to this, I firmly believe, that the British system of annexation by right of escheat was able to go on so swimmingly for a time. The collateral or other claimant has been so accustomed to stand behind the claimant by adoption, that he did not think of putting himself forward; it would almost have seemed a sacrilege to him to do so. Thus, when the right of the one was swept away, the right of the other has shared the same fate. But it is obvious that the tendency of the anti-adoption system is primarily to set up the rights of those other claimants. I have already pointed out that the substitution of such claimants for claimants by adoption is one at bottom not favourable to English influence; since it is putting a dry legal right in the place of one which by custom is bound up with some kind of sanction by the paramount power. And as soon as the natives of India clearly understand that we do mean permanently to break in upon their law of succession by adoption, let us rest assured that other claims will start up under our feet, in greater plenty than we could have wished.

A little reflection will indeed shew the enormous improbability that death without heirs can ever take place among any class of men at the rate at which it would seem to have occurred among Indian sovereigns of late years. Let any one consult his own experience; nothing is more unfrequent. I might say that, technically, escheats are almost unknown to the law in practice, except in the case of illegitimate children, who have no lawful heirs but lineal ones. Nor is this owing to the right of testamentary disposition, or to the extreme concentration of landed property amongst us; for if we look to personal succession, where intestacy is of daily occurrence, how seldom is it that the Crown has ever established a claim to personalty as *bona vacantia!* We may hear every now and then of a locked-up fortune, pending the discovery of next of kin to some runaway errand boy who has become a *millionnaire* on the other side of the globe. We may see advertisements in the "Times" calling on the next of kin of Jones or Thompson to make their appearance. But is it conceivable that a sovereignty should go a-begging for want of claimants—with title enough and to spare?

Suspicion therefore meets us, so to speak, on the very threshold of any annexation by right of lapse. Is it possible, we must ask—even were the adoption and its peculiar consequences entirely out of the way—that sufficient inquiry can have been made, that due notice can have been given to claimants, that their claims can have been fully weighed? Is it possible that English fair play can have been allowed by an English government, to all and sundry who might speak up against its own claim? One would think that no precaution would be omitted by honourable men to make sure of the right in such a case. The most careful legal opinions should be taken, before any claim is shut out; if the technical right is to be enforced by the supreme power, all the majesty of the law would not be too much to shew that that technical right is on its side. But where do we see a trace of any such practice in late annexations? A report or despatch from the Resident or other political—perhaps a paper from some subordinate—such is the staple evidence; if a petition from a Ranee is appended, it will be all that appears on the other side. The Judges are Governors, Councillors, Governors-General, Directors, Presidents of the Board of Control. Of really disinterested, of really judicial investigation, there is not a trace. Every decision is visibly tainted with an interest; if now and then some one rises above it, all honour to the giver of it!

To suspicion as to the fact of lapse we must add, therefore, suspicions tenfold greater as to the mode of ascertaining it. And now let us see whether the evidence before us—the *ex parte* evidence of the Blue-books—does not justify such suspicions.

For this is evident, that in every single instance of annexation on lapse, there *were* collateral claimants. How the rights of these were dealt with, let the Sattara case shew. Lord Dalhousie, Mr. Willoughby, simply left them on one side, treating the question as one between the British Government and the adoptive son only. Mr. Reid, more clumsily, stumbled over the fact of their existence, and disposed of it in this manner:

> "Our treaty of 1819 was with Pertaub Sing, his heirs and successors. All his ancestry, and those springing from them, were passed by. No right was confirmed to them. The other branches of the family springing from Kelojee Babjee, the great-grandfather of Sevajee . . . have no part in the settlement. They might perhaps claim the titular dignity of Raja of Sattara, but they can have no pretension to the territorial sovereignty which was created in favour of Pertaub Sing. By the arrangement of 1839, his brother was specially admitted to the benefit of that settlement." . . *

To which reasoning this simple answer has to be returned: It is *false*,—false in its premises, false in its conclusion.

Let us test this by a simple example.

* Sattara Annexation Papers, p. 83.

Mr. Reid writes on the 25th April 1848. Three days before (22nd April 1848) Her Majesty's assent was given to an act "for the better security of the crown and government of the United Kingdom" (11 and 12 Vict. c. 12). It enacts (s. 2) "that if any person whatsoever after the passing of this act shall, within the United Kingdom or without, compass, imagine, invent, devise, or intend to deprive or depose our Most Gracious Lady the Queen, *her heirs and successors*, from the style, honour, or royal name of the Imperial Crown of the United Kingdom, or of any other of Her Majesty's dominions and countries, or to levy war against Her Majesty, *her heirs or successors*, . . . or to arouse or stir any foreigner or stranger with force to invade the United Kingdom, or any other Her Majesty's dominions or countries under the obeisance of Her Majesty, *her heirs or successors*, and such compassings, &c., or any of them shall express, utter or declare, by publishing any printing or writing, &c., every person so offending shall be guilty of felony, and being convicted thereof, shall be liable, at the discretion of the Court, to be transported beyond seas for the term of his natural life, &c."

I shall not stop here to examine how far Mr. Reid's minute may come within the letter of the enactment. But let us suppose,—which God forbid!—a failure of issue of Her Majesty, and the accession, we will say, of the Duke of Cambridge or some of his descendants. Imagine an offence against this act under the new reign, and the offender brought to trial. Imagine the countenances in Westminster Hall,—I will not say even of the judges, but above all of the prisoner and his attorney, when his counsel, well versed in Indian minutes, gets up and delivers himself somewhat after this fashion:

"Gentlemen of the jury, I submit that whatever facts may be proved against my client, you will unhesitatingly record a verdict of acquittal in his favour. The case lies in a nutshell. He is indicted under an act passed in the reign of Her late Majesty Queen Victoria, directed against persons who should devise the deposal of that Queen, her 'heirs or successors,'—who should levy war against her, her 'heirs or successors.' Well, what then? The act was passed for the protection of that Queen, her heirs or successors. But—to use the words of a late illustrious Indian statesman—'all her ancestry, and those springing from them, were passed by.' No protection was given to them. The other branches of the family, springing from her grandfather, 'have no part in the settlement.' I am far from denying the title of His present gracious Majesty to the crown of England. He may claim this 'titular dignity'; but he 'can have no pretension' to the rights which were created in favour of Queen Victoria. Practically speaking, no doubt, His Majesty is the successor to that Queen. But, to use always the words of the high authority before quoted, "we can have no concern with a successor who is not an heir."

Is there a man out of Bedlam who would expect an acquittal on such a plea? Yet on such pleas are Indian sovereignties annexed. I am really ashamed of reasoning upon points like these. But I remember the money, the misery, the lives which they have cost, and may cost yet, and I resume my tedious task, till such time as I shall see England roused to a due sense of the enormities which have been committed—may yet be attempted—in her name.*

That the word heirs confers a fee simple, or in other words an absolute estate, belongs as a cardinal principle to English jurisprudence. It never has been

* Perhaps I may be told that my reasoning is beside the point; that the question is one of native law. Native law and custom are indeed the cloud under which the goddess of annexation (the "Maha Kalee of Annexation," as she is already called in India) frequently shelters her darlings when hard pressed, though, as in the Sattara case, they repudiate the shelter with contempt when they think they can do without it. I have not here space to go into the question. But I assert after examination that the whole argument upon native law turns upon the two following sophisms, the first of which rests on a perversion of Sir Charles Metcalfe's distinction:

Jagheers are dependent sovereignties;

Jagheers are granted in tail male, and escheat for want of male issue to the grantee;

Therefore, all dependent sovereignties are grants in tail male, and escheat for want of male issue to the grantee;

And:

Jagheers are created by grant;

Jagheers descend in tail male, and escheat for want of male issue to the grantee;

Therefore, all sovereignties created by grant descend in tail male, and escheat for want of issue to the grantee.

Whereby it would be just as easy to prove, from the fact that Sir Jeffrey Hudson was a dwarf, that all men are dwarfs; or from the fact that fishes breathe by gills, that all animals do so.

I need hardly observe that the two facts of an inheritance being dependent, and of its descending only to male issue, have the same well-known connexion as Tenterden Steeple and Goodwin Sands. Thus copyholds are an essentially dependent inheritance, but the bulk of copyholds descend in fee.

supposed that the words meant only "issue of the first taker." A man comes into possession of an estate "to him and his heirs," it matters little whether by purchase or devise. He has no parents living; no children; only nephews or cousins. Is there a boy or girl above twelve years of age in the neighbourhood who does not know that if he dies without a will, a nephew or a cousin will succeed? Say that the estate is Lestock Park,—that the devisee in fee dies intestate, leaving for next heir a second cousin, Mr. Lestock Reid. Would Mr. Reid submit meekly, if told that he had no claim, since "all the devisee's ancestry, and those springing from them, were passed by in the devise"?

Such then is a type of the reasoning upon which the claims of heirs by blood are set aside on annexation. The story of Sattara is in principle that of Jhansee, of Nagpore, as indeed that of Colaba, of Mandavie were already. The extraordinary notion pervades them all, that a sovereignty can only pass to the lineal heirs of the first taker.* And in order to

* So absolutely contrary is this to the rules of English law, that until of late years the broad distinction between title by "descent" and "purchase,"—the latter word meaning simply "personal acquisition,"—was that land owned by a purchaser was inheritable indifferently among the descendants of any ancestor, whilst land owned by descent was inheritable only in the line of descent to or from the original purchaser. (Blackstone's Commentaries, p. 243.) So that the very fact of the Sattara raj, we will say, having been set up by the British, rendered all the relatives of the first Raja by an ancestor capable of inheriting, whilst the son of the first Raja could only claim through his father. And the alteration which has been introduced into our law by the statute "for the amendment of the law of

square treaties to the notion, the two following means are used: First the word "successors" is treated as surplusage; Next, the word "heirs" is construed to mean "issue." In other words, the corporate character of sovereignty is first reduced to a private inheritance, then that inheritance from being a fee-simple is cut down to a fee-tail. We need not wonder if annexations by right of lapse have become frequent of late years.

In the Sattara case in particular, these monstrosities told with peculiar force. For, apart from any consideration of adoption, the claims of collaterals had been long present to the people's minds, and had been even, to all appearance, officially recognized. On the deposal of the first Raja, the enthronement of his brother, under a treaty which simply confirmed the previous one, so far as its articles were not abrogated or modified, and which did not touch upon the question of succession, was itself the most obvious recognition of such claims, whatever Mr. Reid might say about the brother being "specially admitted to the benefit" of the treaty. But in addition to this brother, there was a cousin (Balla Sahib Sennaputtee), of whom it had been written as early as 1833 in the *Asiatic Journal*, that he was "the man on whom all fix their eyes," if the first Raja should die without issue. Sir Robert Grant, when Governor of Bombay in 1837,

inheritance," (3 and 4 Wm. IV. c. 106) has been to extend the operation of title by purchase. Every Indian civilian is supposed to have read English law at Haileybury. I must say that members of Indian Councils evince a rare power of forgetting what they should thus have learnt.

had spoken of both the brother and the cousin as being "in the immediate line of succession;" of the cousin as being, after the two brothers, "the proper representative of the family." It was this very cousin whose son the deposed Raja adopted.* And it would be amusing, if it were not painful, to observe the quoting against this child of that very Hindoo law of adoption which was being set aside,—one of its rules being that the adopted son loses all claim to the inheritance of his real father. Turned into plain English, the argument stands thus: The adoptive heir cannot succeed, because the adoption is not sanctioned. The heir by blood cannot succeed, because there is an adoption. In other words, the adoption is void against the British Government, good in its favour. No doubt by virtue of the well-known legal rule: "Heads I win, tails you lose."

But this is not all. The claims of Balla Sahib and of his children, according to Mr. Frere, the last Sattara Resident, were not really the primary claims by blood. Although the relationship was unquestionable, there were at least *thirty* branches nearer of kin than the one to which those claimants belonged. And the Resident,—with boldness most unusual,—thus wrote (23rd September 1848):—

* "And why not the father?" some one may ask. Because, when accompanying the deposed Raja to Benares, under the charge of a Lieutenant Cristall, being taken dangerously ill, he had sent to request a halt, as being too ill to be moved, and the Lieutenant had refused the request, "imagining it only an excuse for loitering on the road." The Prince died on the road that day, the Lieutenant was reprimanded.

8. "I would take this opportunity of respectfully, but *very earnestly*, pressing on Government the risk of pronouncing any final decision, whether in favour of one adoption against another, or of the British Government against both, and against all other claimants, without allowing any party whose claim may be negatived the fullest possible opportunity, not only of himself stating the grounds of his own claim, but of answering all objections.

9. There is at present, as far as I am aware, no claimant to be heir of the late Raja, who would think his own claim sufficiently strong to be put in competition with that of an adopted son of either the late Raja or his brother; because all other relations, who might otherwise be claimants, believe both adoptions to be regular.

10. *But there are many who might have asserted their claim, had no adoption taken place; and who may possibly assert it now, should they hear that both adoptions are invalidated;* and ANY OF THEM, as far as I can judge of the facts of the case before me, would, were other competitors, save the British Government, out of the field, *be able to establish a very good prima facie claim,* IN ANY COURT OF JUSTICE IN INDIA, *to be the Raja's heir by blood,* AS AGAINST THE BRITISH GOVERNMENT, in its character of heir to all who die leaving no natural heirs* of their own; which appears to me the only character in which our Government can, consistently with the treaty, lay claim to the Sattara state.

11. None of these claims having yet been put forward, none of them can have been tested; and the case of the adopted sons is not very different. They have as yet had no opportunity, as far as I am aware, of stating the precise grounds on which they claim to be heirs, nor for meeting the objections of those who deny that any adopted son can be heir in the sense intended by the treaty till recognized by Government.

12. It may be that both sides of the case have been already very fully argued in the proceedings of Government; but *no man is likely to admit the justice of a decision which negatives a claim to an inheritance, when his case has been nowhere stated but by the counsel for*

---

* Mr. Frere, it is clear, does not confound "natural heirs" with "lineal."

his opponent, and when he, the defeated party, has had no opportunity of answering the objections taken to his claim.

13. Moreover, in the possible case of the ultimate decision being in favour of the lapse to the British Government, that opponent will have necessarily been judge in his own case. It is surely not desirable to add to the necessary and inevitable invidiousness of such a position, the circumstance of the judge having been also the self-constituted counsel for the defeated party."*

Of course it is difficult to see, after an annexation on pretence of lapse in the face of such a warning, what could possibly have thrown the "shadow of a doubt" upon the right of the British Government in any case whatsoever, in which it might please the ruling Governor-General to allege it.

The cases of Jhansee, of Nagpore, are reproductions in this respect of that of Sattara. At Jhansee, the adoptive son was himself a claimant by blood, and the representative in the male line of a branch of the family older to the one which had hitherto enjoyed the chiefship. There were, writes the Resident, two other claimants; one, a nephew by a sister of the chief with whom the treaty of 1817 was concluded; another, a representative in the male line of a branch junior to the reigning one, but more closely related. It was ruled, that as there was "no male heir whatever"—meaning, of course, "no male heir of the body," a very different thing—"of any raja or soobadar of Jhansee who has ruled since the first relations of the British Government with that state were formed," there was, "*therefore*, no male heir whatever existing to the hereditary chiefship of Jhansee."†

* Sattara Annexation Papers, p. 149.

† Jhansee Annexation Papers, p. 22.

At Nagpore, it will be seen from a genealogical tree supplied by the Resident, there were equally several collaterals, such as a nephew by adoption, son by adoption of a sister of the late Raja; two grandsons by blood in the female line of the same sister, a grandson by blood of a sister of the first Raja. It was actually declared, that there was "no male heir who by family or hereditary right" could claim to succeed,* the fact being that the late Raja was himself only a descendant *in the female line* of the late Raja, so that his grand-nephews,—of the elder of whom, Yeswunt Rao Ahey Rao, the Resident wrote, that he "would decidedly be preferred by the mass of the courtiers to any other youth for the musnud," that he was "amiable," "sensible," and "tractable"—would have claimed in precisely the same right as himself!†

The Tanjore case is remarkable, as introducing us to a new class of claimants, whom the setting aside of the right of adoption tends to call forth,—the widows, namely, of princes dying without issue, the senior of whom, it has since been clearly proved, is at least entitled to all the private property of her deceased husband. The Resident in this case, Mr. Forbes, in a letter of the 6th November, 1855, pointed out the remarkable fact, that in 1737 the widow of a deceased Raja of Tanjore was raised to the throne, and stated that he was informed that similar successions had taken place, at the latter end of the last century, both in Sattara and Kolapoor—twice indeed in the latter,—all three states moreover being not only Mahratta, but ruled over by

* Nagpore Annexation Papers, p. 36. † Ibid. p. 20.

different branches of one and the same family; whilst many like instances occur in Hindoo history. Singularly enough, however, Mr. Forbes concluded by recommending the maintaining the Raj in the person of a *daughter* of the last sovereign, dead without male issue. The Court of Directors in their despatch, overlooking (shall I say, carefully?) the widow's claim,—address themselves only to Mr. Forbes's recommendation, and declare that "by no law or usage has the daughter of a Hindoo Raja any right of succession to the Raj, and it is entirely out of the question that we should create such a right, for the sole purpose of perpetuating a *titular* principality." * But what has since happened? The claim of the senior widow to the private property has been heard before the Supreme Court of Madras, and has been unreservedly established. And although the Court was precluded from entering into the political question of the sovereignty, it is observable that the authorities quoted to prove the widow's right to the private property *go all to the case of the sovereignty itself.*†

In connexion with this case should be mentioned that of the Nawab of the Carnatic,—a Mussulman sovereignty, not therefore subject to the same rules of law as we have been lately considering—but in which, as we have seen,‡ the claims of an heir by blood, officially recognized as such by the Court of Directors on several occasions, were set aside.

"Even as a matter of policy," writes Mr. Norton, "let alone

---

* See Mr. J. B. Norton's "Rebellion in India," pp. 107—118.

† See Mr. J. B. Norton's "Case of the Tanjore Ranee."

‡ See ante, p. 49.

honesty, I fancy the Government would at the present moment give a good deal to have acknowledged the Nabob of the Carnatic; at least, the only danger which has been apprehended in Madras has been from the disaffected Mussulmen inhabitants of Triplicane, angry at the degradation of their prince, and poverty-stricken by the withdrawal of his resources."*

We see therefore that, slashingly as the Hindoo right of succession by adoption was treated by the annexation policy, rights of succession by blood or marriage fared scarcely better at its hands. In cases of Hindoo succession it happened indeed to refrain from attacking those of a lineal descendant in the male line, provided these could be traced to the founder of the house, or the prince first recognized by the British Government. But the claims of all collaterals, descended from a more remote ancestor, however well recognized the relationship; the claims of widows; the claims even of collaterals in the female line to a founder, where the last ruling prince was nothing more, were set aside.

It is evident that there was not a landholder in India who would not feel himself struck by the blow thus aimed at native princes. It may be,—I shall have to shew hereafter that this was the case,—that the rights of succession to private property had ere this been no less glaringly invaded than those of succession to thrones and chiefships; that the fallacies which we have seen practised upon sovereigns, had their precedents in those which had been practised upon subjects. But I apprehend that even if it were so, the absorption of private rights would become, not less, but more galling when

* Rebellion in India, p. 102.

magnified into the annexation of states and territories. *For this cut off all hope of better days.* The human mind is so blessedly constituted, that its tendency is always to limit its despairs, to discover ever new horizons of hope. Especially in ruder natures, it will curse the instrument that strikes, that it may yet hope for redress from the hand that wields it; it will curse the hand, and yet say, the head could not have meant the blow. Under the worst of tyrannies, the bulk of the suffering multitudes will always be found muttering to themselves, "If the prince only knew!" The full weight of despair only settles down upon the sufferers, when they are forced to identify their sufferings with the supreme power itself; when these are found to be but the logical and necessary consequence of a policy laid down from on high, and not a mere accident crying upwards for redress. Then, when there is no outlook beyond earthly things,—no deep faith that there is "One higher" than the highest of kings, to Whom vengeance belongeth, Who will repay,—every individual wrong seems multiplied by all other wrongs of the same class, swells at least to the proportions of that which is hugest; the pettiest dispossessed landholder becomes the type of a sovereign despoiled.

LETTER XI.

A SAMPLE OF THE DETAILS OF ANNEXATION:—NAGPORE.

BEFORE however we can fully appreciate what the new policy has yet to undo, it is necessary to go into the details of some particular annexation. Let us take, for instance, that of Nagpore. There is an issue of Parliamentary papers on the subject,* later in date than the one from which I have hitherto quoted. It will be seen from them how, by the 29th April, 1854, Mr. Mansel the Commissioner, and former Resident, admitted that the family of the late Raja "would prefer to retain the actual musnud in the hands of some heir selected by adoption;"† how he himself urged the maintenance of the state as a titular principality under British management, declaring that "it is the bitter cry on all sides that our rule exhibits no sympathy, especially for the native of rank, and not even for other classes of natives;" that "the improvement of the

* Return to an Order of the House of Commons, dated 22nd February, 1856, for copies or extracts "of the correspondence which has taken place between the Government of India and the Commissioner of Nagpore, relative to the annexation of the Berar territory to the British territory (in continuation of former returns);" ordered by the House of Commons to be printed, 5th March, 1856 (to be quoted as "Further Nagpore Annexation Papers").

† Further Nagpore Annexation Papers, p. 5.

native prince is in our own power;"* that the argument of the natives was that whatever blame might attach to the government of the late Raja should be shared by the British Residents themselves, for want of the due carrying out of the system of "advice and check" contemplated by the last treaty.† It will be seen with what "surprise and dissatisfaction" the Governor-General and his subservient Council treated his proposals;‡ how his Lordship cut down allowances to widows, minuted on the sale of jewels;§ how Mr. Mansel's name as Commissioner disappears henceforth from the record; what remonstrances were addressed to the Supreme Government by the Banka Baee, the head of the Nagpore family, and the widows, sometimes in person, sometimes by agents, declaring that there were "rightful heirs of the late Maharaja, and successors to the raj or kingdom and territory of Nagpore, entitled to succeed thereto, both according to the customs of the family and the Hindoo law;"‖ how all communications through agents were rejected, and communications from principals directed to be forwarded through the local officers; how the Ranees' agents were told that they "could not of course expect that the Commissioner would pass on any letter" from them to their own employers "in ignorance of its contents," and that their letters would be "unquestionably" returned if not transmitted unsealed;¶ what a hubbub was excited by the Ranees' sending "a vakeel to Nepaul," who turned out to be merely deputed to a

* Further Nagpore Annexation Papers, p. 6.

† Ibid. p. 7. ‡ Ibid. p. 9. § Ibid. pp. 10, 11.

‖ Ibid. p. 17, and passim. ¶ Ibid. p. 55.

former resident at Nagpore, transferred to Katmandoo, entreating him to interfere on their behalf. It will be seen how the sale of property was carried on from day to day amidst the protests of the Ranees;* how the removal of the royal armoury caused "great excitement in the city," and a native British official was maltreated in the palace, and a Free Kirk missionary in the streets by the mob; how finally the Banka Baee recalled her agents in England, and the matter ended with the Supreme Government's approval of the Nagpore Commissioner's proceedings (4th January, 1856).

There might be much to say on this story. But behind it lies another, not detailed in Blue-books, but believed in by the natives of India. I say not which is true; I would almost say, it matters little. For considering late annexations in their bearing upon English policy, on the morrow of a rebellion, I believe we should endeavour to view them, not as swathed mummies in a Parliamentary paper, but as bleeding corpses before the eyes of the multitude, with many a dark skinned Mark Antony to put tongues in every wound.

I have before me a letter addressed, on the the 20th February, 1856, by two agents of the Maharanees of Nagpore—one an Englishman—to the Secretary of the India Reform Society. It is accompanied by a copy of a memorial addressed, on the 26th December, 1855, by those princesses to the Governor-General.

* Such property usually goes for next to nothing, as the natives generally will not buy. The ranees in this instance complained that bullocks worth £10 went for 10*s*., and a horse worth £20 for £2. Further Nagpore Annexation Papers, p. 28.

The latter speaks of other memorials or communications already addressed, on the 18th April, on the 10th October, 1855, by them to the Court of Directors, only the last occurring in the Parliamentary papers. It is asserted in the first of these documents—against the Parliamentary papers—that "the late prince had long intended to adopt one of his near kinsmen, by name Iswunt Rao Ahee Rao." It is asserted—against the Parliamentary papers—that "*immediately* on the Maharaja's decease the Maharanees made known their lord's wishes on the subject to Mr. Mansel the Resident, . . . and that gentleman assured the Maharanees that he would make known their wishes to the Governor-General for the aforesaid Iswunt Rao Ahee Rao being placed on the throne." It is asserted that the princesses, satisfied with this assurance, . . . "were content to postpone the completion of such ceremony," and "with the concurrence of the Resident allowed Iswunt Rao Ahee Rao to perform the necessary funeral solemnities." It is asserted that "in hopeful confidence that their wishes and the intentions of the late Maharaja would be speedily carried out," the princesses "took no further steps in the matter," till in the middle of March, 1854, suddenly came the order for annexation. It is asserted that "in October, 1854, the palace of the Maharanees was surrounded by an armed force acting under the orders of the Commissioner, and the treasures and family jewels of the late Maharaja, estimated at the value of two millions sterling, were forcibly carried away, despite the protests of their Highnesses," and sold by public auction. It is asserted that the princesses had been subjected to personal indignities and annoyances; that they were prevented from holding intercourse "with any of the friends and advisers of the late Maharaja." It is asserted,—and this also is beyond denial—that "their devoted and confidential servant, Mahdoo Rao Tantyah and eight other persons of the highest respectability at Nagpore," one of them "a member of the Bosla family (that of the sovereign) were summarily imprisoned in the common city jail by order of the Commissioner, without being charged with any offence, or informed of any accusation being preferred against them;" that these persons were then in prison since the 21st August last.* It is asserted that the prisoners had been "offered their freedom by the Commissioner on the condition that they should give security not to interfere for the future in the affairs of their highnesses," and that "one individual, not included amongst the above, was actually released upon such security." It is asserted that "Major Ouseley, a retired officer of the Bengal establishment, who was on his way to Nagpore for the purpose of conducting the English correspondence of the Maharanees, was summarily arrested by the Commissioner, who only released him on his promise to quit the Nagpore territory." It is asserted "that four companies of Sepoys with their officers were on the same date stationed in the Maharanees' palace, forcibly preventing all ingress and egress." It is asserted that no effort had been spared by the Commissioner, through his subordinates, by intimi-

* In the Ranees' memorial of the 26th December, 1855, it is stated that "some of their most devoted servants had been placed under close surveillance since the 27th January last."

dation and threats to obtain the Maharanees' signature to such a document as would annul their own rights." It is asserted that, on the 2nd January, 1856, "a letter containing matter totally at variance with the known wishes of the Maharanees was prepared by the Commissioner's own people, and conveyed to the palace" by "the Commissioner's vakeel, and other faithless servants of the late Maharaja, to obtain the signature of the Maharanees,"—that "nine days after such letter was written, as appears by the date, these persons, by means of threats and intimidation, induced the Maharanee Banka Baee," who was "nearly 80 years of age," to sign such communication. The communication itself—a letter of recall—is annexed in a translated shape. It is a month later in date than one to the same effect inserted in the Parliamentary papers as of the 2nd December, 1855,* and varies from it in several particulars, especially in its bearing an attestation by Captain Crichton, Assistant Commissioner, who certifies that the Banka Baee sent for him to hear it read, that it was "read over to her and explained carefully" in his presence,—that she had made it a particular request that he should witness it,—that beyond witnessing it he had had "nothing whatever further to do with the matter."

A strange disclaimer, though one to which one would attach all faith, so far as Captain Crichton personally is concerned. The letter itself indeed—whether we take the private or Parliamentary date or version

* Further Nagpore Annexation Papers, p. 58.

of it as genuine—proves nothing after all, except that an aged woman, struck by a recent bereavement,—the death of Annapoorna Baee the Raja's chief widow,—has no heart for struggling with British omnipotence. There is no renunciation of the right of adoption, no disavowal of the alleged intentions of the Raja in that behalf. Such as it is, however, as we have seen, the Ranees' agents maintained that it was forced upon the Banka Baee,—one only out of five princesses whom they represented, though the acknowledged head of the family,—by the Commissioner's native subordinates. They alleged in proof,—a fact seemingly of much weight if true,—that the letter "is written, not on ordinary foolscap procurable in every bazaar, but on the paper of the Honourable East India Company," as shewn by the watermark, "which corresponds with that in use in the Commissioner's office, as proved by the official letters of that functionary."

This then is a version not to be found in Blue-books, though in many details supported by them, of the Nagpore annexation, and of the working of that "lively satisfaction" with which Lord Dalhousie, in his final minute, stated that it had been hailed "by the whole population of the province." Women trusting that the British Government will take steps respecting the adoption, and therefore forbearing to exercise their right, till they are surprised by the sudden fiat of absorption; protesting then against it; deprived by sudden arrests of the counsel of all their influential native friends, of the assistance of an English officer; themselves placed under *surveillance* in their palace, alarmed by the presence of four companies of

Sepoys, intimidated by native underlings into recalling their agents from Europe, finally casting themselves in despair on the mere mercy of the Governor-General,—such are some of the elements of that "perfect peace and contentment" which was described as prevailing. Nor is this all, for the belief in Nagpore undoubtedly was that actual adoption had taken place,* an impression founded on the fact that Iswunt Ahee Rao had been selected to perform the funeral ceremonies, both to the late Raja, and afterwards to his chief widow. I have had before me the details of the latter transaction, appended to a translated letter from a native confidential servant of the Ranees, dated 28th November 1855, (Annapoorna Baee, the chief widow, having died on the 14th), but am unable to say whether it would amount to a valid Hindoo adoption, though it is stated that on this occasion the youth was brought to the palace "with all the retinues of the late Maharaja," "accompanied by all the nobility of the city," and that all the ceremonies were performed "with the strictest customs and usages practised when a new Maharaja is installed on the guddee."

The same letter contains an account of the Maharanees' consent to recall their agents (two months nearly, it will be seen, previously to the date of the actual letter of recall). On hearing of this, one of the imprisoned nobles sent word to the Ranees that if they sent such a letter, as soon as released he would "kill

* This will be found stated, for instance, in a letter from "a valued correspondent," inserted in the "Morning Herald" of October 23, 1855, in which many of the details above given are also reproduced.

them." Others of the prisoners sent messages urging the poor woman not to give it; confidential servants yet left free did the same. In the midst of her counsellors the old Banka Baee "cried like a helpless child." Do her people consider her senseless? She has sacrificed her son (the late Maharaja), and her Annapoorna Baee "to the cruelties of the Feringees." She has no hope to survive longer. How can she suffer "the three other quite young and inexperienced creatures, (the three ranees) "exposed to all the indignities and cruelties of the Feringees" after her death? "The Vizier also is dead solely by the disrespectful treatment of the Feringees;"* "all the eminent persons of the Durbar" are either confined, or have deserted her and left the city. Perhaps her present advisers will be confined some day. She is now "like a bird bereft of its feathers." What hope has she that her agents will succeed? The bystanders shed tears with her, they are unable to utter a word, when they see the widow of "the great Raghojee Bhosla crying like a poor common woman." They beseech her, however, to wait two months longer, which she consents to. But the letter of recall was signed within little more than a fortnight.

Take from the same letter some further details of the process of annexation. The sale of the late Maharaja's property by auction is daily going on. The Commissioner has issued orders to all the different districts of Nagpore, to sell all the corn hitherto kept in

* There are some details to this effect in another part of the letter.

stock by the prince, "to meet any emergency, such as scarcity, or for supplying provision to the Company" under the treaty, but which was principally applied in distributions of seed-corn among the poorer ryots, to be returned at harvest time with so much more by way of interest *in kind*,—the surplus being given away to Brahmins and beggars. The value of the whole is reckoned at £100,000 or thereabouts, and the ryots are told that they are no more to depend upon Government for seed-corn. "This is the way," the writer breaks out, "the Company boasts to protect the people from the tyranny of the native rulers. Is it not as a butcher protects his sheep?" The same writer writes again on the 12th November, 1855. Still the sale of the property is going on. The princesses have not had the heart to give a power of attorney to sue for them in the Supreme Court. They suppose that the Supreme Court cannot possess higher authority than the Company; if it did, the Commissioners could not exercise such arbitrary power as they do. At any rate, they look upon Lord Dalhousie as "resolved to annihilate the Bhosla family," as their "powerful enemy," against whom it would be folly to move.

When we look at the Tanjore Ranee's case, is it not evident that, to confine ourselves to the question of the sale of private property alone, these poor women have been illegally despoiled? It is not I, but Mr. J. B. Norton, who says of the Nagpore Ranees:—

"Through mismanagement on the part of the family, their rights have never been fairly placed before the public; but we contrived, on the death of the Raja, to commit an act of meanness which, I will undertake to say, there is not a native in India who cannot appreciate. We seized, and sold by public auction at Calcutta, the jewels, valued at one crore of rupees (£1,000,000) . . . and I am inclined to think that by this single act of petty larceny—villainy—*we have covered ourselves with more ignominy in the eyes of the natives than by any other which can be pitted against it.*"*

I have taken the case of Nagpore, precisely because it is one which has been followed with comparatively trifling consequences in the shape of disturbance or conspiracy; because it thus affords the fairest exemplification of the inevitable harshness by means of which the annexation policy can alone fulfil itself, of the heart-burnings which it creates, even in the most peaceable and successful of its operations. Compare with it, if you like it, Tanjore, and Mr. J. B. Norton's *personal* evidence as to the manner in which that pettiest of our annexations was carried out:

"A company of Sepoys was marched suddenly into the palace; the whole of the property, real and personal, seized,—the Company's seals put upon all the jewels and other valuables; the soldiery were disarmed, and in the most offensive way; the private estate of the Raja's mother, of the estimated value of three lakhs (£30,000) a year was sequestered, and still remains so; the occupier of every piece of land in the district, which had at any time belonged to a former Raja, was turned out of his possession, and bid come before the Com-

---

* The Rebellion in India, pp. 97-8. In Mr. Montgomery Martin's "Rise and Progress of the Indian Mutiny," (a work which travels over much the same ground as the present one, but has only come to my hands whilst these sheets were passing through the press,) will be found, pp. 44-9, a more detailed account, compiled from the "Further Nagpore Annexation Papers," than I have here given. If rumour be credible, there would be a sad sequel to the Nagpore story, in the want of faith towards the princesses of the Europeans whom they had the misfortune to employ.

missioner, who constituted himself judge, to establish a title to his satisfaction; the whole of the people, dependent for their existence upon the expenditure of the Raj revenues among them, were suddenly panic-struck at the prospect of being thrown out of employ; and *in a week the Company succeeded in converting Tanjore, from the most respectful, contented place in our dominions, into a hot-bed of sullen disaffection...The very Sepoys have refused to receive their pensions.*"—(Rebellion in India, pp. 114, 115.)*

And what would it be, if I were to dwell upon the stories of Sattara, or of Oude?

LETTER XII.

WHAT THE NATIVES HAVE SAID OF LATE ANNEXATIONS.

WE are far too short-sighted, I fear, in our calculations as to the effect of our acts in India. Ruling hitherto its subject millions avowedly by the maxim of the authoress of the St. Bartholomew massacre, "Diviser pour régner," we are far too apt to dwell and rely upon the jars and discords of race and caste and creed among them, far too forgetful of the common humanity which binds them together at bottom, into which all the deepest emotions of our nature strike their root, from fiercest hatred to gentlest pity. Let

* See also Mr. Norton's account of the Prince Azeem Jah's refusal, although old and "miserably poor," to accept the pension offered to him in lieu of the nawabship of the Carnatic, and of the non-payment as yet of the Nawab's debts after seizure of his property.—(Topics for Indian Statesmen, p. 161.)

us feel assured that no vakeel of a dispossessed sovereign from the interior crosses the country to the Presidencies, takes ship for England, without awakening curiosity, interest at the least. Let us feel assured that no Moslem Queen-mother of Oude can proceed as a suppliant from Lucknow to Calcutta without calling forth pity in thousands of Hindoo mothers' breasts on her way.

The states, the races, the creeds of India are not shut up from one another by impassable barriers. Although an Indian nationality, in the true sense of the word, does not exist, still the feeling that India is *one country* spreads from Cape Comorin to the Himalayas. The mixture of creeds, the scattered shrines and places of pilgrimage tend strongly to keep up this feeling. The Buddhist of the Himalaya, of the Eastern frontier of Bengal, knows well that from Behar or Magadha went forth the Pali, his sacred language; that the monuments of his faith are scattered throughout the whole of India, that Ceylon is still one of its living seats. The wandering Brahmin from the North pays his way to Malabar with Ganges water, taken from time to time, it is to be charitably supposed, from the *cleanest* roadside spring on his long journey. The great Hindoo Bunnia, or merchant, has correspondents on whom he will give bills, from Peshawur on the Indus to Cochin in the furthest South. The holy places around Cape Comorin attract Rajpoot pilgrims from the North-west. Mussulmen from every quarter of India crowd yearly to its Western coast to start upon the haj, or pilgrimage to the holy places of Arabia. Even the Sikh from the

Punjab is attracted to the Deckan by the burial place of his prophet-hero Govind, at Nuderh on the Godavery. The sacred legends of the Hindoo have the whole of India for their theatre. The subject of one of his great epics, the Ramayana, is the rescuing by the Oude hero Rama of his wife from the clutches of the demon-ruler of Ceylon. The historic traditions of the Mussulman have nearly as wide a field—the conquest of Malabar by Hyder Ali of Mysore, in 1765, being as it were the last wave of that tide of Moslem progress, which had reached Mooltan ere the close of the 7th century.

This feeling, not so much of national as of geographical unity, has been observed long since. After Lord Lake had failed at the first siege of Bhurtpore, the tradition of his defeat, to use the words of Professor Wilson, "had impressed upon the natives, *whether prince or people*, the conviction that Bhurtpore was the bulwark of the liberties of India, and destined to arrest the march of European triumph." Even in the Carnatic the saying had gone abroad, that "India was not yet conquered, for Bhurtpore had not been taken." Now the effect of our rule must undoubtedly have been, even by its mere universal overweight, to break down more and more the sharp differences and rivalries between the various races, castes, and creeds; by the centralization of our Government,* by the uniformity of many of its processes, by the common origin and language of its administrators, to develop more and more among the con-

* Major Wingate, on being asked before the Colonization Committee if he did not think considerable danger arose from the present system

quered that sense of unity which evidently possessed the conquerors; whilst the greater facilities which have been afforded for the spread of information, by the printing press on the one hand, by our great lines of road, by our railways and our electric telegraphs on the other, tend equally to feed and strengthen it.

The effect of our foreign wars, draining all India of troops, has been felt and moralised upon in the heart of India. "The sharpest retort that I remember ever having had myself," writes Sir W. Sleeman in his "Oude," "was given to me by a sturdy and honest old landholder of the middle class, whom I had known for a quarter of a century, on the bank of the Nerbudda, in 1843." Sent to inquire into an insurrection in the Saugur and Nerbudda territories, which commenced in 1842 (and which is not even noticed in Messrs. Taylor and McKenna's valuable compendium of British Indian history), Sleeman gathered some fifty landholders together, and complained of their want of support to Government, notwithstanding the previous good administration of the territory, adding, "But there are some men who never can be satisfied." "True," replied the old landholder referred to, "there are some people who never can be satisfied, give them what you will. *Give them the whole of Hindostan, and they will go off to Cabul to take more.*" And he proceeded to explain how, when

of centralization, answered, "I think so; I think that it causes a community of feelings and of aims throughout the whole of India, which may eventually become extremely dangerous to British supremacy."—Fourth Report, p. 67.

our troops had been taken off for distant conquests, the predatory chiefs of the hills had come down upon the defenceless plains, where men, long deprived of their arms, had even forgotten the use of them.* But if such was the effect of the distant Cabul campaign upon the banks of the Nerbudda, with what feverish anxiety must not the operation of Lord Dalhousie's policy have been watched by our native fellow-subjects, even when personally unconnected with its effects!

I have before me a manuscript memorandum, entitled, "Annexations in India." Judging from internal evidence, it is the production of a native hand, and must have been written in the autumn of 1856, after the annexation of Oude, before any dream of the Sepoy mutiny. At all events, it expresses, I am assured, the feelings of an influential portion of the native population of Bombay, and was forwarded home as the exponent of those feelings. The feelings, be it observed, not of men dwelling in remote districts, foreign to the intercourse of Englishmen, to the use of our language; but of men living in or near, or connected with, the city of all others which is most open to European influences; of men in daily contact with Englishmen, familiar with our Blue-books, able to express themselves in our language, appealing, not to their own swords, but—in however intemperate language—to English justice for redress. By what these men have said to us in English, we may be able to form some dim guess as to what, in the far north,

* Journey through the kingdom of Oude, vol. ii. pp. 94-6.

in the heart of the peninsula, the men of Oude and of Bundelcund, the Mahratta and the Mussulman, *must* have said to each other in their own tongues.

The following are extracts:—

"The question of succession since the escheat of the Sattara state and the recent notification of a legislative act regarding the tenures of property, has (*sic*) naturally created much anxiety and alarm among the Hindoos, either princes or peasants. Relying on the faith of treaties and solemn pledges of the British Government, hitherto they had felt themselves quite secure in the possession of their hereditary or acquired estates, but this change of policy makes their minds quite uneasy as to its future intentions as regards the chiefship or private inheritance.

The custom of succession by adoption was always scrupulously respected by former rulers of India both Hindoo and Mahomedans, and is even faithfully observed to this day by the native chiefs within their own jurisdiction. The Indo-British Government even until very lately followed the same rule.

. . . .

In the case of Sattara, as is well known to the world, the adoption legally made was disallowed, and the territory, against the security of solemn pledges of treaty, has been annexed to the British empire. It is not improbable that the power of the paramount authority may easily be likewise exercised from time to time in other cases, not having even the security which Sattara possessed in the terms of its treaty. However the avarice of a foreign government may seem to justify the exercise of its arbitrary power in matters of so vital importance to the interests of the governed, yet the measure, though supported by plausible arguments, is backed neither by the law of the land or precedent. Both are against it.

. . . .

... With the exception of son or sons or grandsons, the heirs of one's own body, the usage of adoption in all other cases, however nearly connected the selecting party may be, according to Shastra is unavoidably observed. A Hindoo destitute of a son is positively enjoined by his religion to adopt a substitute for the sake of the funeral and other solemn rites, or his soul cannot be admitted into heaven.

"Heaven awaits not one destitute of son," as per (!) Hindoo law of adoption, nay an omission is considered an offence. How could then a Hindoo in consistence (*sic*) with his religion and conscience persuade himself to abandon the performance of this solemn duty. To secure his peaceful abode in the heaven, he must have a son, either legal or adopted, and the adopted son in every sense of the law is believed to be as good heir or "warīs" as the legal male issue. To be consistent, if the law of adoption is either altogether done away with or is defined to certain extent with respect to chiefships, as has been done in the instance of Holkar where the male heirs of body lawfully begotten are only to be allowed as legal successors, the same principle should be applied to private property under British rule. In default of legal heir the private property must become therefore an escheat to the British Government as well as a chiefship. What an alarm the introduction of this principle must create in the minds of the Hindoo community may be better conceived than described.

Following the examples set forth by the paramount authority, the native independent princes, such as Scindia, Holkar, Nizam, &c. &c., may in default of legal heirs of body annex the states of their tributaries to their own possessions. With what plausible plea the British Government, who is a guarantee in several instances, can interfere to stop the lesson of destruction which it has taught? (*sic*) . . ... Made wiser by the past experience, the natives have ceased to place any faith in the solemn professions of good will of their governors, and nothing else but the insertion of a clause in the charter act conferring [confirming] the existing princes in their possessions and to their heirs without any limitation as to the male heirs of the body will remove the daily increasing anxiety and alarm under which they labour at present.

. . . . .

Among the thousand misfortunes of India, the greatest, perhaps, is the superior ingenuity of its governors to that of the governed. The apparent plausibility of argument, and the studied dishonesty of purpose lying deep in the smooth sentences by which the rulers attempt in the state papers to justify their vilest acts of plunder and rapine in this country, have long puzzled the unsophisticated natives, have looked incomprehensible and perhaps unanswerable, but the result is, that confidence in the words, engagements, and faith of the

British nation is irretrievably lost, and from the highest king to the lowest everybody is horror-struck at the abominable scene of spoliation all around him.

The process of destroying a native kingdom is now-a-days so simple, so easy, and so summary that, to use the words of a certain writer, "the stopping of a drummer's pay is more laborious in comparison." The dainty morsel of a fat kingdom in the neighbourhood having once been coveted, you have only to get first a "Friend of India," or some of his fraternity, most veraciously to abuse its chief, administering a goodly volley of invectives to his functionaries in a succession of flashing (*sic*) articles in order to prepare the public mind in England, then get your politicals to pitch (*sic*) up a quarrel with your intended victim on the slightest pretext, or even on a common point of etiquette, to take advantage of a family misfortune or of a common row or dacoity in the country, and let him propose annexation; you then sit down in the midst of a tongueless council, record a wordy minute in which any trash will do for argument, provided it is long enough; blow up any colleague or political who dares shew conscience, refute or support the witnesses and opinions of your own officers without even formally consulting the feelings of the people whom your minute concerns; "declare," if you please, aye, swear, if you have any regard for a marquisdom and a fat pension, that you have no other motive in the heart than the good of the "people," or the good of Manchester, then send out a verbose proclamation and the kingdom is yours!

But the farce is not yet complete. The poor chief is not yet entirely ruined. There are yet a few suits of clothes spared, a few jewels left to his wives or his widows, and unless you take a humane care of them "for the benefit of his family," your gentlemen brothers, the barristers and advocates, will at least for the sake of these excite an agitation. But the agitation somehow or other does arise notwithstanding your judicious precautions. A well informed Honourable Member in the House of Commons rises up to denounce your crimes. Some generous Noble in the House of Lords resents your nefarious doings. A few appropriate speeches are delivered,—but what do you care for them? Your prize is firm in your grasp; you have the whole influence of the Cannon Row and the Leaden Hall (*sic*) on your side. You have a Sir James Hogg to deny the existence of torture in India, and the powerful "Times" to make the British nation swallow their sense of justice by promising a surplus of $2\frac{1}{2}$ millions per annum from the spoils of Oude. And here the matter ends!

The opinions gaining ground among the masses in India with reference to the annexation policy of Government are however widely different. . . . . . The starvation of numerous respectable families, the sending adrift and breadless of hundreds which these clean sweeps naturally entail, are to the natives proofs too convincing and visible to create a belief in the honesty of the logic of rulers, and the simplicity of the Indian mind looks rather to facts than to words. They hear for instance that a kingdom has been taken for the ostensible reason to do good to the people, that 70,000 troops have been disbanded, the jagheers resumed, high situations and emoluments distributed among Europeans, ousting out their former holders, the native nobles, and they wonder how the boasted good to the people is to be effected. The newly acquired ryots clearly see in the appointment of so many highly paid foreigners so many siphons as it were to draw the wealth of this country, to pour it into their own; they can easily conceive the "good" done to the other subjects of the Honourable Company in Orissa, Madras, Deckan and Hindostan, and woefully wait to see a similar sort of "prosperity" to be inflicted upon themselves. In short, all the confidence in the good faith and sincerity of Government having been palpably destroyed in the minds of all the classes of the people of India, the rulers will have to trust to their bayonets alone for the future safety of the empire."*

Now the question is not as to the truthfulness, fairness, good temper, good sense, good taste, good English of the above extracts. I ask them only to be treated, as a medical man would say, *pathologically*, as a study of disease. Set them down, if you like, as utterly false, unfair, ill-natured, absurd, ill-written. Will it not need strenuous efforts to eradicate the mischiefs of a policy which provoked such an outbreak of

* Written in 1856, let us recollect.

disease, which called forth such feelings, among such a class as I have described?

I curtail my extracts, solely from want of space. The MS. goes on to treat separately of most of the cases to which I have already referred—the Punjab, Pegu, Nagpore, Jhansee, Oude. It borrows illustrations from our relations with Scindia and with Holkar, with the petty states of Tehsee and Chutterpore in Bundelcund, of Oodeypore in Rajpootana, with the king of Delhi. Though the writer is evidently a Hindoo, yet his sympathies are alive in favour of the Sikh, the Buddhist, the Mussulman. He quotes largely from blue-books, from official papers. In treating of the Nagpore case he says:—

"'The Honourable the Court of Directors,' says the Governor-General [Lord Dalhousie] 'at the close of the discussion regarding the Raja of Sattara, had addressed very clear and specific instructions to the Government of India for its future guidance in cases which involved the principle of adoption. The Honourable Court laid down that *by the general law and custom of India* a dependent principality like that of Sattara cannot pass to an adopted heir without the consent of the paramount power; that we are under no pledge, direct or constructive, to give such consent, and that the general interests committed to our charge are best consulted by withholding it.'

Now could there be a greater perversion of the general law and custom of India? . . . . Would it not be better to order a general massacre of the gentry and nobility of the land, supported by the native states, and of their numerous dependents, than by this one dash of pen to subject them and their posterity to the inevitable horrors of destruction, misery and degradation?

That the 'general law and custom of India' in all the Hindoo families *is* adoption, even the Governor-General himself could not deny; that Government *is* under all the 'pledges, direct and constructive,' to respect and uphold those laws and customs according to their own proclamations, treaties and precedents, requires no proof, and that to withhold their consent from adoptions made in conformity to those 'general laws and customs,' whether in subordinate or insubordinate (*sic*) states, in consideration of the Leaden Hall or Manchester interests (but the Governor-General ingeniously calls it general interest), would therefore be criminal and faithless.

The Hindoo law ordains a subordinate state to apply for permission to the paramount power before it makes an adoption, with the obvious intention to give to the latter the opportunity to judge that the superior right of any other heir is not superseded. The law gives different degrees of kin, the nearest of whom is to be adopted,* and a deviation from this rule by any interested motives on the parties concerned can be corrected or regulated by the paramount power. This is the object of asking permission; but the law does not, we contend, authorize the paramount power to withhold that permission in order to swallow the state itself. On the contrary, we know the Hindoo law denounces the paramount power so offending to go to hell for 6,000 years. But the fear of God or of the next world being no argument compatible with civilization, we will forbear quoting the passage ourselves; but would respectfully challenge all the ingenuity of our learned rulers to publish any passages they may know of to reconcile the abolition of adoption,—or in the language of the Court to 'withhold permission' (*sic*) with the dictates of the Hindoo law."

The following is the writer's version of the Tehsee, Chutterpore and Oodeypore cases, with which I am not otherwise acquainted :

"While the distinguished families coming within Lord Dalhousie's definition of 'subordinate' states are falling fast and disappearing from the face of the earth, as if struck by the magic wand, there are others called independent, or old states, being gradually prepared for the applicability of the same 'principle' twenty years hence; but the simple and confiding people thus being moulded for absorption are scarcely aware of their fate.

Some noise having been made in the papers on the abolition of the old Hindoo rite of adoption, some time ago a sort of defence was put

---

* This seems too absolutely expressed.

forth in an issue of the government organ the 'Friend of India,' of the 17th May 1855, in which the adoption allowed at Tehsee, a small but ancient state in Bundelcund, was paraded to get rid of the charges of an 'insatiable ambition,' and as an exemplification of the government policy in reference to adoption.

The adopted Raja Soojan Singh of Tehsee having died without issue, there remained three claimants to the guddee, one was Dew Singh, his relation, about 30 years of age, whom it is said the dying Raja had declared his successor; the second was the old respectable Suraee Ranee, the adoptive mother of Soojan Singh, about 60 years of age, well experienced and held in great reverence by the raj, having often managed the state with credit; and the third was the late Raja's young widow Doolya, capable of reading and writing, and naturally very intelligent. But as usual the British Indian Government discovered some grand political logic by which they declared that the 'guddee was vacant,' that there was no rightful heir, that none of the above three personages had any right, but that the British Government, through generosity, liberality, and what else (*sic*) had permitted that seven Boondela chiefs of the neighbourhood might choose a boy who must be a near relation, that that boy should be adopted by Doolyajee, and that the chiefship should be administered by Suraee Ranee, while Dew Singh should go to jail for certain crimes in which he is said to have participated with the late Raja. . . .

The grand principle laid down, so often alluded to, could not *at present* admit of any construction to bring Tehsee within its absorbing influence, it being an old independent state, neither given nor constituted by British Government. . . . But divested from the political truth, what is the real truth? Tehsee is told it has no rightful claimant left, that the British Government now constituted the state, and that it has a right to take it at the next vacancy, or, to use a (*sic*) more precise and eloquent language of the most noble Marquis, copied from the Nagpore book, Government say, (*sic*) 'We had once given away Tehsee to a Boondela boy, and the question is, whether we are prepared to give it away a second time. Tehsee abounds in stone and timber, required for our bungalows and railways, and the interests of England and of India are better served in taking it.' . . . . In Chutterpore, another small state in Bundelcund, a worse language is said to have been used at the time of the last installation of the Raja in 1854, and the succession, though always hereditary, is now said to be limited to the heir males (*sic*) of the body.

Oodeypore, the most ancient and the most respectable of the Hindoo Rajpoot states of India, not a subordinate state, does not seem to fare the better. It is tottering on the brink of ruin, a quarrel seems to have existed between it and its feudatory chiefs. As the British politicals are everywhere the paramount lords, prepared to give relief to master and servant alike, destroying all subordination,—complaints must have of course gone to the agents. These complaints, if admissible at all, ought to have been decided upon their own merits.—But instead of that, a proclamation consisting of 29 articles is issued by the British Government, annulling all former treaties with the ancient house of the Rana, transferring all the chief power to the agent to the Governor-General, who thus becomes a self-constituted magistrate and judge as it were between the Rana and his subjects, and whose decision is to be 'final,' and threatening to carry out these atrocious measures by the force of arms. . . . We have an original vernacular copy of this astounding 'predetermination'* before us, and had it not been copiously extracted and translated by the 'Delhi Gazette' of the 15th of December 1855, and copied by the 'Telegraph and Courier' of the 29th of the same month we would have gone the length of translating it again. The Rana and his chiefs are appalled at this decision—some have actually refused to sign it, and the British Government would, in all probability, have carried out its threat of enforcing it by force of arms, had not the more delicious Oude business, and its less delicious noise intervened. . . . . But we think we have said enough about the 'policy,' the 'predetermination' and the 'faith' of the British Indian Government. . . . The mere speeches of a few generous members and the counter-speeches of the East Indian party do not correct the evil. Short-lived agitation in England, counteracted by powerful papers in favour of the stronger party, who begin openly to advocate the violation of treaties as a superior morality, and the destruction of

* The recurrence of this word has reference to a speech of Mr. Mr. Vernon Smith's, in which he denied the existence of an annexation policy, in the sense of a "predetermination" to annex wherever possible.

the native kingdoms as the 'duty they owe to God and man,' is no consolation to our throbbing hearts. The Thugs who have strangled travellers in India always believed they were discharging one of the most virtuous and moral duties they owed to the goddess, and to the man whom they sacrificed for his happiness in the next world."

Bitter words, surely! And yet, angry though the writer may be, he looks avowedly to England, to the British Parliament for redress. He concludes as follows:—

"Let some of these annexed kingdoms be restored. Let the Indian Government be restrained *by an Act* from taking an inch of ground belonging to their neighbours, until a full inquiry is made by a third party into the cause of their proceedings. It is not consistent with any principle of justice to let an ambitious and powerful Government act the part of an accuser, the judge and the hangman; frame principles in a language calculated to destroy others, and to let them carry out those principles with an iron hand, while the victims of those principles go unheard. Let *an Act of Parliament* be issued at once, to reassure the safety of the remaining kingdoms, or let at least an independent Crown court be instituted in India, to whom the Government may apply for permission before annexing a kingdom; that that court must inquire into the grounds, and openly ask the other party for its defence, and pass a just order after the fullest inquiry.

This, we believe, is the only way left open to reassure the Indian public, and to restore the confidence which is now so entirely lost; and by granting only what is just, by thus securing the safety of the weak against the strong, the great British nation is sure to secure, not only the heartfelt esteem and the cordial loyalty of all India, but the prayers of millions, whose bread and honour they shall have the means of saving for ever."

Such, then, was the effect of the annexation policy, not upon the pretenders to the extinguished thrones, upon the disappointed courtiers, the dismissed menials who surrounded the late monarch, not even upon those who were his subjects,* but upon the mere *native by-stander*, upon our own fellow-subjects. Such was the angry cry which it called forth among them, such their bitter, and yet strangely trustful appeal to "the great British nation." Thank God! That cry, that appeal, is at last answered, in the generous promises of the Proclamation.

LETTER XIII.

GUARANTEES OF THE NON-ANNEXATION POLICY REQUIRED FOR THE FUTURE.

"MAY the first acts," writes the "Retired Officer," "of the new Government be directed to reassuring our Indian allies and subjects. It will be vain to hope that this can be effected without undoing much that has been unwisely or unscrupulously done. Let early opportunities then be taken, or made, for treating our native allies like trusted friends of our Government, in respect to their treaties, and as before pointed out; and *let them all be made certain of their territories*

* It is the fashion to suppose that nothing answering to patriotism exists in India, within the separate states of which it is composed. Those who know India best tell a very different tale. See for instance, in Sleeman's "Rambles and Recollections," vol. i. pp. 236-7, the story of the half naked man in Orcha, beggared by a late famine, who "seemed quite melancholy at the thought of seeing this principality, the oldest in Bundelcund, lose its independence."

and thrones descending to their families."* He had already, in 1856, in words which briefly sum up many of my arguments hitherto, shewn what was required; how the right of adoption or succession was formerly respected by us, wherever our intercourse with a native state was regulated by treaty, unless some particular act was likely to disturb the peace of the country. "The principle," he wrote, "was fully recognized, that a state is never without an heir, every state having an usage of its own for supplying the place of a direct heir failing. Our treaties give us no right of regulating successions in native states; and finally, had we in any instance doubted the right of any principality to be enrolled amongst the substantive powers of India, the fact of our making a treaty with such principality would deprive us of the power of treating it otherwise than as a foreign state, whose relations with us were fixed by such treaty. Had there however (which there is not,) been any doubt as to the construction of our treaties, the benefit of such doubt should have been given to the weaker party—a principle of politic generosity and justice ever advocated, and often acted upon, by our former magnanimous authorities in India, and of itself constituting a host of moral strength to our rule." †

It is not therefore enough to abandon the annexation policy for the future. It is not enough of free grace to restore some or all of the annexed territories. That policy must be felt to be permanently, not temporarily

* Supplement to "India and its dangers," p. 26.

† India, its dangers considered in 1856, pp. 9-10.

abandoned. The grounds upon which it has sought to establish itself must be cut away.

It is not the mere granting of a few jagheers to the Rajas of Putteeala or Jheend, to Jotee Persad, or any other of our more prominent adherents, which will suffice for the purpose. If I mistake not, all those jagheers hitherto are granted only to the heirs of the body of the recipients. They involve then no perpetuity of reward; they strike yet at the right of adoption, so dear to the Hindoo; they bear with them, so to speak, the very threat of resumption at some future period.

The right of adoption, so closely interwoven with Hindoo customs and feelings,—the right of free succession—must be fully, officially acknowledged. The limits of those rights are undoubtedly now wavering and uncertain. Let the law on the subject,—let the British claim of escheat (if any) as against native principalities,—let the relations of the princes of India to the British Government generally, be defined by all means. Not however by English officials, nor by English lawyers only; but on the report of a Royal Commission, assisted by native assessors, and those appointed, to the extent we will say of at least one moiety, by the native princes themselves, and after full communication with princes, ministers, jurists, and others.

The next step, I take it, will be the appointing some judicial tribunal to decide on all future cases involving relations *(not of peace or war)* between the Indian princes and the British Government, such as, between individuals, would form the subject of a judicial trial. It has been overlooked by the annexationists, that the further they pushed the doctrine of the paramount authority of the British Government over all native princes, the more they took the mutual relations between the two parties out of the realm of politics, and brought them into that of law. Where two states are each absolutely sovereign, there is no tribunal which they can appeal to; they may consent to submit their differences to arbitration, they may consent to obey the arbiter, yet after all, force is the only authority which they acknowledge. But as soon as one claims authority over the other, the other party has a right to claim that that authority should be, not one of force only, but of law. Until now, the pretext that the acts of the Indian Government towards Indian princes are matters of state policy has been used, as we have seen, with perfectly ludicrous shamelessness. Self-governed Sattara is annexed one day, because it is independent; the eye-squirts of the late pensioner Raja of Tanjore are detained the next, because he was independent. How the new tribunal should be constituted,—whether it should be the Supreme Court in India, or the Privy Council at home, or some new body, will deserve ulterior consideration; but I suspect that native feeling would run in favour, at all events, of a final appeal to England. Native assessors would probably be required in any case, and the Indian princes should have a voice in their selection. If such a Commission as I have suggested be appointed to consider the law of adoption, &c., it might be requested to report on the constitution of such a tribunal.*

* The establishment of a "Court of Appeal for Indian grievances."

The native princes should moreover at once be set free from the trammels under which they now labour. The incubus of the Resident's authority, where the prince is under no disability, should be removed; the supreme authority of the British Crown as paramount should only be exercised protectively, during infancy or other incapacity of the sovereign, much within the limits of the jurisdiction of the Court of Chancery with us in the like cases as respects private life. What mischief is often done by Residents,—how they gall and crush the native princes, can hardly be said in too vivid terms. Lord Hastings's portrait of them in 1814 is true yet to the life.

"Instead of acting in the character of ambassador, he" (the Resident) "assumes the functions of a dictator; interferes in all their private concerns; countenances refractory subjects against them; and makes the most ostentatious exhibition of this exercise of authority. To secure to himself the support of our Government, he urges some interest which, under the colour thrown upon it by

---

—a somewhat wider idea, it will be perceived, than my own,—was very strongly urged by the "Indian News," in the spring of 1857. It enumerated as follows (April 2, 1857) the cases in which, during the (then) last ten years, the suffering party had, in person or by attorney, pleaded fruitlessly to the Home authorities:—

"1. The Emperor of Delhi.—2. The deposed Raja of Sattara.—3. The Ameers of Scinde.—4. Lalla Jotee Persâd.—5. In the Ahmednugger case, the Raja of Marwar.—6. The Parsee Merchants in the Hyderabad case.—7. The Carnatic Stipendiaries.—8. The Arcot case. —9. The Nawab of Surat's case.—10. Mirza Ali Akbar's case.—11. Bajee Rao, Ex-Peshwa's case.—12. The Nagpore case.—13. That of Gholam Mohamed, son of Tippoo Sultan.—14. That of Lukshmee Begum of Jhansee.—15. His Highness Ali Morad Khan of Scinde.—16. The Nawab of Rampore's case.—17. The Oude Dynasty case.—18. The case of the Raja of Coorg."

him, is strenuously taken up by our Council; and the Government identifics itself with the Resident, not only on the single point, but on the whole tenor of his conduct."*

In Mr. Mead's work will be found instances of the galling tyranny of these officials at the present day.† The Travancore Resident actually prevented the sovereign from dismissing a minister guilty of the most horrible misgovernment. As a rule, these unfortunate princes are prevented from corresponding with England; at least, the intimation by the Resident that they "had better not" is far too weighty for them to dare neglect it; and no one who has not experience of the process can conceive of the shrinking timidity with which information is communicated from the neighbourhood of a British political. The feelings of chiefs and Durbars towards our politicals and their underlings, are well described by one on the spot, as those of "terror."‡

* Private Journal, vol. i. pp. 47-8.

† Sepoy Revolt, p. 203 and foll.

‡ Although I do not profess to deal with the Indian question as a whole, the following suggestions, which I find in a letter written from a gentleman residing in India, of great experience with the native character, dated 25th August, 1857, are well worthy of attention:—

"If I were asked what ought to be done, I should say—First and foremost sell land in fee-simple. Have twenty fortified camps with five thousand European troops in each, infantry, cavalry, and artilleay. Let the rest of the army be made up of irregulars,—Rajpoots of Jodhpore, Jeypore, and Oodeypore (and not Poorbeas of the Doab)—Sikhs and Goorkas of course—Mahrattas and Telingas. Destroy all the old treaties with the existing chiefs who have remained faithful to us. Offer new ones on more liberal and equal terms . . . . Give them liberty of action. Let them rule their territories as independent princes. Interfere not with the ancient practice of adoption . . . Prohibit the Residents and political

Together with the enfranchisement of the native princes from their bondage to English Residents,—with the conferring of territory upon all faithful allies and dependents,—should come, for those who have most distinguished themselves,—those honorific distinctions which the Oriental so dearly appreciates. I for one cannot see why Sultan Abdul Medjid should be a Knight of the Garter, and not such tried friends as the Raja of Putteeala, Holkar or Scindia; nor why Sir Jung Bahadoor should stand alone as Military G.C.B., and the equivalent civil dignity should not be conferred on Salar Jung of Hyderabad, Dinkur Rao of Gwalior, and Ramchunder Rao of Indore. Care however must be taken to confer no British dignity on a minister without the fullest approval of his sovereign, lest he should come to be looked upon rather as the servant of the British Crown than of his own master.

Recognition and definition of the law of adoption, escheat, &c.,—establishment of a tribunal to try legal questions between Indian princes and the British government,—their enfranchisement from the control of our politicals,—enlargement of territory and honorific

---

agents from interfering in their internal affairs, or employing confidential Maulavies and Moonshees, Jamadars, and so forth, as gobetweens, or negociators in any way. They are a nuisance, and an abomination to the Durbars. Let all intercourse be carried on in writing. Small notes would answer quite well enough . . . . Sweep away your contingents. Remodel the Civil Service, or abolish it. Coax a couple hundred thousand families from the middle classes, and yeomanry, and trade, and professions to come and settle . . . You need not fear insurrection or rebellion again. Railways, canals, and roads would then of themselves start up as if by magic."

distinctions to our allies and friends,—such, I believe, would be the measures to confirm the allegiance of the native princes of India for the future, to make them feel themselves integral members of our political system. But there remains still the past to be accounted for. Many a smart must rankle yet in the heart of our allies which ought on every account to be soothed. Let me give one or two samples of such.

LETTER XIV.

HOW SOME OF OUR ALLIES HAVE BEEN LATELY TREATED.*

THE little state of Dhar, in Malwa, is situate close to Indore, Holkar's capital, and is included in the jurisdiction of the Indore agency. At the time of the mutinies it was ruled over by a woman and a child,—a boy of 13, the adopted son of the late Raja (whose adoption had just been sanctioned when the outbreak about to be mentioned took place), and the widow of the latter. Its army consisted of 800 men, of whom between 500 or 600 were Mussulman Patans. From the moment of the outbreak (October 1857) the Dhar authorities shewed themselves strictly faithful; protected the post, protected the electric telegraph, kept the roads safe, forwarded elephants, guns, men at the

* The documents as to Dhar and Indore from which this letter is written are entirely supplied by Mr. J. Dickinson, jun.

bidding of the British authorities, a detachment of 50 sepoys with two guns, for instance, being sent for the protection of the British agent at Bhopawar. As ill-luck would have it, nevertheless, the British agent at Bhopawar sent a fakeer from Amjheera to be confined at Dhar. On his arrival the Patans rose and rescued him to the cry of "deen" (faith), and seized the fort of Dhar,—the authorities having just time to place in safety the ammunition and military stores that were in and near the town.

From the day that this blow was struck, constant applications for assistance were forwarded to the British authorities. Assistance however did not come; the troops meanwhile using every means to induce the Ranee and the boy-king to place themselves in their power,—increasing in importunity, and growing bolder in the outrages which they committed upon the towns-folk, in proportion as succour was more delayed. At last the Ranee saw herself compelled to enter into an agreement with them, stipulating the pardon of the fakeer, pay, enforcement of claims, &c., &c., in short, such terms as a mutinous soldiery will exact; but she instantly sent a copy to the British agent at Bhopawnr, stating the circumstances under which it was entered into. The soldiery marched away, marched back again, turned the guns of the fort upon the town, threatening to sack it; intelligence of their movements being still communicated, assistance again implored. At last it came, palankeens and cavalry being sent to bring on the British officers, hourly intelligence being forwarded while the relieving party was on the road. The fort was invested, the Durbar giving lists of the mutineers, supplying persons acquainted with the locality, who gave plans of the works, pointed out the weak places, &c. After ten or twelve days siege, however, the mutineers evacuated the place by night. The agent demanded the keys of the treasury, they were handed over to him. He required that the minister,—a *protégé* of the British government, who held a jagheer under its guarantee,—and other persons, should be put in arrest. It was done. For seventeen days that the British troops remained at Dhar, they were supplied with artificers, and everything that was required.

On the 14th February, 1858, a Mussulman, Meer Mohammad Shahamat Ali,* appeared at Dhar, bearer of two letters to the Ranee and the young Prince from the Agent for Central India. Their contents must have been the same as those of a proclamation which came with them, dated like the letters 19th January, 1858, and which was issued under the signature of the same Meer Shahamat Ali, as officiating superintendent. It declared that the "infidelity and ingratitude" of Dhar could not possibly "be overlooked;" that the prince "having forfeited the Government of Dhar," would "never be reinstated," that arrangements would be made for the maintenance of himself and the Ranee. The proclamation then concludes in the following strain,—which, from the pen of a Mussulman, must

* *Quære,* Is this the same person as the Meer Shahamat Ali who in vol. xii. of the Journal of the Royal Asiatic Society (1852) gave an account of Maulavie Ismael, the Mussulman reformer, with evident sympathy in his undertaking? If so, we may judge how apt was the choice of such an envoy to the Hindoo state in a time of disturbance!

have touched every Rajpoot's pride to the quick: "This proclamation has been issued for your information. It is incumbent on you to understand its contents, and conduct yourselves accordingly, and with sincere and complete submission to be obedient to the officer who has been appointed to the charge of the affairs of the state, in consequence of the abolition of the treaty, owing to *the unpardonable misconduct of the Dhar Durbar.*" The country was therefore provisionally sequestrated,—the treasure in the privy purse of the young prince was confiscated,—the state property of elephants, camels, horses, &c., put up to auction, only a few horses being reserved for the use of the young chief. The Minister's jagheer was confiscated. The lands assigned, by Mahratta custom, to the Ranee for charitable purposes, amounting in value to £5000 a year, were placed under sequestration. Meer Shahamat Ali took charge of the state as superintendent, and the young prince was not allowed to sit on a chair in public!

Now it is most true Dhar has been restored. But has English morality sunk so low as this, that a flagrant outrage upon all justice should be deemed atoned for by simple restitution? The treaty with Dhar of 1819 binds the Rajas of Dhar to act "in subordinate co-operation with the British Government" (art. 2); binds the British Government "to protect the state of Dhar and its dependencies."* In what had the state of Dhar omitted to fulfil its part of the treaty? How did the British Government fulfil it, when after receiving all the help that Dhar could

* See House of Lords' Return of Treaties, p. 412 and foll.

give, it left that state so long without the protection stipulated, at the mercy of the mutineers? And then, forsooth, it must take advantage of its own wrong, without the shadow of a judicial investigation, without notice, without so much as a specific charge;—only those vague ones of "enmity and opposition" which are the very resource of despots in want of an excuse—to declare the treaty abrogated; to annex, temporarily at least, the territory of an ally, to bully a woman and a child,—Hindoos by the hands of a Mussulman,—to confiscate private property, to outrage the feelings of a whole people through those sales by auction of their chief's goods and chattels which invariably prove so deeply galling. Restitution indeed, after such proceedings as these! Why, if you doubled the Dhar territory, it would be barely compensation enough to the state,—let alone the individuals, the Minister for instance, who declares that before the outbreak of the troops their mutinous disposition was more than once communicated by him to the British authorities, and their aid implored. If this be the way our friends are treated after such a crisis as that of 1857, Heaven preserve us from any other!

But take the case of Indore. Perhaps of all the native states of India, there is none better governed,—by an excellent prince, and an excellent minister. Rao Ramchunder Rao may fairly rank as one of the great Indian ministers of the day. Those who know him well speak unanimously of his striking intelligence, of his being far in advance of his countrymen. Both his master and himself are anxious to promote education. Holkar has established a college, where English is taught as well as the vernacular;—there is a dispensary—a library of English books, an "association for the diffusion of useful knowledge," where weekly meetings and discussions are held, and the prince himself sometimes attends. In the year 1856 alone petty customs' duties, &c., were abolished, to the amount of some £4000 a year. A gentleman travelling through the country in the spring of 1857, just before the outbreak, speaks of "the extent of cultivation," "the prosperous state of the inhabitants; perhaps in no part of India will they appear better clad,—in better bodily condition,—and altogether so contented." "You would not meet more substantial farmers." "They are becoming capitalists." Of the benevolence of the ruler let the following instance suffice: "The collector of one of his districts had oppressed the ryots, and extorted money for his own use. The moment it came to the Maharaja's knowledge, the official was removed and the money exacted restored to the owners. They were collected at the palace, and in open Durbar each man had his own handed to him in a bag, and was sent away with an honorary dress."

The outbreak came, and Holkar's firm friendship stood the severest tests. The sepoys at Mhow,—14 miles from Indore—having evinced symptoms of disaffection, as soon as the prince knew of it he proffered the aid of his troops; cavalry, infantry and guns were ready to start at an hour's notice. But the flame of rebellion ran higher and higher. The native princes who remained staunch found themselves at the mercy of their contingents,—men of Oude, commanded by Brahmins and Mussulmen! The minister's life was threatened. On the 11th July, 1857—just as the officiating Agent for Central India was collecting elephants, &c., for his departure, and had declined to place the treasure under the care of the prince, who had offered to receive it at the palace, an attack was made by the soldiery on the Residency, to the cry of "Deen, Deen." A wounded Mussulman came to the palace, saying that "he had begun the work, and the prince must now go on." Holkar replied by ordering him to be put in irons and shot down if he resisted. But no inclination was shewn by the troops to obey the order. The utmost that the prince could obtain was that the mutineer should be disarmed and detained. It was in vain to order troops to proceed to the relief of the Residency. The officers who professed most loyalty all declared that the men were wholly beyond control. The prince sought himself to go to the Residency, but was restrained by his people. In the meanwhile, intelligence came that the British had cut their way out, and had proceeded to Mhow.

Our ally found himself without power in his own capital,—his own men urging him to place himself at the head of his troops, and drive the Feringhee out of the land,—troopers sending in messages to require large guns for attacking the fort of Mhow,—his very menials insulting him in his own palace for his subserviency to the stranger. Yet his faithfulness never wavered; he did still what he could. He refused the demands of the mutineers as far as possible. The very day of the outbreak detailed accounts were forwarded to the Governor-General, to the Governor of Bombay, to the officiating Agent for Central India. Directions were sent to the local authorities to supply the British with everything they required. The advice of the commandant at Mhow was asked as to what should be done. The ladies and others who had taken refuge at the palace were faithfully protected. As the Prince, thrown upon his own resources, began gradually to resume his authority, he took measures for transporting to Mhow the remaining treasure, recovered a portion of it which was in the hands of city plunderers; his Commander-in-chief rescued Captain Hutchinson, Bheel agent in Malwa, from a position of danger, captured some of the advisers of the rebellious chief of Amjheera. Eleven elephants were sent to meet Brigadier Stuart's column, and the officers in the Fort of Mhow were supplied with all that they required. Last —scarcely least—an *English* office was established in the palace, in order that all important secret and political correspondence might thenceforth be carried on in our language. A more signal proof of devotion to English interests, at such a time, could hardly be conceived.* And what was the reward? If rumour speaks true, a letter from the officiating agent to the Governor-General in Central India, warning him that every native chief is held accountable for the hostile acts which his troops may commit against the English Government, and that the principle can only be waived under very extraordinary circumstances! Was ever devotion, personal danger, so repaid?†

* I believe this has since been abolished through Court intrigues, and the "vested interest" of the moonshees, who are required to carry on the correspondence in *Persian*,—a language about as little understood in Malwa by this time as English, at all events by Hindoos.

† While these letters were passing through the press, incredible to relate, the official in question has been *elected* a member of the Council for India!

Now there are those who think that on this occasion, Holkar saved England to India. Instead of resisting the mutineers at the peril of his throne and of his life, had he suffered himself to be placed at their head, 60,000 men with 20,000 horse, it is said, would have gathered round him in a month. The whole of Malwa would have risen in arms and proclaimed him king, and what would have prevented the whole Mahratta race from following the impulse? He was constantly taunted with the memory of Jeswunt Rao, the hero of the Holkar family, with having let slip the golden opportunity of ridding Hindostan of the European. His defection would have been one of those many probable events, any one of which might have rendered all our countrymen's heroism unavailable for the preservation of our Indian empire, the non-occurrence of which has been miraculous.

Indore was indeed not confiscated. But to this hour, I believe, any open recognition of the Maharaja's faithfulness, by letter under the hand of the Governor-General at the least, has been withheld. Yet that faithfulness has continued to be manifested on every occasion and amidst every inconvenience. The traffic of his country has been—probably still is—disastrously interrupted by the pressing of carts and bullocks for the troops. The Opium-sales,—forming the most lucrative branch of Malwa trade—were suddenly shifted from Indore to Mhow. When, by the native authorities, the troops had been disarmed, the offenders put upon trial before a native commission, those guilty blown from guns and shot, or sentenced to imprisonment in irons with hard labour, suddenly it was required that the prisoners should be sent to the Residency. The request was immediately complied with,—the men were handed over to the British authorities,—tried again,—and set at liberty in every instance where they had been acquitted by the native commission; thus conclusively shewing the satisfactory nature of the previous proceedings, as not having let any of the guilty escape. But when a further request was made, when the whole of those disarmed were required to be sent to the Residency, the men took alarm, and the greater part escaped during the night. Is it possible to conceive a course of action more insulting to a sovereign and his officers than this taking away from them their own prisoners and trying them over again, as if their justice were no justice at all?

Now let it be recollected that the Indore state is not one which can owe any particular gratitude to the British Government. It will be remembered that in 1844 Lord Ellenborough and the Calcutta Council, and eventually Lord Hardinge, attempted to reduce it from the rank of a sovereign state, by ignoring the alleged right of adoption of the dowager Ranee, deliberately setting aside the candidate whom she had recommended as having most right to the throne, conferring the sovereignty on another, in order to shew that the will or whim of England was supreme, and then in an official letter limiting the succession to heirs of the body. It is very doubtful, to say the least, how such an act could have any effect. If adoption forms really part of the public law of India, as respects the independent Hindoo sovereignties, it does not appear at all clear (as an ex-Director observed to me some time back) that the British Government can set it aside in any of those states, whatever ground it may allege for doing so in those which are dependent on it. And this seems to have been felt; for it is perfectly well known that, to bolster up the measure, the boy of ten years old who was put upon the throne of Indore was induced to sign his hand to a letter to the Governor-General, accepting the limitation of the succession to heirs male.

Of course such a document, extracted from a child, would have no validity in any Court of Christendom. But it is equally well known that the proceeding has galled to the quick every member of the state, from the highest to the lowest, and that Holkar himself, since he has come to years of discretion, has repeatedly expressed his pain at having signed it, and his earnest wish to see the attempted restriction on adoption removed. The weight of that restraint was however not adequately felt till this last spring, when his only son died, and the possible proximity of annexation was brought home to all. Twins, I believe, have since been born to him, and so the evil day seems again deferred for awhile. But is this a position in which it is fit to keep an ally like him?

I have taken the cases of Dhar and Indore, as belonging to Malwa, one of the chief seats of war in the late rebellion. Space would fail me if I were to attempt to detail other grievances of our allies. Will no one move in Parliament, for instance, for a certain letter of Salar Jung to the Governor-General, in which, I am assured, he complains that while the surplus revenue of the Nizam's cessions was by treaty to be paid over to that sovereign, the administration of those provinces has been actually so managed as to bring him in a debtor, by the expenses, for instance, of huge cutcherries (law courts), palatial jails, and other buildings of which he does not at all appreciate the utility?

One word more:—

There is one of the late annexations to the details of which I have not yet alluded,—that of the Punjab. Lord Dalhousie reckons it among the fruits of conquest. General Low says, that in his conversation with natives in Rajpootana, "there never was any unpleasant remark made respecting the annexation of the Punjab," "they seemed perfectly to understand that an invasion of our territory entitled us, according to the ordinary course of human affairs, both to repel the invaders and to seize the country;"* — an argument, by the way, fully pertinent to the circumstances of the *first* Sikh war, which was *not* followed by the absorption of the Punjab, by no means so to those of the *second*, which *was* followed by that event. I have given elsewhere my views upon this annexation;† I will not here discuss whether it be consistent with any system of municipal law yet recognized, for the guardian to appropriate to himself the estates of his ward, on account of the misconduct towards him of tenants or servants, — or with any system of international jurisprudence, for a state to absorb the territories of a boy-prince under its protection on account of the insurrection of its chiefs or its people. Waiving then all questions of justice,—I quite admit, and am thankful to do

* Nagpore Annexation Papers, p. 42.

† British India, vol. ii. p. 166-7.

so, that the annexed Punjab has been and is most admirably governed by Sir John Lawrence. I quite admit, and am thankful to do so, that Sir John Lawrence and his Sikhs saved India at the outset of the rebellion. But I cannot overlook the cost of his doing so. I cannot forget that an able and earnest writer, in perhaps the most remarkable pamphlet which the rebellion has brought forth,* has not hesitated to say, that "our North-Western Provinces owe all this rebellion and anarchy to the very Punjab;" alleging that the pouring into the Punjab of the whole European force (or nearly so) of the Bengal Presidency, and the depriving the North-West of all its best civil officers, have been the means by which the Punjab has been made a model province, at the risk of the whole Indian empire. I cannot forget that to the hour of my writing this, it has not been possible to spare Sir John Lawrence out of the Punjab, either for the Governor-Generalship, or for the Council at home. I cannot forget that in spite of the efficient services rendered to us by the Sikhs in the rebellion, or rather because of those efficient services, the most serious fears were entertained at one time as to their fidelity; that there are upwards of 80,000 of them in our pay; that they have openly boasted on many occasions that they had fought against us once, and might fight against us again; and "who knows where the *raj* will be?" I cannot forget that the Maharaja of Putteeala, our worthy Sikh ally, has warned us of the danger of trusting in his

* "Thoughts of a Native of Northern India on the Rebellion, its causes and remedies" (Dalton, 1858); edited by M. W. (understood to be Mr. M'Leod Wylie); p. 3.

countrymen; has written—so Mr. Russell related in one of his letters—in express terms to an officer that "the Sikhs, if left idle, will be worse than the Hindostanees." I cannot forget that actual mutiny was on the point of breaking out, in the latter half of 1858, at Dera Ismail Khan, in the 18th Punjab Infantry, who were to have risen and murdered their officers. And I cannot help asking myself whether it would not be safer for us to have at Lahore a faithful native ally, than the ablest of English Governors. And of all allies that I can think of, I cannot imagine one so desirable as that noble young Christian prince, our Queen's frequent guest, once recognized by us as the rightful occupant of the Sikh throne. Nor can I conceive of any event capable of giving so firm a foothold, so vast a development to Christianity in India, as his re-enthronement. A native Christian sovereign in the Punjab, as it seems to me, would be the very pivot of India's future civilization.

PART II.

THE PLEDGES OF THE PROCLAMATION

TO THE PEOPLE OF INDIA.

LETTER XV.

THE PLEDGE OF RELIGIOUS AND CIVIL IMPARTIALITY AND EQUALITY.

I do not know any of the promises contained in the proclamation which is of deeper import, if faithfully carried out, than the one which first deals no longer with allies, but with subjects.

> "We hold ourselves bound to the natives of our Indian territories by the same obligations of duty which bind us to all our other subjects; and those obligations, by the blessing of Almighty God, we shall faithfully and conscientiously fulfil."

The whole idea of Christian, as opposed to Oriental sovereignty, is contained in these words, vague as they may perhaps seem to many. For the tie between the Christian sovereign and his people is essentially that of *duty*, not that of despotic force, or traditional authority, or kinship of race; in the fulfilment of that duty, not in the gratification of his will, his government consists. Who can tell what stirrings of the heart, what deep questionings about true kingship, such a profession coming from the sovereign's lips may awaken in many an Indian breast? Who can tell whether, more than any quotation from Scripture, it may not lead him to the thought of a Kings of kings,—of a Sovereign Wisdom by whom "kings reign, and princes decree justice?"

But the obligations of duty thus professed are not left obscure and indefinite. They are "*the same*" which bind the Sovereign of England to all her "other subjects,"—the same which bind her to us Englishmen, who boast like the Apostle that we were "freeborn." Even without the more detailed assurances which follow, it is impossible to mistake the value of this assurance to the natives. It is the pledge that there is to be for India no distinction between a dominant race and a subject one; that the natives of India are not our subjects, but our fellow-subjects. All that follows is in fact but the application of this pledge in particular instances.

"Firmly relying ourselves on the truth of Christianity, and acknowledging with gratitude the solace of religion, we disclaim alike the right and the desire to impose our convictions on any of our subjects. We declare it to be our Royal will and pleasure, that none be in anywise favoured, none molested or disquieted, by reason of their religious faith or observances, but that all shall alike enjoy the equal and impartial protection of the law; and we do strictly charge and enjoin all those who may be in authority under us, that they abstain from all interference with the religious belief or worship of any of our subjects, on pain of our highest displeasure."

To treat fully of the question which underlies this paragraph—that of the religious relation between England and India—would require a volume by itself. It was the most difficult passage in the proclamation, it was very likely the most laboured; it is not the happiest. I can easily see how some of its terms may be strained so as to give a colour to the old anti-christian policy of those days, when English missionaries found no rest for the sole of their foot on British Indian soil, of those days when a Sepoy could be ejected from the service for becoming a Christian. But if we interpret this paragraph by the previous one, it will lose most of its seeming narrowness. That none should be "favoured," "molested or disquieted," by reason of religion, forms part henceforth, with us Englishmen, of our public law; in pledging this to Hindoo and Mussulman, the Queen simply carries out her declaration, that she is "bound to the natives of India by the same obligations" as to her other subjects. In enjoining all who may be in authority under her in India, "that they abstain from all interference with the religious belief or worship" of any of her subjects, she must, rightly speaking, be doing no more. She must simply be announcing that civil authority must not be used in India, as it may not be used in England, for purposes of religious propagandism. She cannot mean that her officers should be deprived of the freedom there which they would enjoy here, which there she pledges to all her other subjects. She cannot mean that as individuals they should be debarred from the right of communicating the truths which they believe. It may be indeed that from the long continued overweight of authority in the East, acts lawful in themselves, and which would come here within the pale of Christian expediency, may fall outside of it in India; and if warning was needed on this head, it may have been wisely given. But the native creeds must not be allowed to suppose that they are to enjoy any immunity against Christian missionarizing, which Christianity does not enjoy against their own. Nor must they suppose that the pledge of respect to their religious faith and observances is to extend to every corruption which may be grafted on them.

Social order has its rights, which cannot bow to the mere name of religion. Cruelty and obscenity cannot remain scathless in worship, when they are punishable everywhere else.

That some guarantee of religious impartiality was however needed, is but too evident. The "Native of Northern India," a professed friend to Christianity, expressly attributes the outbreak in great measure to disquietude on the score of religion. The people, he says, were "strongly suspicious of the intentions of the Government to take their caste." He dwells upon the greased cartridges, upon the messing in jails. He recalls the riot in Benares when the latter system was introduced; how "the people of the town met publicly and secretly to discuss the question;" how "they insulted the magistrate openly, and contemned the police," and the cavalry were brought down, and "hundreds of the citizens were sent to gaol." He asks whether, if the same system had then been sought to be established in regiments, the same results would not have occurred as from the greased cartridges; whether this was not "a straw to shew the course of the wind," though "the Government did not heed it. *Hundreds of other acts,*" he continues, "*too numerous to relate*, have been committed in this way by the officers of the Government, which convinced the people beyond doubt *that it was the intention of the Government to take their caste.* Many of these acts were totally uncalled for, and without the least gain to the Government or anybody," and, as he truly says, "the natives prefer losing life to the loss of caste; an out-caste in this country is worse than dead."

Yet "IT IS NOT RELIGION BUT THE WANT OF RELIGION WHICH HAS BROUGHT SO MUCH EVIL TO THIS COUNTRY. The people know that the Government is a Christian one; let it act openly as a true Christian: the people will never feel themselves disappointed, they will only admire it. Who can detest 'religion?' It is the order of their own 'Shastars,' that every man is to revere his own religion. *You may have a thousand missionaries to preach, and another thousand as masters of the schools at the expense of the Government, or distribute a thousand Bibles at the hands of the Governor-General.* The people will not murmur out a single syllable, though they may laugh and jeer; *but take care that you do not interfere with their caste, you do not force them to eat the food cooked by another in their gaols, or thrust grease down their throats with the cartridges made by Europeans. I do not think such acts have anything to do with the Christian religion."**

Let it moreover be remembered, in reference to such religious or semi-religious observances as come under the head of caste, that whatever question there might be as to the mode in which caste ought to be dealt with, or even the expediency of actually ignoring it, supposing we were now for the first time to meet with it, that question exists in such a shape no longer. Caste, as a thing within certain limits to be maintained and respected, has been solemnly recognized by Parliament for now more than three-quarters of a century. The act of the 21 Geo. III., c. 70, s. 18 (1781), runs as follows:—"And in order that regard should be had to the civil and religious usages of the said natives, be it enacted that the rights and authorities of fathers of families, and

* "Thoughts of a native of Northern India," passim.

masters of families, according as the same might have been exercised by the Gentoo or Mohammedan law, shall be preserved to them respectively within their said families; nor shall any acts done in consequence of the rule and law of caste, respecting the members of the said families only, be held and adjudged a crime; although the same may not be held justifiable by the laws of England." The next section requires the Supreme Court of Bengal to frame its processes so as to "accommodate the same to the religion and manners of such natives;" and these enactments, which were confined in the first instance to Bengal, were extended to Madras and Bombay by an act of 1797 (37 Geo. III., c. 142, ss. 12 and 13). *They have never been repealed*; and the cry about trampling out caste, which was rife amongst us a year ago, was, therefore, as dishonest as it was senseless. It was upon the condition of respecting caste that we won India. We have bound ourselves to do so, by the most solemn sanction which a free people can give—that of its statutes; we cannot be released from that bond, until the people of India choose to discharge us.

It will be observed, indeed, that the Parliamentary pledge to caste was limited to its observance in *families*. It may be urged, therefore, that the recognition of it in public matters was not guaranteed. It is, however, impossible to deny that the acts of the Government of India have carried the pledge far beyond such limits. For instance—Lord Canning's General Order of the 27th March, 1857, on the disbandment of the 19th Regiment, N.I., made it the chief grievance against the Sepoys of that regiment, that they had distrusted the intentions of the Government in respect to religious observances. "Neither the 19th Regiment, nor any regiment in the service of the Government of India," said his Lordship, "nor any Sepoy, Hindoo, or Mussulman, has reason to pretend that Government has shewn, directly or indirectly, a desire to interfere with the religion of the troops. It has been the unvarying will of the Government of India to treat the religious feelings of all its servants, of every creed, with careful respect." Again, the General Order of May 19 "emphatically" proclaims to the army, "that the Government of India entertains no desire to interfere with their religion or caste, and that *nothing has been or will be done by the Government to affect the free exercise of the observances of religion or caste by every class of the people.*"

This, then, is the complex state of things we have to deal with; these are the circumstances with reference to which we must judge the wording of the proclamation on this head. On the whole,—though there is one expression in it against which I would earnestly protest, the treating of religion as a mere "solace,"—I am not disposed to quarrel with it. Fairly carried out, it should give England's evangelizing full scope to work and to triumph.*

The next paragraph of the proclamation might also be developed into a volume:

"And it is our further will that, so far as may be, our subjects, of whatever race or creed, be freely and impartially admitted to offices in our service, the duties of which they may be qualified, by their education, ability and integrity, duly to discharge."

---

* I am bound to say that this particular paragraph appears to be specially appreciated by the natives. See the note at the end of the volume.

This itself is little more than the reproduction of an enactment in the charter of 1833:

> "And be it enacted, that no native of the said territories, nor any natural-born subject of his Majesty resident therein, shall, by reason only of his religion, place of birth, descent, colour, or any of them, be disabled from holding any place, office, or employment under the said Company;" *

except that the earlier enactment was only negative,—a mere removal of disqualification,—while the latter one is positive, pledging admission to office. I shall not attempt here to go into the question, how far it may be expedient to extend the admission of natives to office in India, nor yet how far the portals of the "covenant" should be enlarged for the English settler. I shall have to make hereafter some observations upon the position of native officials. But whatever jealousies may hem round the admission of natives to office *there*, they must remember that the remedy lies in their own hands *here*. In the civil service,—in the medical,—in the scientific branches of the military,—no patronage henceforth stands in their way, no private Directorial narrowness can avail to nullify the promises of an imperial statute. They have but to will it,—they have but, in the fair open fight of free competition, to win a fitting place, and the administration of their own country falls in great measure into their hands. I am far from over-valuing educational competition in itself,—I know how unhealthy is the stimulus which it too often supplies to the selfish ambition of young and old alike, of the teacher and the pupil. But as a solution of a great political difficulty,—as a key to open a most puzzling lock in Indian statesmanship,—it seems to me beyond price. Nor can I conceive of a grander, nobler boon

* 3 & 4 Wm. 4, c. 85, s. 89.

being ever held out by the conquering race to the conquered than that of self-government, as the reward of self-development,—self-government, not as a favour to be sued for, but as a right to be won, in peaceful conflict with the conquerors themselves. Where in history do we see the like?

And if, indeed, the conduct of local governments, local officials, fall far short of Parliamentary and Royal pledges,—as it certainly has done, as it certainly will do for many a long year yet to come, still let our native fellow-subjects bear up and bear on. Let them cling to those pledges; let them din them for ever in their immediate superiors' ears; let them slowly work them out into fact. If they really shew themselves "qualified, by their education, ability, and integrity, duly to discharge" the offices now monopolized by Englishmen, let them rest assured that sooner or later Victoria's promise will come true—that sooner or later they will be "freely and impartially admitted" to every employment from which they are now excluded.

Not, indeed, that the qualification must be forgotten, "*So far as may be.*" No doubt these words may be so interpreted by prejudice and ill-will as to nullify the whole promise. No doubt that the tendency to play the Jesuit with them, radiating from many a narrow heart and brain in the Indian Council at home, will for many a long year paralyze the hands of officials in India when the native knocks at the door of office. But by nothing can this tendency be more confirmed, more sharpened into bitter hostility to native claims, than if the qualification and its necessity were overlooked, and the native population were to fancy that the very walls of office are to fall before them at the sound of the proclamation, like those of Jericho at the sound of Israel's trumpets. The qualification is a *necessary* one at present. On the morrow of a rebellion fomented by Brahmins and Mussulmen, which has convulsed all India, England cannot, for India's own sake, treat Brahmins and Mussulmen without caution at least, if not without suspicion.

But there is one thing which may be done, and which will carry out the promises of the proclamation for the present far more effectually than any loose and hasty admission of natives to office. It may be shewn by acts that the fulfilment of that proclamation, which declares on the part of the Sovereign that she is bound by the same obligations of duty to her native as to her other subjects, is not about to be idly trusted to men whose conduct, whose speech, has shewn that they place native princes and native commoners on quite another level than that of the white man—sometimes that they are hardly prepared to treat their native fellow-subjects as human beings. The thick-and-thin supporters of the annexation policy, in the Calcutta Council, and elsewhere, are not those who should be promoted to high employ when that policy is abandoned. The men who advocate the confiscation of Mussulman and Hindoo endowments, are not to be made the depositaries of an authority which is to give "impartial protection" to all creeds. Civilians like that Collector at Meerut in 1856, of whom his own sister has told us that he had "a most absurd horror of a native's coming near him," and declared that he could "detect the copperish smell of the colouring matter in their skins the instant they enter the room," and that "he would much sooner be touched by a toad than by one of their clammy hands,"* should be at once removed from a sphere so uncongenial to their olfactory nerves and delicate sensibilities of touch as that of India. And, lastly, men like Mr. Frederick Cooper, who, in the face of God and man, dare to boast of the butchery, or death by suffocation, of nearly 500 of their fellow-creatures as of the "ceremonial sacrifice" of a "Christian," should be made distinctly to feel, at the hands of every one of their fellow-countrymen, from the Sovereign to the poorest of her subjects, that righteous horror which is due to acts which transcend the grasp of human punishment.†

No message of mercy can avail, while it is liable to be belied and perverted by such instruments. "Cooperism," and the Queen's sway over India, are two incompatible things henceforth. Those who choose to perpetuate the one must forego their allegiance to Victoria.

* The Timely Retreat, vol. ii. p. 89.

† See this hideous story in Mr. Cooper's book, the "Crisis in the Punjaub," pp. 152-70. The men in question belonged to a disarmed regiment, whose rising must have been a very panic of self-defence. They were jaded fugitives, craving for mercy. They were more numerous than their captors, and had to be decoyed into their power by a sham of leniency, planned, as such devil's deeds usually are, amidst "intense mirth." Some, on being led to execution, "petitioned to be allowed to make one last salaam to the Sahib." One of the Sikh executioners swooned away at the 150th who was shot. The narrator seems proud to compare the suffocation of 45 with the Black Hole of Calcutta, and the well into which the bodies are thrown with that of Cawnpore. The hasty sanction given by Sir John Lawrence and Mr. Montgomery to such acts cannot absolve them.

LETTER XVI.

THE PLEDGE OF RESPECT TO NATIVE PROPERTY AND USAGES. A GLANCE INTO THE PAST.

"We know and respect the feelings of attachment with which the natives of India regard the lands inherited by them from their ancestors, and we desire to protect them in all rights connected therewith, subject to the equitable demands of the State; and we will that generally, in framing and administering the law, due regard be paid to the ancient rights, usages, and customs of India."

Maintenance of native rights of property—regard to native law and custom—such are the two momentous pledges of this paragraph.* Before considering the former, let us not overlook what the latter implies. It follows from it, not only that, as enjoined by previous Acts of Parliament, we should not senselessly trample down caste, however it may hamper us occa-

* I need hardly point out the emphatic, though implicit disavowal, in the above paragraph, of Lord Canning's Oude proclamation. I expressed fully at the time, in the columns of the *Leeds Express*, my feelings respecting this measure, which have not changed. It is, I presume, sufficient from henceforth to quote, respecting it, M. de Montalembert's words :—"Ce châtiment aussi impolitique qu'excessif, aussi inique par son application universelle que par sa cruelle réversibilité sur la postérité des coupables et des innocents."—Un Débat sur l'Inde, p, 49. Jeffs.

sionally, but that we should take account of native modes of thought and action in our improvements; that we should endeavour on all occasions to place ourselves at the native's point of view as well as at our own, so as to make of him a fellow-worker, and not a mere tool or slave.

I fear we have forgotten this too often, even in our most boasted, our most real Indian reforms. I thank God, for instance, that suttee has been abolished throughout the British territories, and many native ones. But do you think that, except in the minds of a few thinking men, one or two perhaps in a million, the abolition of suttee added one particle to the popularity of the British Government in the hour of trial? Do we not know that the question of the legality of its abolition was fought out in the Privy Council itself, by natives consequently who accepted our rule and its processes, yet protested against that special measure? Nay, what can any of our most benevolent measures for the mere preservation of human life have done for us in the minds of a people in whom religious beliefs are so strong, instincts of self-preservation, as far as the body is concerned, so weak, that Sir Wm. Sleeman was able to relate two several instances* in which women burned themselves as suttees on the death of men of

* See "Rambles and Recollections," vol. i. p. 34 and foll., the case of a Lodhee cultivator's wife, who, on the death of a banker's father, being at the time between 50 and 60 years of age, and a grandmother, declared that she had been suttee with the deceased six times, and would be so a seventh; stole a handful of ashes from his pyre, which she placed in her bosom, and persuaded her husband and her brother to burn her the next day. See also a similar account in vol. ii. of his "Journey through Oude," pp. 318-22.

other castes, with whom they had no kind of connexion, alleging that they had been their wives in a former state of existence; that Lord Hastings relates having received a petition from a native "complaining that the officiating Brahmins, at a temple of Kali, near Moorshedabad, refused to sacrifice him," and soliciting, "as it was unlawful for him to put himself to death," that Lord Hastings "would order the Brahmins to immolate him"?* Take even the case of female infanticide—a practice connected with no religious belief, peculiar to certain castes, odious to all others; having its origin, perhaps, as General Sleeman somewhere intimates, in a feeling which has a noble side to it, the proud Rajpoot's fear of seeing his daughters carried to the harem of the conquering Moslem,† and yet based in the main on the most selfish feelings—supposed social necessities; ostentation at wedding feasts; punctilios about intermarriage; the relative position of father-in-law and son-in-law.‡ Is it really supposed that all these feelings, selfish though they be, are extinguished with the act itself? Is it supposed that the Rajpoot father, accustomed to see no evil in the putting to death of his infant daughters, or at all events to see that evil wiped out as a matter of course by the village priest for a few rupees, really feels

* Private Journal, vol. i. p. 53. "A short time ago," adds Lord Hastings, "I had another petition from a man, who implored that I would order his head to be cut off, as he was in a state of hopeless penury." This, however, looks to me like a highly Oriental method of soliciting alms.

† See Sleeman's "Oude," vol. ii. p. 48.

‡ See Raikes' "Notes on the North-Western Provinces," p. 1 and foll.

grateful and attached to the British Government when he views around him a family of growing daughters, whom it is a disgrace to keep single, whom it will be a ruin to marry, by whose marriage he will be for ever lowered in social position as towards their husbands? God forbid that we should have done any less than we have done—wherever we have done it wisely—to suppress any inhuman practices! Would to God that we had done far more, and that far sooner, so that the feelings which prompted such practices should long since have become dull, if not obliterated; so that gentler, truer feelings should have had time to grow up in their place! But these are precisely the instances in which the good deeds of the British Government have belonged to a sphere of thought and action so foreign to that of the native population, that they stood it in no stead, except with the chosen few, in the hour of trial.

Take again education. Here indeed I believe that, with all its faults, the Government system of education has had for its effect to conciliate to it the minds of a certain portion of the native population,—those young men, namely, who have been brought within its influence. I do not however apprehend that these constitute at present a very numerous, still less an energetic class. And considering the acknowledged effects of Government education in India, in dissolving all beliefs of Hindooism in the minds of the students, I suspect that up to the present time it has excited more disaffection among the bigoted masses than affection among the free-thinking few.

Do we rely upon railways and electric telegraphs as

securing the attachment of the native population? That they were able to see a use in the electric telegraph, the rebellion has shewn, but certainly not the use which we meant them for, since they simply discovered how handy were the hollow cast-iron posts for extemporizing an artillery against us. And as respects railways,—precious though they be for the future development of India,—what are the few miles of railway made, to the thousands of miles of common metalled road needing to be made, of which the construction of high priced railways must necessarily for the time being hinder the making?

I fear truly that of all the very best deeds of the British Government in India a few public works,—such as the Grand Trunk Road, the Ganges and other canals, the Rajahmundry irrigation works—are almost the only ones hitherto that will have weighed much in its favour with the native population when the hour of rebellion came,—and that only locally. The extirpation of the Pindarrees under Lord Hastings aroused unbounded gratitude at the time. But the generation which had witnessed it must have in general passed away at the time the rebellion broke out; and it may not be unfortunate for us if the excesses of the predatory bands whom it has left behind revive the recollection of that great achievement. Even the transit duties, deemed once so oppressive, are beginning to be regretted.*

To fix an alien government in the affections of an Oriental people, depend upon it, measures of a broader,

* See "Thoughts of a Native of Northern India on the Rebellion," p. 25.

more massive character are needed; measures which, so to speak, dint themselves into the daily life of mankind, or weld themselves indissolubly with it. Now a Hindoo is not always occupied with the burning of widows, the murdering of female infants, the sacrificing of human victims to Kalee; he is not always in dread of the Thug's noose; he does not always live near a railway or a canal; he seldom sends or receives telegrams; he generally troubles himself little about literature. His daily life, I take it, is mainly occupied with three things,—worship, which is also for the most part made an occasion of pleasure,—the pursuit of a livelihood, and of its enjoyments or luxuries, so far as they may be within his reach,—self-preservation in its widest sense, as including the preservation of all that a man appropriates to himself. From these three points of view therefore must any given rule be considered, in order to judge of his feelings towards it.

I place the religious point of view first of all, in order to dispose of it the sooner. It will not be asserted, I presume, by the greatest encomiast of British rule, that it can be considered a religious blessing generally by a native of India. It bears no doubt with it in most cases a negative religious gain. British justice is undoubtedly an impartial arbiter generally between Moslem and Hindoo; and it is thus conceivable that British rule should be hailed with satisfaction by the Moslem inhabitants of a province chiefly occupied by Hindoos, by the Hindoo inhabitants of a Moslem district. Still, we must all feel that mere preference, as between rulers of another creed, of the less fanatical, is no real source of strength to the latter, but simply a mitigation of their dangers. And on the other hand we have to take account of the growing distrust of and dislike to Christianity, on the part of both Hindoo and Moslem,—feelings which I believe to be as yet really prevalent only in the large towns, and among particular castes and classes elsewhere,—but which the rebellion, and the more strenuous efforts of Christian missions,* will certainly tend more and more to evolve, and to exasperate where already developed.

If we pass to the point of view of personal profit, though we may assume that there are certain classes,—the trading classes,—which are generally benefited by our rule, which have shewn themselves generally our staunch friends, yet the trade of India is yet so trifling, compared with its agriculture, that the trading classes, except the village bankers, form a very small item,—and of course by no means a warlike one,—in the community; and the trade in money is so much connected with the payment of the revenue, that I strongly suspect the Indian money-dealer is nearly as unpopular with his fellow countrymen as the Jewish publican was of old with his. It is therefore chiefly with reference to the land,—to the right of property in it, to its enjoyment, to the laws and means for securing both, to the demands made upon it, that we must expect our rule to be judged. Most truly therefore does

* Especially when carried to such a pitch of imprudence, to say the least, as in the late case of the Chetty child at Madras. Of course I do not wish to discourage any the most strenuous efforts of missionaries, if rightly directed,—quite the contrary. The exasperation of Mahommedans and Hindoos is, up to a certain point, a homage to Christianity.

the Proclamation testify to the native's attachment to his land; most wisely does it promise him protection for all his rights connected therewith.

To us indeed both the pledge of regard to native laws and customs, and that of protection to landed property, may seem but the merest truisms. From what has the landowner to be protected except from individual outrages? What protection does he need, beyond a few extra policemen, perhaps occasionally the bracing up of some law grown slack by use? What pledge of respect to law and custom would he think of, beyond the assurance that vacancies on Westminster benches will be duly filled up?

But it has not been so in India. There, it has been too frequently the complaint of the native,—of the European settler—that the extension of British rule bore with it insecurity to landed property, and an ever more reckless displacement of the landmarks of the law. Nor is it to be supposed that these complaints apply only to the quasi-mythical days—as we are prone to fancy them in comparison with the present,—of Clive and Warren Hastings. They were rife a quarter-century ago,—more or less, they have been rife ever since. Nor can we judge how much must turn upon the faithful execution, or the neglect and desecration, of the promises of the Proclamation on this head, without exhibiting the state of things to which they apply.

When that well-known public servant, whose signature of "Indophilus" has often honoured the pages of the *Times*,—whose appointment to the Governorship of Madras has been hailed with such deserved and general approval—was simply an Indian civilian, Assistant-Secretary to the Government of India, he wrote a series of letters to the *Bengal Hurkaru*, reprinted afterwards in the *Mirror of the Indian Press* for 1833. In these will be found a picture, which I cannot doubt was a true one, of the then state of our North Provinces :—

"The whole of our provinces west of Mirzapoor," he said, "are at this moment withering under the influence of uncertainty in taxation. No person connected with the land in those provinces *dares* to make any improvement . . . Can there be said to be any property in the land west of Mirzapoor? . . . . . When is the creation of landed property, which is generally the first step in the progress of society, to take place? . . . Is the agricultural population, which forms the great bulk of the community, richer than they were before? Have they more of the comforts and enjoyments of this life than they had under the native Governments which preceded us? I say, most certainly not. The wealth which formerly accumulated in the hands of the upper classes has, with very few exceptions, been drained off into the Government treasury. . . . . But it must not be supposed that the destructive influence of the system has been confined to the upper classes. Several whole provinces have been cruelly plundered by it, and, generally speaking, our assessment has been raised greatly above that which was demanded by the preceding Government. . . . Compare British Bundelcund with what it was at the period when we first occupied it, and, what those portions of the province which have remained under native rule still are. Fertile, smiling Bundelcund, where the cultivation was noted for being more complete and the inhabitants for being more industrious and docile (I am speaking only of that portion of Bundelcund which is under British rule) than perhaps in any part of our dominions. How is it now? Bundelcund has been fleeced, ruined, demoralized. She has been plucked and squeezed till every drop of capital has oozed out of her, and an atrocious measure, by which large quantities of grain were confiscated in various parts of the province for the realisation of an impossible amount of taxation, even after it had found its way into the hands of the wholesale dealers, deprived the zemindars of the resource which they before derived from their credit with the local monied interest, such as it is. . . . Compare the southern district of the Delhi territory with the Bhurtpore country, or with the neighbouring British district of Agra. I never saw misrule delineated in such undisguised colours as she is in that southern district of the Delhi territory. It seems almost as if it had been got up for stage effect. The soil is highly fertile, and the remains of well-built towns and expensive brick houses in every village, show that the district once enjoyed a considerable degree of prosperity. Now, however, you may traverse it from one end to the other, and there is not a single *pucka* house to be seen that is not rapidly hastening to decay. . . . Their clothiug forms a counterpart to their lodging. . . . . Those native states which are most notorious for their misgovernment, can make a better display than this. Cultivation may not always be carried to the same extent, because the people have not an excessive *jumma* [assessment] to pay up by any means, and because the country is often a natural desert. . . . But many infallible signs denote that the people are better off. There are generally several good houses in each village belonging to the lord of the soil and his dependents, or perhaps to some new man who has made his fortune at Court. . . . There is an abundance of cattle, carriages, horses, camels, and of all the necessaries and enjoyments suited to their existing state of civilisation, and in short the people are well clothed and comfortable. . . . Before leaving the Delhi territory, however, I would ask what has become of some hundred families of men learned in the religion, law, and medical science of the country, which a few years ago existed in comfort, and in many cases in great affluence, at Delhi? Their estates, which had in many instances been in the family for two or three generations, and were a support to thousands besides their own immediate family and dependents, have been added to the fisc. Where are the Milkies, a still more numerous and unfortunate class? . . . . These are the descendants of the first Mahommedan invaders, among whom the lands of many towns and villages were parcelled out. . . . As their tenure of the land originally allotted to their predecessors was always respected by the native Governments, it acquired in the course of ages all the characteristics of the most secure property. In fact it stood on exactly the same basis and was just as good property as any freehold estate in England. Can it be believed that these estates were sequestrated . . . by hundreds, I might almost say by thousands together, and hundreds of families and whole towns and villages full of these poor people were reduced at once to a state of the most abject poverty? The pretence on which they were sequestrated was to hold an inquiry into the validity of their tenure, and after such an act of barefaced injustice it may easily be imagined what kind of decision was pronounced. . . . What has become of the numerous thriving and substantial villages to the west and north of Delhi, abounding at the period when we occupied the district with cattle, horses, jewels, and everything which could render the inhabitants comfortable? They have also undergone the collectorial torture. . . . It must be remembered however that these high-spirited zemindars have not lost their native energy and independence of mind with their wealth; and unless we change our system of treatment, we may rue the day when their fettered and sullen but by no means subdued spirit may find an opportunity, on the occasion of some crisis of our fortune, to burst its bonds asunder. . . . Cannot Rohilcund boast of one spirit frank and fearless enough to tell us whether she has flourished most under the rule of Hafiz-Rahmut, or under the paternal care of *her* collector? . . . . I have heard of certain pergunnahs [districts] situated near the foot of the hills, which are lying waste to this day from the effects of one of these assessments. . . . What is the state of Ajmere, that spot which in a moment of good intention was selected as a peculiarly appropriate theatre on which to display the beauty and harmony of a well constituted government to the surrounding semi-barbarous states? . . . In the latter the better classes continue in full possession of their hereditary estates, while in the former their estates have been either wholly or partially confiscated, and all classes connected with the soil are in rapid progress of being reduced to the bare subsistence standard of our revenue system. . . . Have Shajawulpore and Beirsea enjoyed a better revenue administration under us than they did under the Pindarrees? . . . . I assert, without the slightest apprehension of being refuted, that the revenue management of these public robbers . . was infinitely more humane, more considerate, more conducive to the security and enjoyment of the species than that of the British officers."

Such, then, was a sketch of the results of British rule in Northern India, taken 25 years ago. That a vast improvement has taken place since then, in our Northern provinces, I gladly admit. The promise of it was indeed evidently contained in the very denunciations which I have quoted. No man high in office could have been allowed to utter them thus openly, at a time, be it remembered, when the press was not legally free, unless great and fearless reforms had already been resolved upon by those in higher office still. Those were, indeed, the days of Lord Wm. Bentinck, of whom I believe Sir Wm. Sleeman only spoke the barest truth when he wrote, many years after the death of that Governor-General, that "a more thoroughly honest man never presided over the government of any country."* Under him the revenue settlement of the North-western provinces was begun, and well-nigh carried out, by Robert Mertins Bird. This gave to a portion of the landed interest of India the greatest boon that interest had received since the days of Lord Cornwallis in Bengal, that of a fixed land-tax for 30 years. Before understanding, however, the bearings of that measure, it is necessary to say a word as to the principles on which the settlements of the Indian land-revenue have hitherto been based.

* Sleeman's Oude, vol. ii. p. 150.

LETTER XVII.

THE NORTH WEST REVENUE SETTLEMENT AND THE TALOOKDARS.

It is easy to talk learnedly and wisely on the subject of Indian land-tenures. It is far more difficult,—at least I find it so,—to bear in mind, when dealing with the subject, that what is spoken of concerns 180 millions of people. Group together the whole central zone of Europe—Russia, the Austrian empire, Germany, Switzerland, France, and you do not yet reach the same figure of population. And where is the man who would be bold enough to suppose himself familiar with the landed tenures of all those countries, to speak of them as a whole, to generalise them in a common formula? Yet this is what every Indian official, every writer upon Indian subjects, wittingly or unwittingly, is constantly doing. It is idle to suppose that such talk can really be correct. Our generalisations about Indian tenures must evidently represent, not those tenures in themselves, but the state of our own legislation, the state of our own information respecting them; the former, precisely because it is uniform, at least for huge sweeps of country, necessarily imperfect; the latter, precisely because it must be personal and local, necessarily often incorrect and incomplete.

It is necessary that I should address this caution to my readers, seeing that I am myself about to generalise on the subject. I will say then, that as far as I can make out, one form of ownership seems to have lain at the bottom of Indian tenures, from Cape Comorin to the Himalayas, that of a common holding of the land by village communities. But in the course of ages that form has in many instances entirely disappeared; in more still, has become so profoundly modified as to be almost wholly unrecognisable. And amongst other elements which, though not essentially irreconcileable with it, have contributed more or less to modify or to destroy it, must be prominently placed that of the existence, scattered more or less over the whole face of India, of certain individuals called in Bengal "zemindars," in the north-west "talookdars" ("zemindar" having there a more limited meaning), in the west "deshmooks," &c.* Their origin varies probably as much as their rights are found to do. In many cases, no doubt, they represent the warrior chief under whose auspices the village community was first settled, or restored after dispossession, or to whose protection it was obliged to resort when attacked or threatened. In more cases still, perhaps, they represent simply the conqueror or the brigand, who imposed upon the community the recognition of his supremacy. In others, and probably the greatest number so far as the zemindars of Bengal are concerned, especially since the Mahommedan conquest, they represent either the tenant under the Crown by military service, or simply the farmer of the Crown

* In my "British India" I have not assigned sufficient weight to this element in the social state of India, the importance of which has been so strongly brought out by the rebellion. I was misled on the point by Mr. Kaye and other late Anglo-Indian writers.

revenue, who has succeeded in making himself an hereditary position. And to this last type all the others have assimilated themselves in this one great feature, that where these individual rights exist, the holder of them stands between the State and the village communities, responsible to the former for a certain amount of land-revenue, which he levies with additions from the various village communities inhabiting the district upon which it is assessed. On the other hand, the rights of the village communities have, in the north especially, become in many instances centred in certain families, one or more to a village, belonging chiefly to the higher castes, such as Brahmins or Rajpoots, and which we find designated under the titles of "village proprietors," "old proprietors," "village zemindars," constituting thus a class intermediate between the talookdar and the actual cultivator.

To persons imbued with English ideas as to landed tenures, there was much in the position of the zemindars or talookdars to identify them with real landowners, often little to distinguish them from such. We cannot therefore be surprised that such a view pervaded the first great Indian revenue settlement, that of Bengal by Lord Cornwallis in the last century; that the zemindars were deemed to be, and made into, actual landowners. Yet the measure was scarcely accomplished when it was felt that, however benevolent the intentions of its framers, it sacrificed the rights and interests of the great mass of the agricultural population. The recoil was natural; to sweep away the whole favoured class as mere middlemen, to treat the actual cultivators of the soil as alone worthy of consideration.

This view was carried out in two different modes; in the South, in the professed interest of the cultivators, but apparently with equal neglect of the rights of all parties, by Sir Thomas Munro; in the North-west, with some attempt to secure those of all parties, and a very decided endeavour to uphold those of the village communities or proprietors, by Robert Mertins Bird, under the sanction of Lord William Bentinck. And whilst the South was left a prey to the uncertainty of yearly revenue settlements, the North-west received, as I have said, the boon of a revenue settlement for 30 years, made with the village communities or proprietors.

I am far from contesting the benevolent purpose which prompted the village settlements of the North-west, or even the annual settlements with individual cultivators of Sir Thomas Munro in the South. I pretend to no particular admiration for the feudal system of individual property. I share in all the admiration which has been expressed for the Indian village system in itself; I would gladly see it fostered as much as possible, restored whenever possible. But there is one thing that is higher than any system of landed tenures whatever, that is, Right. And I believe there was much that was not right in the revenue settlement of the North-west.

The temper in which it was carried out, in the first place, was not a right one. The question of title to the land was surely one of fact above all. Yet it was turned into an actual party question. A time came when any revenue officer who was supposed in any wise to favour the rights of the talookdars was a marked man, shut out as far as possible from advancement. If

Englishmen were thus treated, natives fared still worse. Sir William Sleeman, writing to the late Mr. John Colvin, declares that—

> "In the matter of courtesy to the native gentry, Robert Mertins Bird insulted them whenever he had the opportunity of doing so, and that Mr. Thomason (a late Lieutenant-Governor of the North-West) was too apt to imitate him in this and in other things. Of course their example was followed by too many of their followers and admirers. . . . . It has always struck me (he says) that Mr. Thomason in his system did all he could to discourage the growth of a middle and upper class upon the land—the only kind of property on which a good upper and middle class could be sustained in the present state of society in India. . . . . Mr. Thomason, I am told, systematically set aside all the landed aristocracy of the country as a set of middlemen, superfluous and mischievous." *

Some of my more democratic readers may very likely deem this treatment of a landed gentry as mischievous and superfluous middlemen a fine thing. Perhaps the systematic crushing of any class of the community is as inconsistent with true democracy as with any other political system worthy of the name. But without entering upon any theories as to land-holding in general, let us consider the effect of such a measure in India. I suspect the most vehement of English democrats, when he takes into account the difference of circumstances between the two countries, will see that the crushing of the landed gentry is not, under British rule, any blessing at all to the Indian peasant.

For there is this broad line of separation between England and India: England is taxed for the benefit of Englishmen, rented by Englishmen, governed by Englishmen; India is taxed, chiefly in the shape of

* Sleeman's Oude, vol. ii. pp. 413-14.

rent, for the benefit of foreigners, governed by foreigners. And whilst with us, in spite of our constitutional grumblings about rates and taxes, taxation is nevertheless generally, and especially in the case of agriculture, only a secondary element in our social life, in India the land-revenue is the primary element in the social life of its people, the leading concern of the agriculturist. Thus Sir William Sleeman writes, that "in India, where the people have learnt so well to govern themselves from the want of settled government, good or bad government really depends almost altogether upon *good or bad settlements of the land revenue.*"* The question is therefore really this for the Indian cultivator: Is it better that a portion of the produce of the land should go to a man of his own race, residing probably in his neighbourhood, spending his income there, and spending it in great measure on articles of native production, or that, going wholly to the British Government, it should be in part abstracted from the country at once in the shape of charges in Europe, in greater part devoted to the payment of high salaries to foreign officers, without root in the country, who either save money for the purpose of carrying it away, or spend it for the most part on articles of British growth or manufacture; the said foreign officers moreover being few in number, and residing only in the chief towns? Will the peasant not easily see that the existence of native zemindars or talookdars, maintained from the land, is better for him than their extinction? For the position of the British Government towards him after all is simply that of an absentee landlord, acting

* Rambles and Recollections, vol. i. p. 125.

by foreign agents. And although modern political economy, amongst other wonderful performances, has sometimes attempted to prove that absenteeism is no evil, I feel satisfied that no man of ordinary sense, who has had the opportunity of observing two agricultural parishes, in the one of which there shall be resident men of property, spending money within the parish, whilst in the other there shall be no wealthy residents, and all the rents received shall be spent on the Continent, or even in London, but will know that the balance of prosperity lies with the former.

The extinction of the Indian landed gentry then could not but be detrimental to the Indian cultivator, whom it might seem to favour. How it was sought to be carried out—what results it has actually produced—we have next to examine. Let it be observed, that whilst the revenue settlement of the North-West was being carried on, those provinces enjoyed the benefit of being under the rule, as Lieutenant-Governor, of a most true friend to the natives, Mr. T. C. Robertson. He was avowedly shocked at the reckless proceedings of the settlement officers. He was not, he owned, "quite prepared to acquiesce in the very summary process" whereby the settlement officers and their superiors got over the difficulty of the rights of the talookdars, which Mr. Bird in his report on the settlement actually omitted to consider. After confirming at the outset the settlements of different districts, he felt at last compelled to postpone all further ratification of them till further information, owing to the symptoms "of precipitation and a craving for despatch" which were discernible. He saw how "the Raja of Mynpoorie, whose predecessor had received the highest acknowledgments from the British Government for his unshaken loyalty," was, "without a reference to Government," through a mere legal construction put upon his rights as a talookdar, "*deprived entirely, he and his successors, in perpetuity, of all power of interference in* 116 *of* 158 *villages included in his talooka* (*estate*) which had descended to him in regular succession before the introduction of the British rule." He observed how another Raja "had his talooka curtailed by the severance of 138 of the 216 villages which it contained;" how, on his "winning one suit, and having the prospect of gaining more (*for the parties sued are stated to be disposed in most instances to admit his claim*), the collector was *ordered* by the Sudder Board [Board of Revenue] *not to carry the decree passed in his favour into effect.*"

I have taken the above from a minute by Mr. Robertson himself, and from the proceedings of the Government of the North-Western Provinces.* Is it not striking to find thus turning up the name of the Raja of Mynpoorie, one of the rebel chiefs in the present revolt? I believe, indeed, that a portion of his property was eventually restored. But the Rajpoot adage, "a man's life for a finger's breadth of soil," will shew how spoliation, to any extent however little, must affect these fierce chieftains. Think also of the second case

* See "Return on the Revenue Survey (India)," ordered by the House of Commons to be printed, 20 Aug. 1853, p. 120 and foll.; and "Return to an Order of the House of Commons, dated 26 March, 1858, for copies of a despatch from the Governor-General of India, dated the 25th day of Nov. 1842," &c.

instanced, and its enormity. Imagine the Board of Inland Revenue here, after an adverse decision to some excise claim in the Court of Exchequer, which should rule the law against the Crown in a whole group of informations against a firm, directing the court "not to carry the judgment into effect!"

But Mr. Robertson struggled in vain for justice. Already when he wrote, his plea for delay before ratifying the settlement in Benares had been overruled from Calcutta, without even an answer to his arguments. He left; and his place was taken by a model civilian, Mr. Thomason, an imitator, as we have seen, of Mr. Bird. The result may be expected.

I have before me a pamphlet printed lately for private circulation by Messrs. Smith and Elder. It is the reprint, by a retired Bengal civilian, whose name surely need no longer be withheld—Mr. Boulderson—of a "Minute on Talookdaree Cases," recorded by him on the 2d April, 1844, when junior member of the Board of Revenue at Agra. The revenue settlement of the North-West having been terminated, if I recollect aright, in 1842, this minute must be considered as a summary of the impressions produced, by the proceedings for its establishment, upon one thoroughly acquainted with all the facts, but happening to stand outside of the pale of received official theories. And such were those impressions, that he felt himself, he says, so far as the Talookdars were concerned, "bound to place on record in the openest manner his condemnation of the proceedings, and to send the same to Government."

The writer admits fully that "it is highly probable

the talookdars were not proprietors of all the estates they held;" "that it was most just and most expedient to admit, in all cases where the rights of others were proved, and where those rights had been maintained and were found in existence, the parties possessing them to settlement engagements with the Government." All he contends for is, that the respective rights of talookdars and others should be determined, not by what they ought to be, but by what they actually are. And he believes he may freely assert, that so far from this plain postulate of common sense being carried out, of many hundred estates which had been alienated from the talookdars, under a so-called inquiry into their titles, the proceedings, *in no particular case*, were ever perused or considered by the Board of Revenue, which simply decided upon general principles. He shews that in carrying out these general principles, there was literally no breach of duty, no perversion of facts to which the Board did not resort. Whilst a young Raja's property was under the guardianship of the Board as a Court of Wards, his estate of 693 villages, and an area of 675 square miles, was "settled" in a single season, and more than two-thirds of the whole was handed over to village officers, whose rights, by the settlement officer's own statement, had been in abeyance for 200 years. Titles sold repeatedly by Government itself, at auctions for balances of revenue, and contested by various claimants in every court of the country, were simply annihilated, and, to use the writer's words, "all the sanctions of Government and of the laws, from our first possession of the country till the present time," were "set aside as vain, or nothings."

With a report before them as to a certain district, shewing the entire disappearance of the primitive village communities, and their replacement by others actually constituted by talookdars, so that "no trace of the original owners" could be found, the Board decided that those original owners had all along "retained their possession of the soil." With a report before them stating that the rights of a certain Raja to 95 villages out of 105, in a district, had been "first formally recognized about 240 years ago,"—possession by his family being established for 258 years previously—the Board treated these rights as *created* by patent at the date at which they were first recognized. With a report before them shewing that the same chief's rights were only contested in 26 out of the 105 villages, and that even in these no tree could be felled without his permission, and the right of fishing was exclusively his, the Board denied those rights in all but six villages of the whole number, which they had the grace to settle with him in zemindarie tenure. In short, the writer charges the Board of which he was a member, in so many words, with "fabrication of evidence," and appears to prove his case.

The pamphlet refers to the case above noticed of the Raja of Mynpoorie, who had yet received no justice. It quotes that of the princess or Ranee of Powayne, who held villages "in zemindarie tenure, recognized and affirmed on our first acquiring the country, and in every successive settlement ever since." Without the slightest complaint against her, an investigation was directed into her title in 1831. It was recognized by the first inquirer, who found that the villagers derived "more than ordinary advantages under the existing management;" that the majority of them expressed "entire satisfaction;" that there were no "heritable and transferable" properties other than her own. Seven years after, this lady, apparently of full age and under no disability, was placed under the Court of Wards, in order that her estates should be "settled" with the heads of the villages as "real proprietors;" and she only escaped from it after the lapse of six years. In the meanwhile, although she paid her revenue with punctuality, even in the year of famine—although it had been reduced by £1,500 in favour of the village head men—about half were already broken down. Let it be observed that the Raja of Powayne has been another of the rebel chiefs of the present insurrection; though he has since sought to buy our forgiveness by sending in the head of the Moulvie of Lucknow, killed in an encounter with his people.

Famine years were precious to "the system." The talookdars failed to pay their revenue. Their estates were instantly sold, *and bought in by Government.* Mr. Thomason even regretted, it is stated, that in one case where an estate had been taken from its owner, through a mistake of law, and a balance accrued before it was restored, such balance was not instantly taken advantage of to sell the property. Possession, by farmers from the Government itself, of 20, 30, 40 years was upset, and a mortgagee in possession since 1795 was turned out by the revenue officer. The mortgagee claimed and established his right in a court of law. In the meanwhile the reinstated mortgagor embezzled half the revenue, leaving the mortgagee the choice of paying for his default or losing the estate.

The cases I have hitherto dwelt upon refer only to the instances in which the rights of the talookdars have been set aside. But the treatment of them, when recognized, has been scarcely less calculated to excite distrust in the native mind. According to the principles of the settlement, an allowance of 18 per cent. upon the nett profit of the land was to be made to them, "in consideration of the loss of management." As a compensation for an hereditary right, this allowance was, of course, naturally a perpetual one. It is thought by many to have been always somewhat excessive. This was, therefore, first limited (17th Jan. 1844), "so long as the settlement may last," with the further provision that "on the death of each talookdar the arrangement becomes liable to revision," and the surplus beyond 10 per cent. may be disposed of by Government "at its pleasure."* Then Mr. Thomason (in Oct. 1851) proposed to give these provisions, issued in 1844, a *retrospective effect*, so that the limitation to £10. per cent. should be applied to settlements effected before that date, as soon as the talookdar settled with should die, holding out the bait to his superiors of a saving of £8500. per annum;† and it was necessary that the Court of Directors, by a despatch of the 2nd August, 1853, should interfere to preserve the allowance of £18. per cent. for the term of settlement, where no reduction was provided for.‡

"I could quote many more instances," says the writer of the "Minute on Talookdaree cases," "opposed to particular laws, and

---

* Minute on Talookdaree Cases, by H. S. Boulderson, p. 19.

† Return on the Revenue Survey (India), 1853, p. 290.

‡ Ibid. p. 292.

more especially to the whole body of the law prescribed for the guidance of the revenue authorities, . . . which is throughout neglected, passed over in total silence, or shuffled over on all sorts or on no pretext, and every illegal interference and assumption of jurisdiction has been made without a check from the Board or the Commissioner, who has indeed been told by the Board not to interfere. . . . I have in vain endeavoured hitherto to rouse the attention of my colleague and Government to this virtual abolition of all law. . . . *The respect of the native public I know to have been shaken to an inexpressible degree;* they can see facts, and are not blinded by the fallacious reasonings and misrepresentation with which the Board have clothed these subjects; and they wonder with amazement at the motives which can prompt the British Government to allow their own laws—all laws which give security to property—to be thus belied and set aside. *All confidence in property or its rights is shaken, and the villainy which has been taught the people they will execute, and reward the Government tenfold into their own bosom.*"

Such was the ruthless systematising, the contempt for all fact and law when they interfered with the application of a favourite nostrum, which turned the precious boon of Lord William Bentinck to the North-Western Provinces of India, the village settlement, into a curse to whole classes, to whole districts. Not without reason, surely, does the author of the pamphlet say, in reference to our long indomitable enemies of the present day:—

"The talookdars of Oude have been lately often mentioned as disaffected. Whether they experienced or only anticipated the same dealings from our Government as the talookdars of the North-West Provinces of India received, they must have had a strong motive to dread our rule. The 'confiscation' which has been proclaimed against them—whether it really means confiscation or something else—could not be more effectually destructive to whatever rights they possessed than *the disgraceful injustice by which the talookdars of the North-West Provinces were extinguished.*"

In connexion with this subject I may at once mention another, as to which I have not sufficient data to do more than simply indicate it. The right of primogeniture is one of those which, however unjust we may consider them in theory, may yet be most valuable to races placed in the exceptional position of being subject to foreign conquerors, who take no root in the soil, but only come to enrich themselves and depart. If once the worth of a native gentry to India under British rule is recognized, the most ardent partisan of equality may well admit, without compromising his principles, that the right of primogeniture is involved in the maintenance of that native gentry. And he will have the less difficulty in admitting its relative benefits, as the right is among the Hindoos confined apparently within very narrow limits.

"Among Hindoos," writes Colonel Sleeman in his "Rambles," "both real and personal property is divided . . . . equally among the sons, but a principality is among them considered as an exception to this rule; and every large estate, within which the proprietor holds criminal jurisdiction, and maintains a military establishment, is considered a principality. In such estates the law of primogeniture is always rigidly enforced, and the death of the prince scarcely ever involves a contest for power and dominion among his sons. . . . In a great part of India the property or the lease of a *village* held in farm under Government was considered as a principality, and subject strictly to the same laws of primogeniture. . . . In every part of the Saugur and Nerbudda territories, the law of primogeniture in such leases was in force when we took possession, and has been ever since preserved. The eldest of the sons that remain united with the father, at his death succeeds to the estate, and to the obligation of maintaining all the widows and orphan children of those of his brothers who remained united to the parent stock up to their death, all his unmarried sisters, and, above all, his mother. All his younger brothers aid him in the management, and are maintained by him till they wish to separate, when a division of the stock takes place, and is adjusted by the elders of the village. The member who thus separates from the parent stock, from that time forfeits for ever all claims to support from the possessor of the ancestral estate, either for himself, his widow, or his orphan children."*

Now the invariable endeavour of the British Government has been to subject these large estates or talooks to the ordinary laws of inheritance, so as to subdivide them, and break down the great native families. It will be seen, from the passage which I shall presently quote, that Mr. Robertson, the Lieut.-Governor of the North-western Provinces, reckoned "the parcelling of talooks" as one member of a threefold agency under which "every trace of superior existing rank will disappear." And Sir Wm. Sleeman, it seems, had himself to resign the charge of the very territories above referred to (the Saugur and Nerbudda) on this account. "Had the Lieut.-Governor known more of the Saugur territories," he wrote to Sir Herbert Maddock (20th March, 1848), "when he wrote the paper on which Government is now acting, he would not, I think, have urged the introduction of the system which must end in minutely subdividing all leases."† And what do we see now? that these territories, of which Sir Wm. Sleeman declared that "there is no part of India where our Government and character are so much beloved and respected," have been one of the chief seats of rebellion during the last twelvemonth. I have no personal information which would warrant me in asserting that the rebellion in this quarter arose from our tam-

* Rambles and Recollections, vol. i. pp. 460-62.

† Journey through the Kingdom of Oude, vol. i. p. xxix.

pering with the rights of property there, but the juxtaposition of the two facts is at least striking.

For the larger Indian landholder then, at least, even the vaunted revenue settlement of the North-West, the only one perhaps of all our fiscal measures which took its origin in an honest effort to adapt our system to the laws and customs of the natives, the facts and necessities of their daily life, was a sentence of ruin. When it is considered that the ryotwar settlement of Madras, professedly conceived from the point of view of benefit to the mere cultivator, had been carried out with far less regard even to the rights of other parties, it may easily be judged how far a similar class of men in native states to the talookdars of our North-West provinces must have looked with favour upon British annexation. I have already given reasons why their interests and those of the cultivators themselves should be less opposed in practice than they might seem at first sight. I shall have to revert to this subject.

LETTER XVIII.

THE EFFECT OF THE SALE LAWS.

"Every trace of superior existing rank will, I apprehend, disappear under the threefold agency of the parcelling of talooks, the resumption laws, and that late act regarding sales by which the Government has placed a restriction on the exercise of its own prerogative of mercy.*

* Return on the Revenue Survey, India, 1853, p. 125. I have been unable, on a cursory survey, to recognize the exact provision to which

So wrote Mr. Robertson on the 15th of April, 1842. Let us examine this time the effects of the sale laws, to which he refers.

Mr. Martin Gubbins, who believes that our rule is popular in Oude, may surely be trusted when he bears witness to its defects. The following is a striking passage from his work:—

"Our revenue system had in native estimation many faults. These chiefly consisted in the severity and lasting nature of the punishment with which we visited default. The landed property of a defaulter was liable to sale by public auction; and when thus sold, he lost for ever what had perhaps been the inheritance of many generations. A milder process was that of 'transfer,' by which a landholder lost possession of his estate, for periods varying from ten to fifteen years. Both of these processes were disliked; *but the former is viewed by the land proprietors of Upper India, with a hatred and disgust almost equal to that which they feel towards our Civil Law Courts.* The former penalty I have never enforced in my capacity as a revenue officer. *And I hold it in almost equal detestation as the native land-*

Mr. Robertson refers, of the numerous acts relating to sales, among which may be enumerated Regulation I. of 1835, XII. of 1841, I. of 1845, and IV. of 1846. The second, latest at the date when Mr. Robertson wrote, is probably the one in question. But the "Acts of the Supreme Government of India" do indeed contain matter to startle a European reader. By sections 31 and 32 of Regulation I. of 1845, the default to make good a bid at a public sale by payment of deposit is made a contempt of Court, punishable by fine not exceeding 200 rupees (£20), or in default of payment, by imprisonment in the civil jail for not more than one month. I suppose that of all legislators that ever were, or ever will be, the Anglo-Indian is the only one that could ever dream of encouraging the sale of property by punishing with fine or imprisonment the dire offence of not holding to a bid, under the ludicrous misnomer of a contempt of Court.

holder himself. That of transfer ought very rarely, indeed scarcely ever, to be used."*

A witness before the Colonization Committee of last Session, Mr. J. O. Brien Saunders, who has resided as an indigo planter in Allygurh, near Agra, for twenty-five years, gives some instructive evidence as to the results both of Mr. Bird's settlement, and of the sale-laws. The outward effect of the measures he states to be most favourable. "The towns in the North-western provinces are increased, and trade is improved;" traders finding an investment of money in land have advanced it on mortgage, have taken possession, and the country appears to be "very much improved;" "a very large proportion of the lands have been sold to capitalists, merchants, and others; the land has passed from the people who have held it for hundreds of years before." But nevertheless, he looks upon the measures taken as a mistake. He was always of opinion, and he expressed it to Mr. Bird himself, "that the breaking down of the talookdars was certain to end in an excessive dissatisfaction and disloyalty amongst the natives;" and that the result of it would also certainly be that the small holders recognized by Government—the village communities—"would all be driven out, that they could not hold their lands under the terms, and that they would be all sold up for debts." And he shews the process by which this has come to pass.

The principle of the settlement was that the management of the land was withdrawn from the talookdar,—whose position Mr. Saunders assimilates to that of one

* The Mutinies in Oudh, p. 439.

holding under a farming lease,—that the rent roll was divided into three parts, of which 66⅔ per cent. was for the Government, 18 per cent. for the talookdar by way of compensation, and 15⅓ per cent. for the recognized proprietor for profit and expenses. The talookdars remained, without influence or interest in the management of the land, with nothing to do "except to idle and squander their money," to "indulge in debauchery and opium-eating." On the other hand, "as small holdings are much less able to meet the risks of seasons than a large estate would be," the newly recognized proprietor had "still less than the talookdar formerly to meet his risks." He had no capital like the talookdar to balance losses; and moreover as he "had never had the management of money," had never "conducted revenue arrangements, and paid money direct to the Government," when he was intrusted with money, he was "very apt to squander it." Thus he ran into debt; he was sold up, or mortgaged the property, and it became transferred in one form or other. The consequence has been, that the village proprietors, for whose especial behoof the settlement, we are told, was devised, have "fallen into the hands of the hard-dealing money-lender," and "have fallen into the position of cultivators of the land of which they were formerly the proprietors." Hence, though the effect of the new policy "apparently was very beneficial," yet "the dissatisfaction and dislike towards our Government amongst the larger number of people, such as the cultivators and landowners, and people of influence in the country, was extreme at the same time;" and "we know the results from the late rebellion, namely, that *the whole of these money-lenders, traders, and people who came into possession under mortgages and sales have been ousted, and more than one of them murdered.*" Nor has the witness any doubt that "the knowledge of what has been done in our territories" has made the people of Oude "distrust us very much" on the subject of the revenue settlement.

Let it be clearly understood that in this examination we have got by this time a step further down in the social state than the talookdars. Let the talookdars be ever such usurpers and oppressors; it is not they whom Mr. Saunders speaks of as dispossessed and ruined under our system. The "old proprietors" whom he speaks of are "the Hindoo proprietors,—Hindoo families;" recognized in the country as men of ancient descent; "Rajpoots and Brahmins;" "highly respected and always looked up to" by the people.*

In corroboration of this testimony, let me give that supplied by a civilian, Mr. Edwards, in his recently published "Personal Adventures during the Indian Rebellion." Mr. Edwards tells us how, at the outset of the rebellion, he could have found a shelter for himself with native friends in the district of Budaon, of which he was magistrate and collector, but could obtain none for the European indigo planters and others who had taken refuge with him, "more especially as some of the party *were at feud with some of the people of the district, in consequence of having purchased estates sold*

* See "Fourth Report" on "Colonization and Settlement (India)," pp. 201-225.

under harsh circumstances by the decrees under our civil courts.

"*To the large number of these sales during the past twelve or fifteen years,*" he proceeds, "*and the operation of our revenue system, which has had the result of destroying the gentry of the country, and breaking up the village communities, I attribute solely the disorganisation of this and the neighbouring districts in these provinces.* By fraud or chicanery, a vast number of the estates of families of rank and influence have been alienated, either wholly or in part, and have been purchased by new men—chiefly traders or Government officials, without character or influence over their tenantry. These men, in a vast majority of instances, were also absentees, fearing or disliking to reside on their purchases, where they were looked upon as interlopers and unwelcome intruders. The ancient proprietary of these alienated estates were again living as tenantry on the estates once theirs—by no means reconciled to their change of position, but maintaining their hereditary hold as strong as ever over the sympathies and affections of the agricultural body, who were ready and willing to join their feudal superiors in any attempt to recover their lost position, and regain possession of their estates. The ancient landed proprietary body of the Budaon district were thus still in existence, but in the position of tenants, not proprietors. None of the men who had succeeded them as landowners were possessed of sufficient influence and power to give me any aid in maintaining the public tranquillity. On the contrary, the very first people who came to me imploring aid were this new proprietary body, to whom I had a right to look for vigorous and effectual efforts for the maintenance of order. On the other hand, those who really could control the vast masses of the rural population, were interested in bringing about a state of disturbance and general anarchy."

Observe again here that Mr. Edwards speaks of our revenue system—*i.e.*, that of the North-West provinces—as having had the effect not only of "destroying the gentry of the country," which, as we have seen, was almost the avowed object of its introducer, Mr. R. M. Bird, but of breaking up the village communities,"—which it was its express object to preserve. And recollect that this was predicted in 1842 by the foresight of Mr. Robertson. So different is logic from fact, when applied to the complicated processes of human society, that the interests of the individual land-owner and the village community, seemingly irreconcileably opposed to each other, have by time become inter-dependent, have worked themselves into so firm a knot that they cannot be loosened from each other without tearing up the whole framework of society, breaking the thread upon which all order hangs. But to proceed:—

"For more than a year previous to the outbreak I had been publicly representing to superior authority the great abuse of the power of the civil courts, and the reckless manner in which they decreed the sale of rights and interests connected with the soil in satisfaction of petty debts, and the dangerous dislocation of society which was in consequence being produced; I then pointed out that although the old families were being displaced fast, we could not destroy the memory of the past, or dissolve the connection between them and their people; and I said distinctly, that in the event of an insurrection occurring we should find this great and influential body, through whom we can alone hope to control and keep under the millions forming the rural classes, ranged against us on the side of the enemy, with their hereditary retainers and followers rallying round them in spite of our attempts to separate their interests. My warnings were unheeded, and I was treated as an alarmist, who, having hitherto only served in the political department of the State, and being totally inexperienced in revenue matters, could give no sound opinion on the subject.

In Budaon the mass of the population rose in a body, and the entire district became a scene of anarchy and confusion. The ancient proprietary body took the opportunity of murdering or expelling the auction purchasers, and resumed possession of their hereditary estates. The danger now is, that this vast mass of our subjects, who are numbered by tens of thousands, and who are the real thews and sinews of the country, will never consent to the restoration of a Government to power which they consider treated them with harshness; whose system tended to depress and dispossess them; and whose past measures, after the return of tranquillity, they consider must be to put back the auction purchasers and evict them. I feel convinced that no amount of force will restore us to power, unless at the same time some measures be taken for undoing the evils of the past, and coming to some compromise by which the old families may be reinstated, and their sympathies and interests enlisted on our behalf, while those of the auction purchasers are also duly cared for. I am fully satisfied that the rural classes would never have joined in rebelling with the Sepoys, whom they hated, had not these causes of discontent already existed. They evinced no sympathy whatever about the cartridges, or flour said to be made of human bones, and could not have been acted upon by any cry of their religion being in danger. It is questions involving their rights in the soil and hereditary holdings, invariably termed by them as *jan se azeez*—dearer than life—which excite them to a dangerous degree."*

Now, although the experience of Mr. Edwards may be local, we should be warranted, I believe, in widely generalising his conclusions. He is a witness for Rohilcund; Mr. Saunders for the Doab further south. The sale laws of which he speaks extend to the whole of India; the laws regulating the civil procedure are the same. Wherever, therefore, there are interests in land worth selling by decree of a Civil Court, there the same heart-burnings, the same discontents, the same dislocation of society must prevail.

Observe moreover, that in consequence of our sale-laws being thus entirely out of harmony with the feelings of the people, they do not succeed in giving security to the rights of the purchaser, whilst breaking up those of the hereditary landowner. This insecurity,

* Personal Narrative, pp. 12-17.

as Mr. Edwards's narrative shews, is not only patent in time of rebellion. It is an abiding one. He speaks, as will have been seen, of the new purchasers as generally "absentees, fearing or disliking to reside on their purchases." Nor is the siding of the peasantry with the dispossessed landholder merely the result of clannish feeling. With singular infelicity, the law has actually bound up their interests together. For the sale of land by decree is held to annihilate, with certain exceptions, all derivative interests; and a draft-law to secure sub-holders not in default in their holdings, notwithstanding sale, brought forward eighteen months ago, I believe, in the Legislative Council of Calcutta, by Mr. J. P. Grant, was defeated on account of some objectionable clauses by the indigo-planters, and has not, so far as I am aware, been yet passed. The planters' evidence before the Colonization Committee of the last session recurs frequently to this point. Mr. Freeman, for instance, reckons it the greatest grievance in the sale law as respects Bengal. *Bonâ fide* leases for terms of years, or even perpetual, which may have been acquired or worked under at considerable expense, are cancelled by the Government sale; so that if the zemindar of the estate, of which the lease covers a portion only, thinks proper to keep back, "wilfully or otherwise," a trifle of the Government revenue of the estate, the whole is sold, and the lessee's money is lost *in toto*.*

* See "First Report" on "Colonization and Settlement (India)," p. 110 and *passim;* See also Mr. Theobald's evidence, *ibid.* p. 61 and *passim;* Mr. MacNair's evidence, Second Report, p. 3 and *passim;* Mr. Dalrymple's evidence, *ibid.* p. 69 and foll.

In theory, perhaps the European witnesses before the Committee may seem to make too much of this point. It is well known that under our own law, where there is a lease with underleases, every underlease is liable to be made worthless by some forfeiture on the part of the superior lessee, giving the ground landlord a right to re-enter upon the whole of the property comprised originally in the lease, however since subdivided among the underlessees. But practice, common sense, common fair dealing, the Court of Chancery, have reduced the exercise of this right within the narrowest limits. We never hear of Lord Portman, or the Bishop of London, or the Duke of Bedford, taking advantage of some default in payment of rent, by one of their lessees of what was originally a field and is now a street or square, to sell the whole as vacant property, ignoring or ousting every tenant for the purpose. If we could realise such a proceeding by actual home experience, we should be able to enter into the practical horrors of the Indian sale-laws, as they have been carried out under British rule. For the Government has done there for years, does there day by day, what appears to us so incredible on the part of a private owner. These sales are not even those of a ground landlord setting aside a term of years for non-payment of rent, but those of a Government disposing (in Bengal at least) of a fee simple for non-payment of land-tax. Now, odious as a distress and sale for rent always seems, a distress and sale for rates or taxes seems always doubly odious. There is not an atom of personality behind the claim; all is dry and formal. Any subtlety used to defeat it is looked upon by many rather as a joke; any fraud even seems to solicit toleration. Can you wonder that amongst a people servile and mendacious like the Bengalees for instance, every such sale is sure to call out all the latent powers of fraud in the race against the purchaser? Mr. Freeman tells us that, after purchasing at a sale for £20,000, and taking possession of a zemindary near Calcutta, false charges were made against him to such an extent that he left the place, and put in a manager at £50. a month.*

And yet, strange to say, though far from favourable to the natives, he states that the insecurity of the purchaser's title (which in spite of the sale being made free from incumbrances is often, it would appear, disallowed after two or three years,) is not owing to the causes above mentioned. "You may say in general," he declares, "that where a sale, after having taken place, is disallowed by the Government authorities (I should say *in nine cases out of ten*), it is owing to *the formalities not having been carried out by the revenue authorities, principally the collector.*"†

I shall not pursue any further this branch of the question which these latter words open. What I would wish all thinking men to reflect upon is the utter social "dislocation," to use Mr. Edwards's word, which this evidence from opposing quarters exhibits.

* First Report on Colonization and Settlement (India), p. 108.

† Ibid. p. 111. In this Report and in the second will be found details of many other grievances connected with the sale-laws, which want of space has not allowed me to enter into. The evidence of Messrs. Theobald, Freeman, Macnair, Wise, Dalrymple and Mackenzie, should be consulted on this head.

A clumsy legislation, devised and enforced by aliens, has put every class interest out of joint. In the North-West, the talookdars have been robbed and degraded, the village proprietors dispossessed and ruined, the money-dealers who have taken their stead placed at the mercy of a popular insurrection. In the North-East, under the permanent settlement, the land-owner, the tenant, the purchaser have got none of them fair play. The land-owner fears to lay out money lest he should see his whole estate brought to the hammer for some default in payment of a monthly instalment of revenue,--perhaps incurred in famine time for the maintenance of his tenants,—amounting perhaps to the merest fraction of the value of his estate, and which the sacrifice of a mere strip of land would cover. The tenant fears to lay out money, lest his landlord's pettiest default should involve his ruin. The capitalist dares not invest in land, or if he invests, fears to reside on his purchase, out of dread of one or both of the two former classes if dispossessed.

LETTER XIX.

THE RESUMPTION LAWS AND THE INAM COMMISSION.

LET us now consider another powerful means employed by the British Government for the destruction of the native gentry, extending to a class very far below the talookdars or great land-owners in social position,—the resumption of rent-free tenures. It appears to have been the practice from time immemorial in India for the sovereign to grant portions of the public land free of tax, or as Anglo-Indians like to call it, rent, mostly perhaps for religious or charitable purposes—often no doubt from mere caprice. These estates, known in Bengal as "lakhiraj" lands, in the Deckan as "inam," or "enam," or by other names, became valuable in precise proportion to the pressure of the land revenue. In many cases the original purposes of the grant became obsolete, were overlooked or deliberately set at nought; religious services were discontinued; lands granted for the maintenance of Brahmins passed into the hands of warriors or merchants. Nor are the people of India indifferent spectators of these diversions from the original purpose. I am assured that wherever a genuine religious or charitable purpose is attached to the grant, the popular feeling is always strong for its being restored to that purpose. A relative of mine has told me that while political agent in a native State, he had an infinite number of grants made for educational purposes, and which had been usurped by private persons, restored to those uses, and that this was done amidst the general approval of the people, though the adverse possession might have lasted for even a couple of centuries. And as respects rent-free grants made unconditionally, for purposes of mere caprice, there is no doubt that under a native sovereign they are looked upon with great disfavour by the people; so that Colonel Sleeman quotes somewhere the saying, that there is "no blessing" upon rent-free lands.

Had, therefore, the inquiry into the rent-free holdings had for its primary object the restoring of all such holdings to their original purposes, where practicable, or to such purposes as the moral sense of the community would have approved of, I believe the proceedings of Government would have commanded the sympathy of the natives of India, instead of arousing their discontent. I believe they had in these rent-free lands the grandest fund conceivable for education, charity, for every purpose of public benefit. Where such purposes have been found subsisting, they have no doubt been respected as far as possible. But otherwise the question has been lowered to one of revenue,—Has the holder of such and such lands the right to hold them free of land revenue, or can we the Government claim it from him?

This was already a somewhat invidious position for the Government to take up. Still, accepting this lower view of the subject, I go indeed entirely along with the Indian Government as to the general principles by which their proceedings, in reference to rent-free lands, have been defended. I quite agree with them in thinking, that where the bulk of the taxation of a country is raised from the land, it is a *prima facie* grievance to the rest of the community that a portion of the land should be wholly exempt from the burthen of the land revenue. I quite agree with them in thinking that in such cases the burden of proof lies *prima facie* with the man who claims the exemption. I am perfectly aware that in a vast number of cases possession had been fraudulently obtained, sometimes under merely colourable titles, sometimes without any title at all. But on the other hand, I cannot believe but that there are other means of making these rent-free holders contribute to the public burthens, besides that of reducing them to the condition of ordinary cultivators. I cannot but admit the force of the argument, that their case is precisely the same as that of holders of land free of tithe or land-tax in this country, except so far that the absent burthen is in India the primary one on the land, instead of being only a secondary one, as tithe and land-tax are with us. And so long as India is governed for the benefit of this country, or rather of a small number of persons belonging to this country, and not for her own benefit,—so long as the bulk of her revenues is not applied to her own purposes,—so long, I think, must any such exemption be looked upon with extreme indulgence, as preserving a given number of estates from the exigencies of an ill-applied fiscal system. And at any rate, when the burthen of proof is laid upon the holders, it should be a reasonable one; a fair period of prescriptive possession should be allowed, and the right founded thereon respected.

The "resumption of all hidden rent-free tenures" formed already in the North-west one of the objects of the revenue settlement in that part of the country. I have no detailed evidence at hand as to the working of this part of the settlement. But it will probably be sufficient if I quote Mr. Robertson the Lieutenant-Governor's observations on its performances:—

"The proceedings in the Resumption Department," his honour observed, "had in these, as in the Lower Provinces, been marked at the outset by a hard and harsh dealing with individual rights, gradually but reluctantly yielding to the tempering influence of the orders which from time to time have issued from superior authorities, especially the Honourable Court [of Directors]. The settlement officer swept up without inquiry every patch of unregistered rent-free land, even those under ten beegahs (rather over three acres), exempted by a subsequent order, and which did not come out before five-sixths of the tenures had been resumed. In one district, that of Furruckabad, the obligations of a treaty and the direct orders of Government were but lightly dealt with, *and in all a total disregard was evinced for the acts even of such men as Warren Hastings and Lord Lake.*"

Fully aware of the tendency of such proceedings, the Lieutenant-Governor further observes, that it is "a fearful experiment" to try to govern without the aid of any immediate agency of native growth. In a short time, he says (in words partly quoted already):—

"All may stand on a new basis; the village watchman and the village accountant may be persons in the direct service of Government . . . while every trace of superior existing rank will disappear under the three-fold agency of the parcelling of talooks, *the resumption laws*, and that late act regarding sales, by which the Government has placed a restriction on the exercise of its own prerogative of mercy."*

I cannot but once more recommend these remarkable words to those who may still see in the revenue settlement of the North-west, as carried out in contempt of the rights of the talookdars, a practically democratic measure. Mr. Robertson, it is clear, saw in it precisely the reverse. He saw in it the destruction of the self-government of the village communities,—the spreading of the yoke of officialism throughout the land.

But let us see the resumption laws at work in another field. In the North-west, the actual making

* Return on the "Revenue Survey (India)," 1853, p. 125.

of a revenue settlement afforded an admirable opportunity for breaking down the native gentry wholesale; the resumption of rent-free holdings formed but a detail in that operation. In Bengal, where the permanent settlement of Lord Cornwallis still subsists, such resumption rose to more substantive importance; and it is by its means that the greatest inroads have been made upon that settlement. The operation of the resumption laws, passed in 1828,* we are told by an English witness before the Colonization of India Committee of the session just expired—(Mr. J. P. Wise)—commenced in Bengal about 1836. A previous law of 1793, by which the Government could resume only on proof of its right to resume, was set aside, and persons who had been 60 or 70 years in possession were suddenly called upon to prove their titles before certain special commissioners. Although these laws have now ceased to operate, their effect still exists. People remember them *as a blight passing over the country;* money was extorted from them in every possible way; the poor natives clung to their ground, and they lost it, and very often lost their money in trying to bribe the officials from their duty. "In the Chittagong district," Mr. Wise says elsewhere, "it was a

* Bengal Regulation III. of 1828; "for the Appointment of Special Commissioners for the more speedy hearing and determination of Appeals from the decisions of the Revenue authorities in regard to lands and rents, occupied or collected by individuals without payment of the revenue demandable by Government under the general law of the country, and for otherwise more effectually securing the payment of the public dues" (modified by Regulation IV. of 1829) is probably the one referred to.

wholesale sweeping away of the rights of the whole population, nearly causing an insurrection."*

In vain did upwards of 20,000 landholders petition against the harshness and injustice of the law. In defiance of a Regulation of 1805, which barred the claims of the state, after sixty years' possession, "to the assessment of land held exempt from the public revenue without legal and sufficient title," a prior Regulation which allowed no length of time to be a bar was enforced, although expressly rescinded in 1819; and enforced so pertinaciously that the rent-free holders actually ceased to quote the Regulation of 1805 in their defence, until, in a celebrated case of the Raja of Burdwan,—a Hindoo nobleman who was rich enough to carry his claim before our English Privy Council,--English justice at last prevailed over the repeated, deliberate, persevering contempt of their own law by the Supreme Government of India, the Board of Revenue, and other inferior authorities, and a period of prescription beyond which the title to rent-free lands should not be questioned was, in 1851, for the first time judicially established.† But what became of the dispossessed owners whose case was similar to that of the Raja of Burdwan? Did the Government take any steps to repair its own misconstruction of its own laws,—to use the mildest term? Quite the contrary. It began by passing Regulations (1852) to hinder applications to the Resumption Commissioners for reviews of judgment.

* Second Report on Colonization and Settlement (India), 1858, p. 44 and foll.,—and p. 60.

† See *Maharaja Dheeraj Raja Mahatab Chund Bahadoor* v. *the Bengal Government*, 4 Moore's Indian Appeal Cases, p. 466.

And when the British Indian Association of Calcutta petitioned that a list should be drawn up from the records of the resumption courts of the cases which had been decided in those courts since 1828, in favour of Government, notwithstanding direct or presumptive proof of sixty years' adverse possession, with a view to restitution, what was the answer of the Supreme Government? That they were unable to comply with the request "with any regard to a faithful administration of the national income."* In other words, that they could not afford to be honest; that the estates which they had got within their clutch, as it turned out, by illegal means, they would only give up to sheer force, according as the parties entitled were able to apply its pressure through the courts of law. Thus, as Mr. McNair, an English landholder, stated in May last before the Colonization Committee, all the rest of the poor natives, who could not like the Raja of Burdwan afford an appeal, "are still taxed for those lands;" knowing all the while, that if they could appeal to England, they would be released from the tax.† Is this the way of securing a people's confidence in its Government?

The resumption laws have indeed ceased to be enforced in Bengal. The presence of many English landholders, united in the same interest with the natives —the position attained by many of the native landholders under Lord Cornwallis's settlement—have no

* See the "Petition of the British Indian Association" (of Bengal) "on resumptions made contrary to the rules of limitation, 1854, and the "Second Report of the British Indian Association," 1854.

† Second Report on Colonization and Settlement, (India,) p. 9.

doubt brought about this result. For it is certain that the evils of the resumption measures were less in Bengal than in any other part of India. Yet if those evils were nevertheless so great in Bengal that the system could not be persevered in, what must they be in other parts of India where there is no permanent settlement, where there are no sturdy English indigo planters to give tongue?

We have seen that the operation of the resumption laws in Bengal was compared to "a blight passing over the country." That blight is still passing over the Bombay and Madras Presidencies. Under the title of the "Inam" Commission, it forms one of the main grievances of the former.

There appears to be no doubt that when we took possession of the South Mahratta country in 1817-18, a large portion of the then existing grants ("Inams" or "Enams") of rent-free lands had been either made without authority or obtained or simulated by fraud. That an inquiry into these titles would be necessary, was intimated in 1819 by Mr. Elphinstone, then Commissioner in the conquered provinces. A valuable means for carrying it on existed in the revenue records left by the Peshwa's government, extending over a period of eighty years. Government took charge of these, but fulfilled the charge in such a manner that, as admitted by a Bombay civilian, Mr. Goldsmid, in 1845, "portions of," and "entire documents" disappeared, "no means were taken to secure the identification of the papers," * &c., and in fact they were for years, to use

* See "Selections from the Records of the Bombay Government," No. xxx. New Series, (1856), p. 43.

the words of another civilian, Mr. Hart, in 1848, "virtually inaccessible, and almost unknown."* In the meanwhile, though desultory inquiries into rent-free holdings had been carried on by a few collectors here and there, a title by adverse possession against the Government had been established in numberless instances, when at last, in 1843, an "Inam Commission," consisting of one European and one native officer, was appointed to investigate the titles to rent-free holdings in the South Mahratta districts. The native Commissioner soon disappeared; and the carrying out of the purposes of the commission was entrusted, as a Bombay civilian, Mr. J. Warden, stated lately before the Colonization of India Committee, "not to any judicial officer whatever," but to "young gentlemen of the civil service, and captains and subalterns," so that, "at this moment, the head of the Inam Commission is a captain of native infantry."† This Commission carried on its proceedings for nine years (1843-1852) "even without the sanction of an act of the Indian legislature;" and was in fact so illegal, that in 1848, the law officer of Government at Bombay recommended that Government should keep it "out of sight." By a Regulation, which one is surprised to find emanating from such a man as Mr. Elphinstone, the former subjects of the Peshwa had been deprived of the right to sue the Government in the courts of justice. And now, in 1852, thirty-five years after the occupation of the country, Lord Dalhousie's nefarious

* Selections from the Records of the Bombay Government, No. xxx. p. 58.

† Third Report on Colonization and Settlement, (India,) p. 73 and foll. See also Fourth Report, p. 30 and foll.

Calcutta Council passed an act which, "instead of simply extending to the Deckan the laws in force elsewhere," re-enacted the provisions of a law rescinded on account of its inconvenience, by which 60 years of enjoyment were required to constitute a title by prescription, instead of 30 years, as previously allowed, and such 60 years were to reckon before the introduction of the British Government, consequently 95 years before the date of the act; whilst "females were altogether deprived" of the right to inherit, the burden of proof being moreover "thrown upon the holder." *

Now I have compared these rent-free tenures to tithe-free land in this country, or land on which the land-tax has been redeemed. I believe English landowners would stare, and more than stare, if they found a captain in the line appointed to investigate their titles to such land, without any appeal to a court of justice, but only to some revenue authority, and in the last in-

* The amount of badgering which Mr. Warden underwent, in his second examination before the Colonization Committee (Fourth Report, pp. 29-46), at the hands of the Director Members of the Committee, Messrs. Mangles and Willoughby, for this simple assertion, is almost incredible. The process is, that the holder is called upon to prove his title; he rests it in the first instance on possession, and appeals to the district officer's accounts,—*i.e.* to evidence in the Government's own hands—to shew that he, or those he claims from, have held free of rent for the required space of time. If there is no evidence to the contrary, his title is confirmed. Of course this is an *onus probandi* laid upon him; his only privilege being that his possessory title is to be deemed primâ facie sufficient, without proving the origin of it. Messrs. Mangles and Willoughby are both now members of the Council for India.

stance to one or other of the Ministers; and if they were required, one and all, to shew 95 years' title previous to 1852, or now 103 years. But this comparison would only hold good in Bengal, where, under the zemindarie system, property in land actually exists. It is not so, really, in Bombay. Mr. Warden distinctly states that, with the exception of the inam lands, and in spite of all the boasted revenue improvements of which we have heard so much, the land in Bombay has no saleable value for an English or for a native capitalist; that he "never heard" of its being sold as "an article of commerce, on which capital can advantageously be laid out."* So that the case is simply as if two-thirds, say, of all England being rack-rented by Government, the infantry captains before referred to were appointed to decide all questions of title in the remaining one-third, consisting of fee-simple estates.

Are you surprised that, in a rack-rented country, thousands of these rent-free titles should have been fabricated? Are you surprised that, with such measures taken against their holders, every means should have been resorted to which the weak can invent to defend themselves against the strong—abstraction and concealment of documents, fraud, forgery, perjury?†

* Third Report on Colonization and Settlement (India), pp. 86-87.

† See, for instance, the "Selections from the Records of the Bombay Government, No. xxix. New Series; correspondence regarding the concealment by the hereditary officers and others of the Revenue Records of the former Government." (1856.) But who could be surprised at the attempt to withhold title-deeds from a Government which, by the confession of its own officers, had been so careless of

Those who are engaged, like myself, in the handling of our real property law, know how rare it is, after our long years of internal peace, to find a *legally* flawless title for 60 years, and yet how rare is a *really* bad title. What would it be, if 100 years were required? What would it be, if our country had been, within that hundred years, torn by as many wars and social convulsions as Western India? What would it be, if the question at issue were not as between one private claimant and another, the nature of the holding remaining unaffected, but the momentous one between fee-simple and a tenancy-at-will at rack-rent, and Government the claimant of the rent? What would it be, if all "nice points" in conveyancing were to be decided by a captain of infantry? I verily believe that if such a state of things were conceivable in this country, there would be, ere long, as much fraud and forgery committed for the purpose of setting up un-

them when obtained, that "portions of" and "and entire documents" had disappeared from its custody? Nor is this all. I have had before me a copy of a petition recently presented to the Bombay Government by claimants to an inam, in which they declare that when "they requested the Inam Commissioner and Government to give them copies of certain documents in the possession of the authorities, and which were calculated to prove the validity of their claim, or to allow them to have access to such papers," this request was "*refused.*"

It is impossible indeed not to see that the mere concealment of documents, though mixed with whatever lies as to the possession of them, is no necessary evidence of fraud, but rather of insecurity and distrust. Fraud would in many cases destroy title-deeds rather than secrete them.

founded fee-simple titles, and bolstering up good titles unbacked by sufficient evidence, as any that the Inam Commissioners have detected. On the other hand, the proceedings of these Commissioners, as related to me, are almost incredible. Parliamentary pledges of respect to native usages have been directly violated by the powers given to the Commissioners, and freely used by them, of breaking into any man's house at night in the search for documents; of entering into the very *zenana*, or women's apartment, and carrying away all the papers they can find, for the authorities to keep until they have time to investigate them.* And the efficiency of the Commissioners is said to be estimated

* The following is an extract from a memorial presented to the Managing Committee of the Bombay Native Association, by the Inamdars and other inhabitants of Poona and other towns:—

"We believe it was never the intention of Government that the Inam Commissioner should authorize his people to enter the house of the ryots forcibly, and occasion destruction of furniture, breaking open the locks, to seize all documents relating to Inams and vuttuns, sunnuds, copies of accounts, papers relating to the Government of districts by contracts, in fact papers of every sort that may be in the possession of the officers of villages, and carry them away without passing a receipt of these papers, or mentioning the amount of Dufturs. . . . The taunts and insolence of these people of the Inam Commission and the oppression and force they have exercised, we blush to mention. They have even gone so far as to enter the houses of people in their absence, force open the locks, and carry away the documents." And they quote instances in support of what they say.

I have been told that an Inam Commissioner, on being asked whether allegations of the sort were true, answered, "Of course they are; do you think we'd give the niggers a chance of cooking their papers if they expect us to overhaul them?"

in the exact proportion of the revenue they bring in by resumptions.*

But the magnitude of the evil is not even measured by its nature. To the year 1856, 108,199 claims to Inams had been recorded—of these only 6,002 had been decided on, and more than 100,000 remained to be so. That is to say, that in thirteen years (1843-1856), these claims had been decided on at the rate of 461 a year; at which rate, any national schoolboy may calculate that it will take more than *two hundred years* to go through the remainder. But in the meanwhile, the value of *all* such land is practically annihilated; so that, as Mr. Warden says, whilst forty years ago a man might have gone to the Bombay Presidency, and, by purchasing an *inam* village, have purchased an even better title to land than an English fee-simple, and thus obtained good security for laying out his capital, at present "nobody would take inam land unless these special courts for adjudicating titles to inams were abolished."

We must however distinguish two different branches in the proceedings of the Inam Commission. The inquiry, whether lands claimed to be held rent-free are really entitled to such exemption, forms the one. The other, and no doubt the more galling of the two to the native population, relates to the determination of the rights of the rent-free holder, recognized as such. I have said that as between the *claimant* of a rent-free holding and the Government, the question is that be-

* At any rate, an Inam Commissioner is understood to have considered himself entitled to promotion for having, in a short time, resumed lands to the amount of £80,000 a year.

tween a fee-simple and a tenancy at will at rack-rent. But between the recognized *holder* and Government there is a further question, scarcely less momentous. He claims a *bona fide* fee-simple. "Language is exhausted," says Mr. Warden, in the title-deeds of the grantee or inamdar, "in its attempt to carry to him the proprietary right in the soil;" and "when a native of India wishes to convey to you that he has a proprietary right in anything, he says, 'this is my inam.'" Yet in spite of this, under the British Government, the holder of an inam is now precluded from aliening it from his family, and it is seized as an escheat if he does; or in other words, Government cuts down his fee-simple to an inalienable estate in tail male, with reversion to itself.

The process by which this revolution in landed property is being carried out, deserves to be considered in a separate letter.

LETTER XX.

THE INAM COMMISSION, AND THE GOVERNMENT PRACTICE AS TO ADOPTIONS AND ALIENATIONS.

Mr. Elphinstone—who weighs out his words like gold—whose most hesitating beliefs are worth more than most men's confident assertions—speaks thus unequivocally of Hindoo crown alienations of lands held free of service.

"Other alienations are, to temples or religious persons, or to meritorious servants and to favourites. Though very numerous, they are generally of small extent: often single villages; sometimes only partial assignments on the Government share of a village; but in some cases also, especially religious grants, they form very large estates. Religious grants are always in perpetuity, and are seldom interfered with. A large portion of the grants to individuals are also in perpetuity, and are regarded as among the most secure forms of private property, but the gradual increase of such instances of liberality, combined with the frequency of forged deeds of gift, sometimes induces the ruler to resume the grants of his predecessors, and more frequently to burden them with heavy taxes. When these are laid on *transfers by sale*, or *even by succession*, they are not thought unjust; but total resumptions, or the permanent levy of a fixed rate is regarded as oppressive. The reaction must have begun long ago; for the ancient inscriptions often contain imprecations on any of the descendants of the grantor who shall resume his gift."*

Even as respects jagheers, or lands held for military service, he says:—

"Lands held for military service are subject to reliefs in the event of hereditary succession, and to still heavier fines when the heir is adoptive."†

Most people, I should think, in this country, not being interested in the matter, would consider the authority of the historian of India irrefragable on the question of the character of such titles as those he refers to. And it is deserving of especial remark, that he must have had prominently in view, as one of the fields of such alienations, the Bombay Presidency, and the South Mahratta country,—the country, namely, which he had known in its independent condition, while Resident at the Court of the last Peshwa, and in the an-

* History of India, Book II. ch. ii.

† Ibid. note Q to Book II. ch. ii.

nexation of which he had taken a prominent part,—the Bombay Presidency generally, which not only includes the districts in question, but of which he had been himself the Governor. Now it is precisely the South Mahratta districts of the Bombay Presidency, as I have stated, in which the Inam Commission has been at work. It is, therefore, of the inams or grants free of service in these districts, that he tells us that all religious grants, and a large portion of all others, are in perpetuity; that he implies clearly that they are capable of transfer by sale, since it is not thought unjust to tax such transfers; characterizing beforehand the proceedings of the Inam Commission by saying that total resumptions of such grants are considered "oppressive."

The mode in which the security of this sort of property has been impaired leads us round again to the annexation policy in itself, and will shew how completely the interests of prince and landholder have been identified by common grievances. For the main leverage for the breaking down of native property—in the Deckan at least—has been the same as that which has been used for the breaking down of native sovereignties—the curtailment, namely, of the right of adoption: First, by turning the formality of notice to the superior into an essential condition of obtaining that superior's sanction; secondly, by concluding—law and sense to the contrary notwithstanding—from the sanction to the power of resumption as an alternative for it.

It was not so in the days of our great Anglo-Indian statesmen. When we took possession of the Peshwa's territories, it was on a purely conservative ground that we continued the practice of insisting on the Government sanction. Thus a proclamation by the Bombay Government, issued 12th August, 1820, bade all landowners wishing to adopt give notice to the authorities, and then, "after an inquiry shall have been made into the rules of the Shasters and the usage applicable to the case," an order was to be issued. "Should any one make an adoption without permission, the Sirkar [Government] will not recognise it."* So far, there was nothing in the action of the Government that the Indian races would not willingly accede to. And although two years later we find the rein already beginning to be tightened, though as to adoptions by widows only,† still on the 3rd June, 1825, the Government admitted as a general rule in the Deckan, that "children adopted with such forms and sanctions as may have been usual should succeed to inam lands, or whatever may be considered private property,"‡ and this rule was again repeated in a circular dated as late as 24th October, 1831. By 1836 however the rule was already disregarded. Then the Inam Commission was appointed. Increased stringency in the proceedings of the Government is at once observable. The essential necessity of Government sanction to all adoptions is assumed as an axiom by 1848.§ By September 14, 1852, the Bombay Government recorded their opinion that they had "a right to reserve in all cases the power of granting or refusing such assent to an adoption as may confer upon the adopted son a title

* Selections from the Records of the Bombay Government, No. xxviii, new series (1856), p. 4.

† Ibid. pp. 5—8. ‡ Ibid. p. 15. § Ibid. p. 11.

against the state." Still, for the present, they directed that all applications for adoption by holders of inam lands, &c., should be assented to, except when there were special reasons for refusing assent, declaring however that "the only question in any adoption case for Government to decide is, whether or not there is any reason on the part of the Government to admit the liability of the state to the demand against it of an adopted son, as though he were born in wedlock."* When rummaging the records of the Mahratta Government, the Commissioners discovered that under that rule,—which, when we wish to contrast ours with it, we invariably describe as a pattern of rapacity and tyranny,—one inam was resumed because the holder quitted the Peshwa's camp without permission,—another without reason assigned,—a third because the holder's brother had not paid a Government fine,—a fourth because the widow of the late holder had adopted a son;† and upon this evidence, as reported by the military Assistant Commissioner, the Court of Directors (1855) declared it to be "conclusively" established, "that under the Government of the Peshwas the consent of the ruling power was invariably required for the adoption of heirs to all rent-free holdings."‡

* Selections from the Records of the Bombay Government, No. xxviii, new series (1856), p. 27. In Madras, it would seem that an order of 1846, which came into operation on the 11th February, 1847, required all adoptions to be notified to the collector six months previous to the decease of the adopting party,—as harsh a proceeding as one which would require all wills to be registered six months before the death of the testator. See Mr. J. B. Norton's "Topics for Indian Statesmen," p. 174.

† Ibid. p. 43 and foll.

‡ Ibid. p. 60.

See, then, the complete inversion of Government practice since the first occupation of the country. In 1820, Government required notice of adoption, in order that a legal inquiry should be made into the laws and usages applicable to the case. Then, if the adoption were not sanctioned, the adopted son was to lose his rights, those of collateral heirs being impliedly confirmed. In 1852, the "*only question* in any adoption case for Government to decide is, whether or not there is any reason on the part of Government to admit *the liability of the State* to the demand against it of an adopted son," the implication being, as the fact undoubtedly is, that for want of adoption the land is treated as escheated to Government.

Take a recent illustration of the practice. I have already alluded to the chief of Nurgoond, in the South Mahratta country, lately executed at Belgaum for the murder of Mr. Manson. The *Bombay Gazette* of June 8, 1858, contains a memorial by this chief (reproduced by the *Star*) addressed to the Court of Directors, for permission to adopt an heir. He urged that for nearly 200 years his family had held the estates of Nurgoond and Ramdroog by a tenure (called *suwasthan*) giving an absolute estate of inheritance, which descends of right to all lawful heirs. He told how in 1820 his father entered into a treaty with the East India Company, by which his right was acknowledged to hold his estate to himself and his heirs for ever, and the Government authority for the succession was to be renewed each time without any present being demanded. He declared that "all former Governments have given their sanction as a matter of course, except under very unusual circumstances; only keeping up the custom of applying for and granting their permission as a convenient mode of obtaining *nuzzurs* [presents], they never in the most disorderly times or under the most rapacious Sovereigns or ministers made use of their power of refusing to sanction adoption, for the purpose of putting an end to the succession, and so securing the property for themselves." He memorialised in vain, Mr. Manson reporting against the sanction being given. The Brahmin brooded over the wrong for years. The rebellion seemed to give him an opportunity for revenge. He rose, and murdered the European officer. But who first robbed *him?* Or can you wonder why his kinsman of Ramdroog, holding under the same title, was said to be implicated in his rising?

If it be now remembered that Sattara, Jhansee, Nagpore were all annexed on the ground of absence of adoption, or of sanction to an adoption, it will be felt on what a scale the claim of escheat under such circumstances has been enforced by the British Government.

But it is not only in the case of unsanctioned adoption that estates are confiscated. Unsanctioned alienation affords the same pretext.

"If," says Mr. Hart, the Inam Commissioner of 1845, "the more solemn ceremony of adoption, (which vests in the person adopted a far stronger right to the whole of his adoptive father's property than he could have obtained to it by any other means), be in the eyes of Government an insufficient title to an Inam, it follows *a fortiori* that the less solemn transaction of sale or gift must be so. . . . It can only be concluded that, according to the existing rules, an Inamdar's rights to prejudice Government by alienating in *gift* or *sale* to a stranger an Inam hereditary to his family, is as little to be recognized as his right to do so by adoption."*

I confess it is difficult for me, as a lawyer, to deal patiently with this chop-logic system of confiscation which our Indian authorities have adopted, most especially when the logic used is of the character of the above. For an adoption, as distinguished from a gift or sale, is, as I have shewn, a disposal of property to take effect after death, instead of during life, analogous therefore to a disposal by will amongst ourselves; and no possible conclusion can be drawn, from a restraint upon disposal after death, to a restraint upon disposal during life. Amongst ourselves, centuries elapsed from the time when free alienation during life prevailed, to the time when free testamentary disposal was allowed. We are probably the only nation in Europe where it exists entire; where a man can will away his whole property from his family. In France, even in Scotland, children have their *legitim* (as it is called north of Tweed), as against the claimants under a will; yet in France, as in Scotland, a landowner in fee may sell out and out without saying "by your leave," or "with your leave" to any one. And yet, everywhere, without exception, the disposition to take effect after death only is surrounded with greater solemnity than the disposition to take effect during life. A scrap of paper with a signature is all that the Court of Chancery with us requires to enforce an immediate trust, even respecting land; it cannot look at a will until it has been ascertained by a different court

* Selections from the Records of the Bombay Government, No. xxviii. new series (1856), pp. 1 2.

that it has been attested by two witnesses in a certain manner, and under certain conditions. With Mr. Hart's logic, (embodying in italics my variations from his language), I will prove in a sentence that every sale of goods requires probate, under penalty of forfeiture to the Crown; for "if the more solemn ceremony of *testamentary disposal*, which vests in the *executor* a far stronger right to the whole of his *testator's personalty* than he could have obtained to it by any other means, be in the eyes of the Government, *without probate*, an insufficient title to *goods*, it follows, *a fortiori*, that the less solemn transactions of sale or gift must be so." . . . When shall an Englishman feel shame enough for handing over our Indian fellow-subjects to the fangs of such law and such logic?*

It may be objected, that Captain Cowper has disinterred eighteen instances in which, before our occupation of the country, the sanction of the Peshwa's Government was given to gifts or sales of inam lands. Certainly, he might have adduced 500 such instances.

* Mr. Warden, in his second examination before the Colonization Committee (4th Report, p. 29 and foll.), seems to have given as his opinion that under the native Governments inams were not saleable (pp. 35, 6). Whether correct or not, this statement would in nowise affect the character of Captain Cowper's logic. We have however to the contrary Mr. Elphinstone's statement, and that of the Commissioner in the Deckan, on the 19th May, 1825, that the practice of the Peshwa's Government as to inams was that "the holders could dispose of them by will, *in sale*, or in any other way they chose." I quote this from a letter by Mr. Warden himself, dated 9th December, 1852, to be found in the "Correspondence of the Inam Commission on the Deckan Surinjams" (Bombay Government Selection, No. xxxi, 1856), App. B. p. 7.

The court rolls of any manor in England will shew him thousands in which a copyholder has come into court, and "prayed" to be admitted tenant on the surrender of another, and paid dues and steward's fees for his admittance. He may find more still; he may find a so-called "forfeiture" enforced for alienation against the custom, or even from the so-called forfeiture. But if, from the "prayer" of the copyholder he were to conclude, that the English lord of the manor has really the right to refuse his consent to an alienation, and then take possession of the land for his own benefit, he would be drawing a most preposterous conclusion, since every one knows that nine-tenths of the copyholds of this country are, or were ere they were extinguished, as they are now fast becoming, as secure at least in point of title as freeholds.*

Never forget that this false logic "*is being carried*

* The following custom would astonish the steward of an English manor. It is related by a collector, and for aught I know may be still in force.

"It has of late years been the practice in this collectorate to *attach the lands of Inamdars on the death of the incumbent, however valid his title may prima facie be, pending the orders of Government for their continuance or otherwise.* In some cases the proceeds of such lands have been credited to Government, and in others kept in deposit. Under the Government circular dated 18th August, 1845, No. 4084, this practice has been discontinued as regards Inam *villages,* because the holders, by virtue of their tenure, have claims to money payments in compensation for liquor farms, but is retained in the case of Inam *fields,* as the holders are not entitled to money payments of any kind from Government. I have not hitherto ventured to interfere with what had become an established practice in the collectorate before I assumed charge of it, although apparently not derived from any express order of Government." Selections

out." In Mr. Warden's evidence before the Colonization Committee will be found a letter from Jafur Alee, of Surat—in which district also an Inam Commission has been appointed—giving instances of Government seizures under this plea. Hundreds of such cases, he says, have taken place at Surat, and the Government has always taken possession, after the death of the purchaser or mortgagee :—

"And the people are too poor to go to law against the Company, in the Company's courts, presided over by the Company's judges. Their rights are thus lost for ever. The Company is, as I have said, fast taking possession, under one pretence or other, of lands which people have, in various ways, from their former governments ; and as it does not give nor sell land to the people, *it is clear that very soon will disappear from India all who once held land, and could call it their own.*"*

The Inam Commission has quite lately (Sept. 1, 1858) been extended to the Madras Presidency, yet Mr. Warden tells us that, on a proposal to extend it "from the patient and submissive inhabitants of the Deckan to the more warlike and independent people of Guzerat, the officer conducting the survey in this province declared his opinion that the measure would produce a

from the Records of the Bombay Government, No. xxx. new series, p. 104; letter by Mr. J. S. Law, Collector, dated 22nd Oct. 1847.

You hold land free of land-tax. Imagine on your death the land-tax collector entering into possession of all your fields, "however valid your title may primâ facie be, pending the order of Government," and either crediting the proceeds to Government, or keeping them in deposit! And imagine his doing this, not only not by virtue of any law, but without even "any express order of Government!"

* Third Report on Colonization and Settlement (India), pp. 83-4.

rebellion.* And he expressly attributes the existing disaffection of the South Mahratta country to the Inam Commission, which has made the people "mentally fraternise with everything that has been going on against the Government."† So a recent traveller in the Deckan, writing to myself, states that he "found everywhere the same hatred of our rule, and the same causes ascribed for that hatred,—our confiscations under the Inam Commission, and our administration, or rather mal-administration of justice." I have still more recent letters from India, referring to the deep-rooted discontent of the South Mahratta country, and attributing it equally in the main to the Inam Commission. We have extended similar proceedings even into the Nizam's ceded districts, of which our possession is professedly only temporary. Incredible as it may seem, I am assured that on our occupying these districts the rule was laid down, that no tenants were in future to pay rent to private landowners, till the titles of the latter should have been approved of by a commission, *to be appointed* for the purpose, which was not appointed for about five years, in spite of urgent yearly remonstrances, petitions, representations by our own officials of the distress and starvation of the land-owners. "Our proceedings in the annexed districts," writes the distinguished traveller before referred to, "in which we set to work in our usual reckless way, ignoring the just rights of natives and dispossessing them of property long enjoyed, have given rise to a very strong feeling against us." In Madras the latest news (as may be seen from a letter of Nov. 27, in the

* Ibid. p. 77.

† Ibid. p. 93.

" Morning Star " of Dec. 30th) represents the feelings excited by the introduction of the Inam Commission as being of the most bitter description. Compared with the measure for Madras, the Bombay Commission is termed "an act of justice, of mercy, of grace, of tenderness unspeakable." The Mahratta country, it is urged, did not come into our possession until 1818; but in Madras inamdars have remained in possession of their tenures for considerably more than half a century. And the measure is pointed out as being " brought forward in utter contempt of that part of her Majesty's proclamation which declared her respect for the attachment with which the natives regard the land inherited by them from their ancestors."

The uncertainty prevailing in the proceedings of the Government with respect to inams is scarcely less complained of than the proceedings themselves. In the memorial of the Bombay Inamdars, before referred to, it is alleged that in one instance (the Pinglapoor district of the Poona collectorate), a grant actually confirmed by a political agent, in pursuance of a rule laid down by him on the 19th Feb. 1846, as conferring a perpetual inheritance, descending both to the male and female lines, and subsequently also confirmed by the Governor of Bombay in Council, on the 12th August, 1849, was cut down by the Inam Commissioner to a life estate. In the Madras Presidency, on the other hand, Mr. J. B. Norton relates the instance of two soobadars of a native regiment who, at the time of the Vellore mutiny, gave information of it to their commanding officer, and received in reward grants of inam land in two adjoining districts, Trichinopoly and Madura. In the one, the sons have been allowed to inherit; in the other, the widow only was allowed to hold the land as a special favour after her husband's death; it was then resumed by Government, and the faithful officer's child turned adrift, to curse perhaps his father's faithfulness.*

This, it will be observed, is a case not connected with the direct operation of the Inam Commission. Mr. Norton quotes another, yet more frightful, that of an adoption set aside after "*twenty-seven years' open recognition by all parties;*" although among the claimants by blood one had actually disputed it at first, but had afterwards admitted it; the adopted son having been all this time "in open notorious possession and management" of the property, and having been cut off by the adoption "from all succession to the estate of his natural father." And the sole plea, apparently, on which this was done, was the order of 1846, ordering adoptions to be notified six months prior to the adopting party's decease,—this order being applied *retrospectively*, the adoption having taken place in 1827! It is true this statement is taken from the claimant's petition; but it is printed by Mr. Norton as exhibiting "a fair average specimen" of the working of the Government policy. At any rate, it is shameful to relate that a petition containing such statements should have remained unanswered.†

And now let us observe that the practice thus introduced, with respect to private property, is not only identical in principle with that pursued of late years

* [illegible] n Statesmen, p. 169.

[illegible] pp. 170-176.

with respect to native sovereignties, but was made a foundation for it. In Mr. Willoughby's Sattara minute, Mr. Hart, the Inam Commissioner's Report of the 27th March, 1847, as to the necessity of the sovereign's consent to an adoption, was expressly quoted to justify the annexation of the Sattara state.*

But to conclude: A recent eye-witness speaks of the Inam Commission as "that general confiscation of proprietary rights, carried through with unexampled harshness and contempt of law," which "has put the entire population against us" (he is referring to the Deckan). Such language may be too strong; I trust it is. But the results of that Commission certainly shew us how a chain of sympathetic discontent has been established between the prince and the poorest inamdar; how annexation has tended to give chiefs, and the resumption of inams soldiers, to any rebellion that might have started into flame within the Deckan. And do not let us suppose that that danger will ever pass away so long as its causes are not removed.†

* Sattara Annexation Papers, p. 86.

† I have confined my observations respecting the Inam Commission to the case of Inams properly so called, or grants free of service. There would be much to say also respecting jagheers, or grants upon conditions of service, and "surinjams," or grants to nobles for the maintenance of their dignity. Respecting the last, in particular, I have had before me a thick volume entitled "Correspondence by the Inam Commission on the Deccan Surinjams" (Bombay Government Selections, No. xxxi. 1856), of which I will only say, that such a mass of spoilt paper and wasted ink, such a hopeless chaos of official prolixity, I had never yet met with. Practically, the whole volume, of Heaven knows how many pages (for the paging begins again and again, with EE appendices), consists of a long wrangle between the

LETTER XXI.

GOVERNMENT PURCHASES OF LAND.

General revenue settlements,—laws for the resumption of rent-free lands, and special commissions to carry such laws into effect,—suppression of the custom of primogeniture,—of the right of posthumous disposal by adoption,—of the right of disposal during life, by gift or sale,—and as a consequence, an enormous extension of the claims of Government by escheat,—such appear

Inam Commissioners, Capt. Cowper in particular, and Mr. Warden, whose evidence I have above referred to, and who, in the capacity of "Agent for Sirdars," had drawn up certain lists of native claimants for Government, as to the accuracy of these lists. Thirteen pages (Appendix X) are devoted to the case of a single village, worth £250. a-year, subdivided among an infinite number of claimants, some of them actual cultivators, and whose shares fall as low sometimes as £1. 14*s* between three! Whilst the time of Indian officials, and the money of the natives of India, are wasted upon such futilities, it will hardly be credited that an Inam Commissioner (Mr. Hart) actually annexes to an official letter to the Government of Bombay (Appendix B, p. 105), in illustration of the obligations of the Court of Directors towards the people of India, and the Bombay Government reprints without note or comment, a leader of the "Times" newspaper dated 9th February, 1853, speaking of the maintenance of native Sovereignties as "a scandalous misuse of those opportunities which Providence has given us!" The animus of the Inam Commission may be judged by such a fact.

The "Bombay Times," Nov. 9 to Dec. 9, 1858, contains an elaborate series of articles on the Commission, which I have not had leisure to make available for the purposes of this work. On the other side may be read, amongst other documents, a letter signed "Observer," in the "Overland Bombay Standard" of Dec. 24.

to have been the principal means by which the Government of India, whether wittingly or unwittingly, has hitherto destroyed the native landowners, and, where practicable, the native princes, so to speak, by wholesale. I must now give some instances of the way in which those landowners have been rooted out one by one.

For this purpose, I shall carry my readers into a different quarter of our Indian empire from that which has hitherto formed the subject of my observations. We have seen a little of what has taken place in the North-West, in Bengal, in Bombay. Let us now turn to Madras.

Madras, like Bombay, enjoys generally the blessings of what is termed the *ryotwar* system of land revenue, —*i.e.* that of fixing from year to year with every cultivator the assessment payable by him in respect of every field in his holding. The result of this system in Madras may be stated in few words. With the exception of a very few large estates, chiefly held by Englishmen, or by the representatives of former native sovereigns, who have become our pensioners, all large holdings whatever have disappeared. I find in a letter of the Court of Directors to the Madras Government of the 17th December, 1856, that out of a total number of single holdings of 1,409,729, no less than 834,190 (or more than 59 per cent.) were assessed at sums below £1. giving an average of 7*s* per holding.* Now as respects the rate of assessment, Lord Harris, the present Governor of Madras, in a minute of the 26th October, 1854, says—"At present, in this Pre-

* "Papers relating to the Revised Survey and Assessment of the Madras Presidency," &c. 1857, p. 17.

sidency, I hear *that it is often* 50 *per cent. or even more,"** *i.e.* of the gross produce; so that, at this rate, the gross annual value of 59 per cent. of the Madras holdings might be taken at 14*s* per annum. But take a lower standard of assessment,—33 per cent. instead of 50,—the average gross income of the ryot will yet be only about a guinea a-year. Then as, according to a rate of calculation which Lord Harris refers to, 33 per cent. of the gross produce are reckoned to give two-thirds of the nett profit, it follows that the nett annual profit of 59 per cent. of the Madras holders of land in 1856 might amount to the munificent income of 10*s* 6*d* per head. How far they are likely to become good customers to our manufacturers, out of an income so superabundant, any one who pleases may speculate. No wonder that the Indian Government have been of late anxiously considering the means of diminishing "the evils arising from the existence of very small holdings, and consequently of a class of ryots *scarcely, if at all, above the grade of paupers,"*—to quote again the Court of Directors,—or that Lord Harris proposed at once to reduce the Government demand to 25 per cent. on the gross amount, to be fixed for a term of years—a boon, it will be observed, which would raise the average annual income of the aforesaid 834,190 landholders to less than fourteen shillings, sterling money; a week's wages of a Suffolk labourer!

It will hardly be credited that, with these facts before their eyes, not only Lord Harris and the Madras

* "Papers relating to the Revised Survey and Assessment of the Madras Presidency," &c. 1857, p. 6.

Government, backed by their superiors, uphold the ryotwar system, but every effort has been made by the Government, up to the latest time of which I have any record, to eradicate from the Madras Presidency the traces of any other.

It so happens that, in the Northern extremity of the Presidency, through the districts called generally the Northern Circars, originally part of the Bengal Presidency, the Zemindaree system,—*i.e.* that of large landed estates, owned by individuals, and permanently assessed in the bulk to the land revenue, had been established. A Madras civilian, Mr. P. B. Smollett, has lately published a book under the title of "Civil Administration of Madras, in 1855 and 1856," founded on the writer's experience of these districts, as compared with the rest of the Madras Presidency. His aim has been, he tells us, to shew "that the system of landed tenures in Madras is the great social evil of the Presidency, and that coercion and the ill-treatment of the native cultivators are the necessary consequences of its continuance," and to illustrate "the manner in which this detestable land system is carried out—demoralising the revenue servants, degrading the agricultural classes, and devoting the private possessions of the native gentry of Southern India to ruin and confiscation." Yet his work says nothing of resumption laws, Inam Commissions, escheats, rights of adoption, or any other of the subjects which we have hitherto considered. It simply deals with individual cases, and shews how, by a skilful use of legal machinery, this man and that has been, in plain English, jockeyed, or positively swindled, out of his property. The chief means by which this result has been attained, has been simply—Government purchases, at Government sales.

I dare say that amid the strange farrago of Indian legislation some enactments may be fished up which bring such proceedings within the pale of legality. But certain it is, that according to the law of England, for the trustee or agent for sale to become the purchaser of what he is selling is illegal. The characters of vendor and purchaser are inconsistent. A man cannot fairly act out the one when he is seeking to put on the other.* Nor is this view one of the insular peculiarities of English law. The American jurists have admitted the same doctrine to the full.† The Code Napoleon does the same by specific enactment.‡ Nor is there, that I am aware, the slightest ground for supposing that the principle would not be applied to the Crown as well as a subject. It probably never occurred, since there have been judges in England, to any adviser of the Crown to recommend that the Crown should buy that which the Crown had to sell. But so little disposed have our Courts shewn themselves to derogate from their principles of action in favour of the Crown, that the Court of Exchequer refused, at the suit of the Crown, to enforce a Crown sale under an extent, on the ground that a bidding had been reserved by the conditions, and that according to the strict rule of the Common-law (mitigated by Equity) the employment of a puffer in an ordinary case would

* See, for instance, Lord St. Leonards' Vendors and Purchasers, ch. xix. § ii.

† See, for instance, Story's Equity, vol. i. p. 154 and foll.

‡ Code Civil, Art. 1596.

vitiate the sale,—"*there being no reason why the Crown should be subject to a different construction.*" *

It is then the practice of this "constructive fraud" (to give it its technical name) by the Government of India which we have now to consider.

I must let Mr. Smollett speak, as far as possible, for himself, or I suspect few of my readers would believe what he has to say. The doctrine, he tells us, that native zemindars are "oppressors, plundering middlemen, successful robbers of the public estate," and that it is "a dereliction of duty" to "omit taking every fitting opportunity to eject them,"—this doctrine

"Occasionally acted upon by the Government 30 years ago, . . . is now, in 1856, openly avowed and inculcated even where the greatest native chieftains are concerned. Former circular orders enjoined the sequestration of landed estates whenever 20 per cent. of arrear was reached, in order to obviate the necessity of sale; but the policy of the day now is, to wink at disorder, to decline interference during the official year, and to sell up the owner peremptorily at the end of the season. With this view *we see constantly large estates exposed to sale in the gross for small revenue balances, although, if these possessions were subdivided, as the law permits, the sale of a few villages would fetch a price that would discharge the arrear of revenue; but then the Government would miss the opportunity of acquiring a large territory for a song.* Now, as there are few capitalists in the Madras districts to compete at such sales, and as many lands held on feudal tenure are really unsaleable, *Government, in most instances, acquires these valuable possessions at* 1-10*th of their real worth.* . . . .

Meet a ryotwar collector in his own house, at his hospitable board, he will admit that the sale of a great zemindary which he has just achieved was brought about by dexterous management; that *the owner had been purposely permitted to get into the meshes of the collector's net beyond his power of extrication;* that the sale could easily have

* *Rex* v. *Marsh*, 3 Young and Jervis, 331.

been obviated, nay, perhaps was uncalled for. He will not deny that the unconditional sale of an ancient zemindary, entire, for a small balance of taxes, when the subdivision and disposal of a part would have met every requirement, is a questionable transaction, barely honest. He will hear, without being offended, an unprejudiced person stigmatise the purchase by Government of an ancient patrimony sold thus in the aggregate without necessity, as a robbery, as spoliation under the pretence of law; but *he will excuse himself by saying that it was the anxious desire of the Government to obtain possession of the dispossessed zemindar's inheritance.*"* . . . .

And Mr. Smollett proceeds to give instances,—a few, he tells us, out of many,—of "the improper confiscation of property," during a long series of years. He shews how twenty years ago an ancient estate in Tinnevelly, yielding now a clear surplus revenue of £3,000 a year, was obtained by Government "for absolutely nothing,"—the owner having been arrested and thrown into prison, without any specific charge whatever being brought against him, at a time when he had voluntarily come to see the collector and settle terms for payment of his arrears,—no person having dared to bid against the Government after such an act.† He shews how in 1840, another estate—the Woodiagherry jagheer—in Nellore, worth £8,000 a year, was appropriated "in even a more summary manner, without a reasonable excuse, and without recourse even to the forms of law,"—the owner, "a Mahommedan nobleman and a man of 70 years of age," having been arrested and made a prisoner for life, and his estate confiscated, on a report of his treason by a Commissioner, made without seeing the

* Civil Administration in Madras in 1855 and 1856, pp. 72-74.

† Ibid. pp. 75-6.

accused, "or hearing his defence, or telling him of what he was accused;" although "every inhabitant of the Nellore district believes that the charges were unfounded," and the Commissioners at the time had opportunities of knowing that some of the papers on which the owner was condemned were forgeries.* He shews how in Guntoor, in recent times, large estates (the Dasareddy), paying a revenue of *sixty thousand pounds* a year were sold in the gross, and were bought in by the Government salesman for *five hundred pounds*, "this being the only offer. *The pretext for selling these estates was the existence of an enormous balance which had accumulated during twenty years, created chiefly through the mismanagement of the officers of Government, who as trustees had administered the revenues all that time*, the lands being under judicial sequestration owing to a disputed succession." And this monstrous advantage taken by Government of its own wrong was moreover directly contrary to law; for "the highest courts of the Madras Presidency have ruled repeatedly, that lands secured by a deed of permanent settlement are not answerable for arrears of revenue accruing under Government management; but *the heavy expenses of litigation against the state and the poverty of the family have prevented this illegal act from being sifted and exposed in a Court of Law*;" while the Court of Directors, as Mr. Smollett delicately phrases it, were "erroneously informed," that the arrears of taxation had been caused by the personal

* Ibid. pp. 76-7. See also Mr. Mead's "Sepoy Revolt," pp. 223-4. He states that the alleged conspirator was "bed-ridden," and had lost the use of his limbs for twenty years.

extravagance of the zemindar, though he had not been in legal possession for twenty years!* In Masulipatam, three years ago, says the author, apparently writing in 1856, other estates which he names were purchased by Government for about £1,200, "at a mock auction," the value of them being perhaps £3,000 a year.†

"In Vizagapatam, some years back, the ancient zemindary of Golgondah, which yields about 10,000 rupees (£1,000.) of clear surplus annually, was sold, and bought by Government for £10. sterling. *The collector who sold the estate, and the then Board of Revenue which authorised the sale, advised its being restored* to the member of the family who seemed best capable of administering the zemindary; *but the Government said it was a valuable acquisition, and desired that the subject of restitution should on no account be ever entertained:* . . . *Six years afterwards, this act of spoliation was the cause of a local insurrection, which it took three years to suppress, with a great sacrifice of life and property.*"‡

But indeed "there are other ways of securing the decay and confiscation of landed proprietors besides that of selling them. There is, for instance, the policy of abnegation, or non-interference, now being carried out in Jeypore. This ancient zemindary or fiefship in Vizagapatam, is held under the usual deed of permanent settlement, by which *the Government* is bound to preserve the peace of the country, and is charged with the maintenance of an efficient police. *For more than half a century the duty has been wholly neglected in Jeypore.* . . . The zemindar, who is styled the Raja of Jeypore, when active and capable, apprehended criminals, and punished misdemeanours, *although he had no authority to do so*; but of late years he has become old and foolish, . . . and a sort of anarchy

* Ibid. pp. 77-8. † Ibid. p. 78. ‡ Ibid. pp. 78-9.

universally prevails." In 1855, a Commissioner for the suppression of human sacrifices, with his assistant, visited Jeypore, and finding this state of anarchy, quietly recommended the removal of the zemindar on a life pension, and the confiscation of his estates, worth £15,000 a year. The local agent however,—apparently Mr. Smollett himself,—recommended "that the long and discreditably neglected duty of maintaining an efficient police force in Jeypore should be at last undertaken," and that the zemindary should be administered in trust for the owner. The Madras Government acquiesced in these suggestions, but a reference to the Supreme Government was necessary, and Lord Dalhousie "at once" overruled them. A pledge to abolish widow burning had been given by the incompetent zemindar, and it would be well to wait and see if he fulfilled it. The anarchy spoken of seemed exaggerated. He saw no sufficient grounds for interference; but "if the Government did interfere *it must be once and for ever*." Whereon Mr. Smollett observes, and not I:—

"The plain meaning of this is, the pear is not quite ripe, the rich man is not yet *in extremis*, but in a little time, upon a proper representation being made, confiscation will be had recourse to. At the same time *it is strictly enjoined that no reform shall be commenced upon, and the responsibility of Government to introduce a police system*, and to maintain tranquillity, by which alone order can be re-established, *is quietly ignored*. The Governor-General's admirers consider the annexation and absorption of independent kingdoms in the British Indian empire as the highest proof of his administrative ability . . . but *this angling for the confiscation of private estates is contemptible petty larceny in a ruler*."*

---

* Civil Administration in Madras, pp. 98-9.

One more extract to conclude:—

"The landlords in the Northern Circars, as a class, have no faith in the security of possession of their lands. They look on themselves as a doomed race, and believe that their families will, sooner or later, be beggared under British rule. They see daily the endowments of their temples practically removed from the protection of the law, their landed estates confiscated, and their noblest families reduced to starvation. If not at present absolutely disaffected, the population in these parts view the British dominion with fear. *Our empire is certainly not one of opinion. It is distasteful to all classes of the people.*"†

The question indeed naturally occurs,—if confiscations of the nature above described can take place, not only against the spirit of English law, but sometimes against the letter of Indian Regulations, is there no recourse? The Privy Council compelled the restoration to the Raja of Burdwan of his rent-free lands, when resumed in violation of prescriptive rights; could it do nothing for the dispossessed Madras landholder? A natural enough question, but to which the Vasareddy case, before referred to, otherwise that of Lutchmeputty Naidoo, gives answer.

In Mr. Mead's "Sepoy Revolt"† will be found a full account of this most extraordinary judicial farce, for it can be called little else,—given perhaps in somewhat too highly coloured a style, but which is vouched for as correct by Mr. J. B. Norton.‡ It will there be seen how, when the Privy Council had decided in favour

* Ibid. p. 105. † Pp. 276—284.

‡ "I can vouch for the literal accuracy of every word of the narrative." Topics for Indian Statesmen, p. 169, *n**.— Mr. Danby Seymour, too, I believe, when at Madras in 1853, was rendered fully cognizant of the case.

of Lutchmeputty Naidoo, as sole heir to the Vasareddy estates and their £50,000 a year, the Madras Suddur Court would not put him in possession until he had paid the Company's bill for costs, amounting to £32,000;—how, when he had been sold up to pay these costs, he was told there was nothing to give him. The Company had bought, as before stated, the bulk of the property (in Guntoor) for £500. He might have the remainder in Masulipatam on payment of £280,000 of arrears. But before six months from the filing of the Privy Council decree in the Suddur Court, the Masulipatam property was put up to auction *as belonging to his competitor*, and also bought in by Government (1849). Lutchmeputty applied again to the Privy Council, and in July 1854 obtained an order for being put in possession. But the Suddur Court refused to put him in possession, telling him that he must proceed through the lowest Court, the Zillah, in three suits, one for each estate, and one for money deposited. "The first sheet of paper used in each cause would cost £100, and each separate page of the proceedings would cost 4*s*." The Raja is out of possession to this day. Thus the Government, having first, as it turns out, illegally sold and bought one property, as belonging to a man who was not the owner, next, in the face of the Privy Council decree, instead of restoring that one, proceeded illegally to sell and buy another; and the highest Company's Court of justice, instead of carrying out the decree of the Queen's Privy Council, which reversed their own proceedings, bade the suitor begin all his proceedings *de novo!* If you can imagine a man required to proceed in a County Court for a sum which the House of Lords has declared to be justly due to him, you will have some idea of the mere absurdity involved in the affair, though scarcely of the insolent denial of justice which it involves. Let it always be remembered that the original sale was illegal, even against the wrongful claimant, as the estate had passed into the hands of the Government unincumbered, and with a surplus fund of £50,000, and Government had sold the estate for a debt of which £140,000 had been accumulated *by itself*. Mr. Smollett, it will have been seen, openly charges the Madras Government and its officers with wilful abuse of the powers of the law, wilful contempt of its provisions, for the confiscation of native property in land. Himself a Madras civilian,—coming forward to us, so to speak, from behind the scenes,—he is surely the most trustworthy of all witnesses, a witness against his own interest. I leave it to others to consider how far such a course of conduct can be attributed to the Government and its officers in other Presidencies, to the "young gentlemen," for instance, as Mr. Warden calls them, of the Inam Commission of Bombay. Mr. Robertson's observations on the North-West, and particularly on the case in which the Board of Revenue of those provinces "ordered" a collector not to carry a judicial decree in favour of a landowner's claim into effect; Mr. Boulderson's mention of the estates bought in by Government in famine-time, may shew that such conduct has not been, if it is now, entirely without precedent in that part of India. Mr. J. P. Wise, in his evidence before the Colonization Committee, shews equally that it is not without precedent in Bengal. He there relates how in 1833-4 a purchase by him of an estate at a Government auction was reversed upon three grounds,—two of them purely formal, and if correct (which he denies) arising out of the default of the Government officer himself,—the third, that the collector was a relation of his, and had favoured him by accepting Company's paper (!) as security for his bid, which also he states was incorrect. But the Acting Commissioner who recommended the reversal, advised also the purchase of the estate,—as it was "a very valuable one"—"on behalf of Government at the next sale." The Board of Revenue to whom the report was addressed, adopted both the recommendation and the advice, purchased the estate on the next sale day, "and that estate is now held by Government." It does not indeed seem to have been purchased at a gross undervalue, but at no advantage to the original vendor certainly, since the difference of the Government figure over that of Mr. Wise was only that of "the increased revenue up to the date of sale."* Still, I must own it, I would fain, fain hope that the "benighted Presidency" exhibits in this respect monstrosities not to be equalled elsewhere.

Perhaps you will say—and the plea is the one always urged in India—that however harsh or iniquitous may be the conduct of the British Government towards the native landowner, the change to the cultivator from tenancy under the former to tenancy under the State must be a beneficial one. Dark indeed, I must own, are the colours in which the native zemindar is painted in Bengal by the missionaries, by the ryots

* Second Report on Colonization and Settlement (India), pp. 38-9.

themselves; scarcely less dark those in which the English planters, rival members of the same class, represent him before the Colonization Committee. And yet, if we are to believe Mr. Smollett, there is a landlord far more oppressive to the native cultivator than any heathen or Mussulman zemindar,—and that is, the Christian British Government. Let us hear how he describes the transition from the one form of landlordism to the other, in the case of those estates in the Madras Presidency which are wrested from their owners by the Government, through processes of which I have quoted some instances from him.

"In estates so acquired the first thing done is to introduce the equivocal blessings of a ryotwar [annual] settlement. All alienations of rent or reduced assessments on the villages made subsequently to the permanent settlement are set aside, the old standard of land-rent is enforced, a scrutiny into rent-free holdings is ordered, and all private and acquired property within the zemindary is thus put in jeopardy. The local village establishments of the zemindars for maintaining order are discontinued, and in lieu, a stipendiary police, who find their own clothes and arms, and who receive a salary of 6*s*. or 8*s*. a month only, are let loose upon the people. Over all is placed a native collector, who is also a magistrate within his limits, with power to commit all criminals to the courts without reference to his superiors, and he possibly gets from £5. to £6. sterling a month. Under such supervision the inhabitants of the zemindary soon learn to sigh over the downfall of their easy, though possibly dissipated native landlord. . . . . In all the ancient zemindaries which have descended in the family for some hundred years, the permanent settlement is moderate. In general the country is thickly peopled; ploughing cattle abound, *the rents of land to the farmer are easy, when compared with the cultivators' rents in Government villages;* the fields are well tilled, and *there are in these estates no large tracts of rich soil left uncultivated for years because the rent is too high.* . . . . In the modern estates, where the Government permanent settlement is sometimes oppressively high, the ryots are not so favourably situated; but *even in those estates the condition of the people and the management of the cultivation are immensely in advance of any ryotwar Government district in the Madras Presidency.* In the town of Vizagapatam you will meet natives with fine houses, who own good conveyances, and who have handsome furniture in their dwellings, and there are many landlords who live upon their estates, and who spend their thousands per annum as rationally as gentlemen of fortune spend their incomes in England or Scotland. *In what ryotwar district will you meet with anything like this? There, a merchant or banker worth* £10,000 *is a wonder, and capitalists there are none.* In Vizagapatam there are several natives worth 10 lacs of rupees (£100,000) each, and in the district there are a score with a lac of rupees (£10,000) and more at their command.

There are only two talooks (estates) in the Vizagapatam district managed directly by the officers of Government. These talooks were once private property, since acquired by Government, by purchase and dexterous management. . . . . *It is not an exaggeration to say that* 90 *per cent. of the complaints made to the Commissioner in the Vizagapatam district come from the Government talooks.* The complaints are of over-assessment—of taxes illegally levied—of oppression—of moneys extorted—of lands taken from the cultivators against their will—of coercion, and every other villainy of ryotwar management. Compare the condition of a Government village with that of a village in a zemindary, and take the Madagole zemindary, which adjoins the Government lands, as a sample. The owner of this estate is a gentleman of ancient family, always on the brink of ruin; and it might be supposed that fiscal mismanagement was rife there, if anywhere. But the zemindar's people are well off, his villages are flourishing, and the rents are collected not only without distraint, but sometimes they are paid a year in advance. I will take it upon myself to affirm, without fear of contradiction, that not one petition from Madagole has reached the Commissioners' office complaining of coercion or exaction in the revenue collections during the last six years; whereas from the neighbouring Government estate of Survasiddy, during that same period, the complaints presented on the same score may be computed by thousands.

. . . . *The districts where zemindars still flourish are the only provinces in the Madras Presidency that exhibit any symptoms of vitality*, in the presence of capitalists, a wealthy aristocracy, enterprising native merchants, respectable bankers, and a peasantry more contented and less harassed in their occupations than can be found in ryotwar districts. . . . When the estate is bought by Government, the same land-tax is collected from the villagers, generally under a much more grinding system than the zemindars followed. The revenues, instead of being spent as heretofore on the spot, are swept into the general treasury . . . perhaps to build a university at the Presidency, estimated to cost one-third of a million sterling.* . . . . Gentlemen who fancy that agricultural operations cannot proceed regularly in village communities, and that fair rents cannot be collected punctually without the aid of an accurate and scientific survey of each field and holding, might be sent to learn their duties as land stewards, with benefit to themselves as well as to the Government, from the practice of native landowners, whose management is in most instances vastly superior to that of their European masters."†

* Civil Administration of Madras, in 1855 and 1856, pp. 85-94.

† Civil Administration of Madras in 1855 and 1856, p. 127. The whole of the chapter from which the last extract is taken, (IV. "On the revenue management of the Vizeanagrum zemindary in Vizagapatam during the last twenty years,") is well worth notice. It shews how the owner of a great estate, having fallen into private difficulties, proposed to resign the management into the hands of the Government officials in 1826, the collected rental being then £86,000 a year; how with the gradual but ultimately complete introduction of the ryotwar system, the rental fell to £62,800 by 1846; how the introduction of the village system sent the rental up to £98,900 by 1852, discharged all debts, and placed the zemindar in possession of an unencumbered estate yielding a nett surplus of £60,000 a year, which continues to prosper since that time under his management. See pp. 107-127. Mr. Smollett's book, however, is disfigured by abuse of the Madras engineers; the *bêtes noires*, indeed, of many a civilian, but who ought not to be such to him.

Remember that the witness before us is a Company's civilian, writing on the spot in 1855. Remember that he has had before him the native landlord, not in his best days, but in his worst. For just as British protection, and above all, the policy of annexation of native principalities, once put forth, tends fatally to degrade the character of the native sovereign, so is the character of the petty native chief deteriorated by British rule. "There is a great tendency," says Mr. Smollett, "to dissipation in these chieftains, from their having, under British rule, been deprived of their military and political powers, and from their being reduced, from feudal tributaries of the State, to the class of landlords only;"* though "physically, there is no finer race of men than that of the ancient zemindars of the Northern Circars; and in the very few instances in which their education has been at all cared for, they have turned out remarkably well in after life, managing their estates with economy, and living creditably in the midst of their own people."†

I have no reason for supposing that these zemindars of the Northern Circars are either above or below the average of other native landlords. Put them above, if you like it. Suppose it is only in every other instance that the ordinary native landlord reaches their level. Then we are justified in saying, that if the 108,199 Bombay inams were recalled to-morrow, in more than 54,000 instances there would be an immediate change for the worse to the cultivator, in passing under the British Government as a landlord. Add

* Ibid. p. 101.

† Ibid. p. 103.

this to what has been already stated as to the result of the Inam Commission in Bombay.*

Of course the details of Mr. Smollett's picture are not universally applicable. The ryotwar system will only be applied where the ryotwar system exists. It is sufficiently disliked by officials themselves out of its own sphere of operation to make us rest assured that it will not be extended, in its unmitigated shape at all events. But it is observable that in Bengal, where the Permanent settlement exists, it is at once set aside as soon as land gets into the hands of Government. It is then, not sold out and out, but let "generally in farms for a period of years, *from five to ten years*."†

"I cannot admit," wrote St. George Tucker, "that the zemindars, who have an interest in the prosperity of their estates, and in the well-being of their tenantry, are likely to be more oppressive functionaries than the officers of revenue, who have no such interest. The over-zeal of a young and inexperienced collector (and there are many such I fear) is supposed to have caused 50,000 beegas of land to be thrown out of cultivation in a single year in one of the Baroach districts. No zemindar could have been guilty of such gratuitous folly, for he must have perceived that his own ruin would be the inevitable consequence."‡

---

* Did space allow, the case of the "Desaees," and other zemindars of Baroach, might here be quoted. It brings out in a remarkable manner the destruction by our late proceedings of the inheritable rights of females.

† Second Report on Colonization and Settlement (India), p. 39, qu. 2660. It need hardly be added that inams are not granted by the British Government, except in very rare instances. One of the exceptions is that of "Ballajee Punt Natoo"—whether the same individual as the treacherous Brahmin of that name, to whom Raja Pertaub Sing, of Sattara, owed his downfall, I cannot say.

‡ Selections, p. 21.

Elsewhere he says, of the Talookdars of the North-West:—

"We cannot destroy the memory of their past, or the consciousness of their present state. They were once prosperous, and they and their descendants must feel that they are no longer so. They are silent, because the natives of India are accustomed to endure, and to submit to the will of their rulers; but if an enemy appear on our western frontier, or if an insurrection unhappily take place, we shall find these Talookdars, I apprehend, in the adverse ranks, and their ryots and retainers ranged under the same standard."*

LETTER XXII.

DECAY OF THE WEALTHY AND RESPECTABLE CLASSES IN GENERAL.

As the wealth of India is mainly in the land, it follows that the destruction of native land-owners is really the destruction of the wealthy classes in general,—so far as wealth does not consist merely in money, and does not flow from the traffic in it. This fact and its consequences are perhaps nowhere better set forth than by Colonel Low, in his first Nagpore minute.

* Selections, p. 19. I have not space to dwell on the case of the Carnatic jagheerdars, which is referred to by Mr. Mead, p. 221 and foll. of his "Sepoy Revolt." The summary of it appears to be this,—that a sum of money, set apart by treaty in 1801 as one of two "*permanent deductions in all times to come* from the revenues of the Carnatic" for the maintenance of the family and officers of the Nawab, is being gradually cut down to nothing by curtailment of pensions on every successive death of a pensioner. The pensioners, I believe, only ask to receive land instead of the pensions, being confident of being able to turn it to good account.

10. *"So far from increasing or keeping up the previous number of wealthy and influential men in those native states which we annex to our own territory, we uniformly and immediately diminish the number of such men in these countries. . . .*

11. The general effects which I have described of the number of men of wealth and influence being immediately diminished when we take possession of a new territory, have probably been produced by various causes; such, for instance, as that of our remitting large portions of the revenue for pensions and salaries in England (which bring no return to India), instead of spending such revenues within the countries which produce them, as all national governments do. And again, our not employing natives in high military commands, or in very important civil offices, must also have the same general tendency; and so must the fact of being foreigners, who never associate with or make personal friends of natives of India.

12. *I could cite in detail, were it necessary, several instances in time of famine,* which have occurred at different times within my own personal knowledge, in the Deccan, in the Saugor territory, and in the North-Western provinces, *of our having suffered heavy losses in revenue, and very extensive losses in human lives, owing to the want of wealth among our native subjects; while in the neighbouring native states, which had experienced exactly the same drought, they did not suffer nearly so much,* either by the death of their subjects or in revenue, solely because the wealthy jagheerdars and zemindars, and other men of property (and as far as regards Oude, even farmers of districts) made large advances of money from their private funds, whereby great numbers of men, by digging new wells, were enabled to raise sufficient grain to keep them alive for the season, and who but for these advances of specie, must assuredly have died of starvation."*

---

* Nagpore Annexation Papers, pp. 39-40. It will hardly be credited that Lord Dalhousie took no kind of notice of all this part of Colonel Low's second minute. See his Lordship's second minute, *ibid*. pp. 53-5.

The following passage from Mr. Gubbins is almost as strong as that from Colonel Low:—

"It cannot be denied that the native gentry of Hindostan have not much to thank us for. In the early years of our rule, many old

Colonel Low's reasonings go obviously much further still than his words, for they not only apply to wealth and influence, but to talent, and learning, and energy, and ambition, and every faculty and impulse which tends to raise man above his fellows, whether in civil or military life. On one side of a boundary line a man may hope to rise to the highest dignities of the state; on the other, he must limit his ambition, if a civilian, to some subordinate judicial office; if a military man, to a so-called command in which he shall be subject to the orders of any foreign boy with a white face. We are far too prone to slur over this point, which has an important bearing upon the mutiny itself, and has been so referred to by others than myself. I have, for instance, before me a valuable pamphlet, on the "Re-organisation, Discipline, and Future Management of the

families were ruined by the severity of our assessments. In later times the settlement operations, while they greatly remedied the first defect, have yet much diminished the power and consequence of the Talookdars. . . . Again, the native gentry, especially the Mahomedan portion of it, in India, look chiefly to the service of the state for a means of subsistence. But as all the chief offices in British India are monopolized by Europeans, the minor ones only are open to them. In fixing the remuneration of these, we have too much followed the scale of pay we found to prevail in the native Governments which we succeeded; forgetting that with them, bribes and pecuniary gratifications were not forbidden. Under our system they could not openly be received: and in consequence several departments of the public service have been grossly underpaid. In the police service this was so particularly the case, that it has been found difficult to induce natives of good family to enter it at all. . . . The native gentry were becoming daily more reduced, were pinched by want of means, and were therefore discontented."—Mutinies in Oudh, pp. 55-7.

Bengal Army," by Lieutenant-Colonel Hunter,* an officer familiar with native feelings, and noted for having brought a corps of wild Bheels into a "perfect and wonderful state of discipline." He speaks, in terms almost exactly answering to those used by Sir John Malcolm nearly fifty years ago,† of the present system of the Indian army, which always keeps the native officers in the back-ground, "and subjects them to the authority, not only of the youngest and most inexperienced European subaltern in the regiment, but, what appears a strange anomaly, also to the authority, and not unfrequently to the vulgar and unmerited rebukes of the European non-commissioned officers." He writes as follows:—"The feelings of disgust, *and sometimes of bitter contempt*, which such a system is likely to engender, have, it appears to me, been altogether overlooked in accounting for the extraordinary disaffection of our native soldiers."‡ Nor is the case

* Published by Acton Griffith, 1858.

† See "Sketch of the Political History of India," p. 511.

‡ "Suggestions relative to the Reorganization," &c. pp. 2-3. Let me quote another weighty passage from Mr. Gubbins:—

"Sir Henry Lawrence was strongly impressed with the opinion that the native officers of our Sepoy army were underpaid. . . . . He would compare the status and emoluments which a native gentleman could attain to under native governments with those attainable in the British Indian army, and he thought that the disparity was too great. . . . . Let it be fairly considered whether the means of honourable employ held out by our Government to the better classes are sufficient to excite loyalty and to maintain contentment. . . . . Under native governments, such as that of Runjeet Singh in the Punjab, or those of Nagpore and Oude, natives, be it remembered, held the highest civil and military offices, and received emolu-

less glaring as respects civil employment. At this present moment it is perhaps not too much to say that the maintenance of our empire in India has been owing as much to the wisdom and genius of three great ministers —Salar Jung at Hyderabad, Dinkur Rao at Gwalior, and Rao Ramchunder Rao at Indore—as to the valour of our troops. Do you really think it would be more hopeful for India if such men had no other prospect than that of becoming, say, Principal Sudder Ameens in our Native Courts of justice? Have we many administrators equal to them? I strongly suspect, indeed, that much of the undue influence, and intrigues, and corruption which are attributed, and justly no doubt, to the native *omlah*, or officers of our magistrates, are due in great measure to the very pressure of our rule, keeping down talents and faculties which demand a wider scope. Beyond all question the native officer is, at least frequently, an abler man, a better lawyer, a more experienced officer than his European superior; * yet he is dependent and irresponsible. Can

ments not inferior to those received under our system by Europeans. The father may have received 1000 rupees (£100.) per annum as commandant of cavalry under Runjeet Singh; the son draws a pay of 80 rupees (£8.) as sub-commander in the service of the British Government. . . . . *No doubt the upper classes of natives, both Hindoo and Mahomedan, on this account viewed with regret the extinction of the dynasties of Lahore, Nagpore, and Oude.* They were used to repair from our provinces to seek the prizes obtainable in these native Courts. Though these were few, and not easily obtained, nor perhaps often long enjoyed, yet they grieved to see them abolished, and everything reduced to the almost dead level of Anglo-Indian service."—Mutinies in Oudh, pp. 97-9.

* "Many of the native tahsildars, and several sheristadars in the Madras territories are, for the work they have to do,—viz., the ad-

you conceive a situation more full of temptations, more void of checks than this?

But, indeed, it is well known that the gentry of India generally do not accept office under our rule. "Have the landholders," it was asked of Mr. Saunders, before the Colonization Committee, in reference to the North-West, "become officials under the Government to any extent?"

"*Not one of them.*"—"They have not become judges?"—"*No.*" —"Then none of the old families of that part of India came under the employment of the Government of India?"—"When Lord William Bentinck first introduced the system of employing natives as judges, he was very anxious to get the old families to accept appointments, and some of the old Mahomedans who reside on the northern side of the Doab were employed indeed, at Agra and Allygurh; but they very soon found the rules irksome, and threw up the appointments, and they gradually fell to the lot of the class of people who had been brought up in the inferior departments of the Courts."

It is not, unfortunately, only "the rules" which are irksome to native gentlemen when they accept office under us. The last chapter of Mr. Smollett's book, "On the treatment of the native servants of the State under the Madras Government, more particularly in the Northern Circars,"* reveals other causes for their declining to serve us. He tells us that if

"In the judicial department a few respectably paid appointments

---

ministration of a province,—superior in capacity to their European superintendents, and a district is often wholly managed through their instrumentality, the collector himself being quite a non-entity in everything except his official emoluments."—Smollett's Civil Administration of Madras, pp. 19, 20. This is but one testimony out of a multitude.

* "Civil Administration of Madras in 1855 and 1856," p. 128 and foll.

have indeed been thrown open to natives, ... in the revenue department not only has nothing been done for native advancement, but the office of native collector or tahsildar has greatly deteriorated. The tenure of power has become more and more precarious, and the highest situations attainable are falling into disesteem in public opinion. . . . . *When a head of police, or stipendiary magistrate for a county, receives less pay than an English footman gets in a gentleman's family, and when the deputy superintendent of a division draws less pay than an ordinary black cook, honesty in the native service is not to be expected.* The wonder is, that with such instruments so much work is done, and that on the whole it is so creditably performed. Under a good system a great number of the present subordinate servants might be dispensed with; the salaries of the rest should be trebled. *They should be treated like educated gentlemen, and not trampled upon like menials.* . . . . The Local Government, so far from endeavouring to improve the condition of these overworked men, has been continually imposing more work and greater labour, and has been tasking its faculties to degrade the appointments. . . . . *Inquisitions are annually made into their private circumstances; the possession or acquisition of lands is held to be a disqualification for office in the districts in which they live, and all the superior native servants are vexed and harassed by constant investigations to this end. Their small salaries are in every month attenuated by fines for every trivial mistake, or for delay in furnishing the ever increasing multitude of returns called for by half-a-score of departments.* . . . . Everything, in short, is done to disgust respectable natives with the service of Government, and nothing is listened to that tends to improve their condition, or to render it respectable."

And, clinging where his teeth are set, like a true British bull-dog that he is, Mr. Smollett proceeds to quote instances.

"Fifteen months ago an application was made to have the pay of two native collectors, in the district of Vizagapatam, *raised* to £10 *a month*—no great thing for a magistrate and land-steward over a hundred thousand men, with *a revenue of at least* £12,000 *a year to manage*—but the Commissioner in the Northern Circars refused even to entertain the recommendation; he thought £8 a month ample! So far from these appointments being generally held for years together, half a dozen tahsildars are frequently discharged in a month."

What is the consequence? "So far from the situation of tahsildar being coveted or sought for by the ablest and best of the native population, in these parts it is often extremely difficult to get a decent and creditable person to accept the office at all." "*We go to the bazar here for Tahsildars*" was the saying of a European assistant. This insecurity extends to the higher offices of head and deputy Serishtadars of districts. Mr. Smollett details at length the case of Cumbrun Nursingarow, head serishtadar of Rajahmundry, who, after 27 years of creditable service, was summarily suspended, sent to jail, and kept incarcerated for 16 months on charges which turned out to be utterly unfounded,—dismissed from office *pending his trial* as "unfit for government employment,"—and after being fully acquitted, not only was not compensated by the Madras government for the wrongs he had endured, but was refused by them any recognition of his fitness for employment. To the credit of the Home authorities be it said, his exclusion from public employment was cancelled by them on his appealing to England. But we have lost his services for ever. He is now in the employment of one of the few great remaining zemindars, the Rajah of Vizeanagrum, "and admirably conducts the revenue administration of that princely estate." In another case mentioned by Mr. Smollett, a head serishtadar of 40 years' service, "who was about to retire on his full pension with an honorary distinction to be conferred by Government for some acknowledged political services," was apprehended and committed to trial by a newly installed civilian jack-in-office—the same who had dismissed C. Nursin garow—on a charge "so frivolous and vexatious," that the judge refused to entertain it, and struck the cause off the file, yet could obtain no redress months, and only obtained at last, from the C Directors again, the payment of his full salary.

"In my judgment," concludes Mr. Smollett, "the high uncovenanted servants are treated, year by year, with gr greater indignity by their superiors. The orders issued fro time by Government, pretending to enforce an opposite cour ceeding, seem to me to be shams, for those officers of the covenanted service who treat them most as waste paper, and who violate them systematically both in the letter and the spirit, generally rank the highest in Government favour, and are most frequently singled out before others for promotion and advancement. *There is nothing, in my judgment, that renders the British Government in India so distasteful to the educated classes as the want of courtesy which most officials shew to native servants of eminent capacity, and who, but for our domination, would fill with credit the offices of governors in the provinces afflicted by ryotwar maladministration.*"

That this picture from Madras would become an exaggerated one, if applied to the whole of India, I gladly trust. But I see the leading lines of it on all sides. Mr. Gubbins in the North, as we have seen, admits that in the police service, owing to the inadequacy of the pay, it is found difficult to induce natives of good family to engage themselves in it. Of the revenue service he says that "a native officer, responsible for collecting £20,000 per annum, might receive a salary of £20 per month," adding, "The natives complain, and with some justice, that in the earlier years of our government we had shewn more liberality; and that a native collector had then been used to receive a commission of 10 per cent on his collections, which would give him ten times the salary which has been latterly allowed."* The unanimous outcry of all the planter witnesses before the Colonization Committee against the corruptions of the native officials ıgal, and for the employment of a larger number ·opeans, proves, I suspect, at least as much that ;ive officials are as a class degraded and void of pect through the conditions of their employıs that the native character is itself intrinsically and corrupt. Indeed, these witnesses when essed admit often as much. "There are very many trustworthy and intelligent natives," says Mr. McNair, "but the class of court-omlahs are not generally trustworthy."† Mr. J. P. Wise says of the police, "They are very often turned out of employment; the situation is not very certain; petitions are often put in against them, and they consider the place unsafe, and take advantage of that to get as much money as they can."‡ Yet the same witness says, "You find a good number of very superior men in India, men of great intelligence and worth."§

The enormous difference of salary between the alien and the native must indeed be of itself, to a man of self-respect and spirit, a sufficient bar to the acceptance of office under the British Government. The native judges do 95 per cent of the civil business. Yet of

* Mutinies in Oudh, p. 56.

† Second Report on Colonization and Settlement (India), p. 27.

‡ Ibid. p. 58. § Ibid. p. 59.

2846 employed, 2109 get salaries under £240. per annum—*less than the pay of the youngest civilian;*—and only 49 get salaries of £600. per annum and upwards, while the European zillah or district judge gets £3000.* And I do not know anything which brings out so strikingly the contrast between employment by the British or by a Native Government so strongly as the list given by Mr. Norton, in his "Topics for Indian Statesmen," of the situations held by natives educated in our institutions. In the column of salaries, one only stands prominently out from the mass, of which only 22 upon 239 exceed *ten pounds* a month. It is that of T. Madava Row, acting Dewan (or finance minister) of the native state of Travancore, whose salary is *two hundred* pounds a month, whilst no other exceeds *thirty-five* !† And who is Madava Row? Read his history in the same work, "by the affectionate hand of one of his own royal pupils" (he had been tutor to the Travancore princes before becoming a minister of state).‡ Let it be recollected that this was the same native state where the most frightful misgovernment had previously existed for years under a minister, supported by the English Resident, whom the Raja *could not obtain permission to depose.*§ Read how this great minister, though but of a small principality, suppressed corruption and violence, caused all notorious criminals to be apprehended, carried on irrigation works on a large scale, trebled various branches of the revenue, rendered himself familiar with every detail of the

* Second Report on Colonization and Settlement (India), p. 58.

† Topics for Indian Statesmen, Appendix B.

‡ Ibid. pp. 360-3. § Mead's Sepoy Revolt, pp. 205-8.

districts which he administered. And then consider how precious, I will not say to the natives of India, but to God's universe itself, is the existence of even such a petty native principality as Travancore, which allows to such men as Madava Row the full exercise of their powers for the benefit of their fellow creatures, instead of mewing them up,—like the highest paid of Madava Row's fellow pupils in the employ of the British Government (there is one of them rather better paid in the Supreme Court)—in some office of "head-serishtadar" at £28 a month!

And now let it not be forgotten that the same sympathy, the same bitterness, which are excited on a large scale in the minds of the mere spectators by the annexation of a state, by the beggaring of a race of kings, by the spoliation, as it is deemed, of a ranee or an adopted prince, are excited equally on a small scale by the absorption of a talookdaree, by the ruin of a petty chief, by the application to private property of the same technical rules which avail us to annihilate kingdoms. Such a sight has ere this struck the European observer with a sort of amazed pity, when he has come across it. Thus Indophilus, in his letters to the *Hurkaru*, speaks of the ruined noble "who considers himself fortunate if his banker, more out of respect to the hereditary claims of his family than from any expectation of repayment, doles out to him the means of appearing once a year in a *khimkaub* (embroidered silk) coat before the collector, like a *lifafah* or empty envelope, or like a shade unwillingly evoked. I have seen," he continues, "these apparitions of the prosperity of former days stand trembling before that all powerful magician a collector, and have fancied I heard them say, like the ghost of Samuel to Saul, 'Why hast thou disquieted me, to bring me up?'" Yet these eloquent words cannot convey a tithe of the feelings which the same sight must keep up in the men of the same speech and colour, the neighbours, the kinsmen, for whom every such apparition has its own special name and history, connected with perhaps the most glorious, or the most precious local recollections. As it has been truly observed by Mr. Russell, "There is among the Hindoos, as there is among all nations which possess great antiquity and historic families, a profound respect for old houses, and for the descendants of those who were coeval with the early records of their race, no matter in what positions fate may have placed them, or their own personal insignificance." It is of no use to discuss the reasonablness or unreasonableness of such feelings. They *exist*; and, aliens in a foreign country, we must take account of them, if we do not choose to spoil or even throw away, by our narrow headstrong folly, the most glorious empire that the arm of man ever won, the most glorious opening that God ever granted to a nation for the enlargement of His kingdom.

LETTER XXIII.

THE LAND-REVENUE.

We have seen how deep a meaning for the native of India must have the proclamation pledges of respect to native property and native usages, considering the inroads which have been made by our rule upon ancestral usages, the whole classes which it has swept away. There is another side to the question,—one which Indophilus treated of 25 years ago,—one which is still of momentous consequence. We have destroyed property in land where it existed. Have we helped sufficiently to create it where it did not?

To judge of this, I will confine myself to the one main test of the land-revenue. I will leave aside the salt duties, the excise, the Madras Moturfa (falsely spoken of as suppressed by the Court of Directors in their late "memorandum"), and other grievances alleged by the native population, the consideration of which would carry me much too far, and which I have indeed glanced at elsewhere. I will merely, in the briefest manner, endeavour to shew what the real nature is, of the pressure of the land-revenue. I believe indeed that, since the days of Lord Cornwallis, it has been a constant object of the Government of India—in one or other of its branches—to lighten that pressure. But I believe also that to this hour, except in Bengal, the land-revenue is breaking India's back.

How is this to be accounted for? Whence these constant efforts to relieve the burthen, and their as constant failure? Whence the anomaly of a taxation so light in numerical amount, when compared with that of other countries, and yet felt to be so heavy?

I have come to the conclusion that the main cause of the pressure of the Indian land-revenue lies far below the range of any of the experiments that have yet been tried to relieve it. I believe it takes its origin chiefly in the scarcity of money-capital, created by the levy of taxation in specie, and not in kind, increased by the constant drain of home-charges, and rendered more galling by the suppression of local mints, and the ruin of local centres of trade and luxury. The excess in the *rate* of the tax beyond what is reasonable—which alone is what in general has been sought to be alleviated—has been comparatively a mere accident. I am not the first to express this opinion. It has been set forth, in all its main features, with great clearness and ability, by Major Wingate amongst others, a Bombay Engineer officer, afterwards Revenue Survey Commissioner for the whole Presidency, in certain passages of an article in the "Bombay Quarterly Review" for 1857, which are made part of his evidence before the Colonization Committee.*

The principle of the Hindoo land-revenue is, beyond all question, payment in kind. Menu, treating of the king's dues, does not give the least hint that they are to be paid in money. Of grain, he says, the king may take "an eighth part, a sixth, or a twelfth;" of cattle,

* Fourth Report, pp. 59-61.

of gems, of "*gold and silver*," a "fiftieth."* The precious metals are thus treated, not by any means as representatives of wealth, as standards of value, but simply as peculiar forms of wealth, the increase of which is apparently assimilated to that of cattle, and is thus supposed to be more than four times as low as that of the produce of the most unfruitful soil.

The Mussulman conquest no doubt tended to break up this state of things. The first rush of Mussulman invasion left, so to speak, but little silt behind it. The invader was an armed missionary, ever pressing onwards to make the war-cry of Islam heard in new lands; or he was an armed rover, looking still back to his own country, intent on shewing some day at home the fruits of his forays. In either case, a drain of money-capital must thus have set in. The Mussulman came not to buy and to sell; he must have money, or the metals which can be turned into it; some part he would carry on with him from land to land, some he would take or send back to his own country. Even when the process of settlement began, the same influences must have continued at work. For a length of time the Indian Mussulmen were recruited by new comers from the East, many of whom no doubt remained in the country, but many of whom also departed again after a certain period of service, laden with India's wealth. On the other hand, the precarious tenure of the conqueror's power, the antipathies of race and creed yet hot, the contempt of the faithful for the usages of the heathen, must have tended to render galling, it may even be said, to both parties, that collection of revenue in kind which, by introducing into the administra-

* Code, ch. vii. s. 130.

tion of public affairs many of the practices, renders them subject also directly to the necessities of trade, such as time, and peace, and security, and mutual forbearance, if not mutual goodwill. Hence, I suspect, in great measure, the rise of the great revenue farmers, —the talookdars of the North-West, the zemindars of Bengal. The prince wanted money; the ryot had none to give, but produce only. Between the two there grew up these middlemen, possessed of capital, of power, or of influence, who, collecting from the ryot, more or less, in kind, rendered account to the sovereign in money, taking percentages to themselves. At any rate, it is in Mussulman countries, such as Bengal, and Oude, and Rohilcund, and generally round Delhi, the seat of the Mogul empire, that I find the talookdaree or zemindaree system most completely developed.

By the time the Mussulman system had become fixed, I take it, there was practically not much change in the condition of the people at large. A certain drain of money-capital from the Mussulman part of the population was no doubt always going on,—in the shape of the expenses of the *haj*, or pilgrimage to Mecca, which every true believer is bound to perform once in his life, pilgrims' donations included, which are often very large,—in the shape of offerings to the holy shrines, and contributions to charitable or religious foundations in the holy cities, such as are still remitted from India by Mussulman princes and nobles. On the other hand, the cultivator of the soil would have to yield up a larger portion of his produce, both to defray the necessary expenses of the intermediate agency of the talookdar or zemindar, his unauthorized exactions, and the rapacity of the alien despots to whom he was accountable; the middleman himself, to play his part more easily, would endeavour to raise in specie the revenue for which he accounted under that shape. Still, in the main, I believe that the condition of things in general, and in particular that of the cultivator, though worse in degree at the period when the English power grew up, than in the best Hindoo times, was the same in its nature as it had ever been.

The pressure of the land-revenue, however great, was not a money-pressure upon the cultivator. His dues to the state were paid, in the main, in produce or in labour.* Money-capital was, so to speak, scarcely an item in the world of agriculture,—that is to say, in the leading occupation of the great mass of the people. It only came into play in the world of trade, properly so-called, or in that of enjoyment. It accumulated as specie in the hands of the trader, in the coffers of the state; it was melted down, and hung in jewels and bangles on the person of the woman and of the child.† Hence the phenomenon of enormous outward wealth, which so struck all early European observers in India, traders and adventurers, which seemed for a long time inexhaustible. The pa-

* "The Anglo-Indian financial system differs from that of the native governments in the following most important particulars: the payment of the army, police, and other public establishments in cash; the collection of the land-tax in money, instead of wholly or partially in kind; the transfer of a portion of the Indian revenues to England for the payment of the home-charges . . . the creation of a funded public debt, of which the interest has to be paid in cash." —Major Wingate's evidence, Fourth Report on Colonization and Settlement (India), p. 60.

† To this day, the itinerant jeweller in India finds his material in the coins with which he is supplied, and which he melts down.

goda-tree was no doubt laden with golden fruit; it was not unnatural to suppose that the soil was charged with gold. Judging from the European point of view, in which a money-circulation lies really at the basis of our social economy, and only the surplus gold and silver beyond what is needed for all the daily wants of all the population becomes accumulated in a few hands, or turned into ornament, the affluence of the precious metals on the coasts, in the towns, in the hands of the merchants, or used by way of ornament, seemed to indicate a perfectly limitless store. But the real fact was, that behind all this outward affluence there was nothing of what was imagined; a teeming soil indeed, but one of which the resources could only be made available by the utmost possible development of the means of communication, by the opening of export markets, by the removal of burthens.

In levying the land-revenue in money, we in the first instance forcibly called back to the land the money capital locked up in trade. For, if we take the land-revenue at half the produce, and suppose that the other half was actually exchanged for money, the demand for money in agriculture was instantly *doubled.** Up to this time, in the cultivators' relations to the state, produce had been money; and this money-value of produce towards the largest of all his yearly creditors tended at the same time to give that produce

* "Under the native system, the sale for cash of a small part of the agricultural produce of a district sufficed to provide for all its liabilities connected with taxation and commerce. Under the British system on the contrary, twice, or perhaps three times the quantity of produce had to be sold in order to provide for the same objects, owing to the whole amount of the land-tax being demanded in cash." —Major Wingate's evidence, *ubi supra,* p. 61.

a money-value also towards the smaller ones. Now, produce was, to use a modern French expression, *demonetized*; a vacuum to that extent was created in the circulation, which trading capital of necessity rushed in to supply; we, on the other hand, not endeavouring to moderate, but accelerating the movement, by subjecting Indian articles to heavy import duties at home, and restricting Indian trade with foreign countries; by raising loans in England, and paying the interest of them from India, or even remitting tribute to the mother country; by proprietors' dividends, Leadenhall Street and Cannon-row salaries, pensions, &c.; by discouraging the settlement of Europeans, or, in other words, forcing those who had made fortunes in India, to go and spend them in England; by letting roads and canals, tanks and embankments, run to ruin. Hence on the one hand the enormous and undeniable falling off of the commercial activity of India, properly so-called; the decay of those flourishing marts with which the whole coast was once studded; and on the other, the equally enormous development of the purely monetary activity of the country, if one may so call it, the substitution of the village shroff for the great banker. But with the contraction, and in a great measure, ruin of trade and the neglect of public works, came also the depreciation of agricultural produce, which (except of late years in Bengal) is observed to be a marking feature of our rule; which has hitherto falsified all the revenue calculations of the most benevolent settlement-makers. With the extension of our rule this evil always increased. The numerous local mints, which the existence of so many independent principalities had scattered over the whole face of the country, and which, in the absence of a paper circulation, were of immense value in facilitating the transformation of fixed metallic capital, such as jewels, &c. into circulating, disappeared one by one, depreciating by so much to the possessor the value of his uncoined metallic wealth, placing him by so much the more in the dependence of the money-lender.* The numerous local markets created by the existence of the native sovereigns and nobles, and which by serving as centres of money circulation enhanced the value of produce on the spot, disappeared in like manner, and with the like effect. Everything combined to make the pressure of the land-revenue heavier and heavier, in a far more rapid ratio than that of any lowerings of the Government demand.

That that demand on the part of the British authorities has itself been excessive, is not to be denied. This may be maintained, without in the least denying or blinking the fact, that such excessiveness was characteristic of the revenue demands of the native princes whom we succeeded; that they took all they could get. Their exactions, corrected as they were by a thousand checks and counter-influences,—payment in kind, prodigalities to favourites, liberalities to religious persons or foundations, fear of insurrection, &c. &c., bore no very permanent effect. The rapacity of one sovereign might fill his treasury with idle gold, beggar a given number of landowners or employers of labour, lay

* Major Wingate seems to overlook the effect of the abolition of mints. They are forcibly pointed out by "Indophilus," in his 6th Letter to the *Hurkaru* (Mirror of the Indian Press, p. 164 and foll.) with reference to those only of Benares and Furruckabad.

waste a province. But the next reign would probably scatter the hoard broadcast over the land, create new landed estates and wealthy families, re-people the waste by liberal offers to cultivators. With the British Government the void created by the money-demand of revenue was not supplied; the drain for home-charges, &c., once begun never ceased; no new families were built up in the place of those broken down. To keep the land-revenue from pressing unduly upon the people, under such altered conditions, enormous reductions would have been needed; instead of which, for a length of time there prevailed what "Indophilus" in his admirable letters vigorously denounced, what was termed the "whole-rent theory,"—the theory, namely, that the state was to demand the *whole rent* of the land. What the consequences of that theory were in the North-West, I have shewn already from his letters. But the idea upon which that theory is based—that of state landlordism, has embodied itself in the ryotwar system, which prevails still through the two Presidencies of Madras and Bombay, where we have seen already some of its fruits.

It is indeed very difficult for an Englishman to realize the fact, that throughout the greater part of India, the Government claims to be the actual landlord of the soil, to grant it out on leases, which seem never to exceed thirty years, which throughout nearly two whole Presidencies are yearly ones. I have to rub my eyes, and make sure that I am not reading some translation from a continental socialist, of what may be called the official or centralist school, when I see, in a minute by the late Governor of Madras, Lord Harris, dated 26th October, 1854, a sentence like the following:—"*I consider that the land of a country belongs to the Government de facto, and should be held by it, and should be distributed by it amongst the population*, in such a manner as to cause it to be most beneficially cultivated, both as regards the interests of the cultivators and of the whole community." (Para. 78.) Imagine, O ye landlords, and eke tenants of England, Mr. Ernest Jones and Mr. Bronterre O'Brien become "government *de facto*" of this country, and proceeding upon my Lord Harris's theory, of considering that the land belongs to them, and distributing it with a view to beneficial cultivation! Nor is the sequel less startling: "There may be," says his Lordship, "and we know there are, many hindrances to this principle being even openly allowed, much more to its being fully carried out, in all countries; *but in those cases wherein the opportunity is afforded of starting from first principles it should not be neglected.*" Wretched French provisional Government of 1848, what an opportunity of "starting from first principles" in re-distributing the whole land of France did you not neglect! I certainly shall not discuss "first principles" of the law of property with his Lordship. I express no opinion, whether the land of a country ought to belong to the Government *de facto*, or to the Government *de jure*, or to private owners. But I do say, it is very hard that of three men professing the self-same principles, one may be sent to rot at Cayenne, another, perhaps, to hard labour at Portland, while the third proclaims and carries them out on a splendid salary as Governor of Madras.*

* I am bound to say that I have not the slightest sympathy with the theory which makes the state a mere policeman. But to entitle

Now, although other Indian Governors may be shy of setting forth Lord Harris's theory of state-landlordism with the same frankness as his Lordship, I must say that there is too much of the practice of it everywhere. What its final results are, in Madras, may be easily shewn. It is not I, but Mr. J. P. Grant, member of the Calcutta Council, who says, in explanation of the affrays about land so much complained of in Bengal, "In most Madras districts *land is valueless, by reason of the revenue system there in force*; the contentions there being when a ryot is forced, not to give up, but to take land." Mr. Mead, from whom I quote the above extract, tells us that "in Cuddapah, Bellary, and Guntoor, three of the naturally richest districts in the Madras Presidency, land is wholly unsaleable, whilst in Chingleput it is only worth six months' purchase."* And Mr. Smollett informs us,—

it to meddle with those great social labours of agriculture or industry, it is at least essential that it should be itself truly national and social. Almost any form of individual property in land is probably better than the land-ownership of a government at once alien and despotic, as the Anglo-Indian Government necessarily has been till now.

* Mead's Sepoy Revolt, pp. 323, 338. In Coimbetore,—said to be the crack ryotwar province—it appears from the "Madras Athenæum" of Dec. 7, 1858, that, of 5649 rs. compensation awarded during the first quarter of 1858 for lands taken on account of the railway, 2271 represented the "value of land," 1209 the "loss of produce," the balance being made up of the items of "trees," "wells and ponds," "houses" and "pagodas." If we suppose the produce lost to be that of the whole year, the land would thus be worth less than two years' purchase. If the "loss of produce" be simply that of standing crops, of which there may very likely be three in this rich province, the fee simple of the land would be literally valueless.

a fact indeed fully recognized—that only one-fourth of the cultivable land in Madras is brought into actual cultivation under the ryotwar system, whilst he can quote the Vizeanagrum zemindary as an instance in which, since the discontinuance of that system, nine-tenths have become so.*

In the other ryotwar Presidency—Bombay—Mr. Warden, as we have seen, equally asserts that the land has no saleable value. This appears, from Major Wingate's evidence before the Colonization Committee, to be incorrect as respects the land brought under the new survey, which would seem to flourish in a remarkable degree.† But even there it is only worth six years' purchase—in Bengal alone, under the Permanent Settlement, twenty or twenty-two.‡ So far, therefore, as the ryotwar system prevails, we may say that the pressure of the land revenue (at least when not alleviated by public works) has either actually reached its utmost limits, or has only slightly receded from them,—for how short a time we cannot tell, as even the new survey settlement in the South Mahratta country is professedly not permanent, and the example of the North-West shews us how thirty years' settlements can be infringed upon ;—that the Government demand absorbs practically, whatever governors and civilians may choose to fix as its proportion, the whole, or nearly the whole, surplus value of the land.

* Civil Administration in Madras, p. 127.

† Fourth Report on Colonization and Settlement (India), p. 46 and following.

‡ Ibid. pp. 84-5. But even in Bengal, "where the assessment is moderate," Mr. Dalrymple tells us that the Government rent is "in many instances" excessive. Second Report, p. 74.

In the favoured North-West land has undoubtedly a value, for it is bought and sold. Yet the mere introduction of the survey and settlement into the best managed district was equivalent itself, Mr. Robertson says, to a direct impost of at least £10,000 on the agricultural classes.* And Mr. Saunders tells us that if the settlement is "not excessive," it is "full," and that it is "scarcely worth while for any one to purchase" mortgaged estates, "so little is their profit," so that the mortgagee has practically no remedy but to foreclose, which is "just a little better than leaving the native in possession and losing their debt."† Hence the substitution of the trading classes for the agricultural, as respects the ownership of land, of which we have seen the effects already. I should gather from Mr. Saunders's evidence that such sales of land as take place must be chiefly on account of Government, for payment of revenue arrears.

And Mr. Gubbins,—though he declares our revenue system to be good,—yet with his North-Western experience declares also that "the pressure of the Government demand is in many districts greatly too high. It is too high in Agra, in Allygurh, in Mynpoorie, in Boolundshuhur, and throughout the greater part of Rohilcund. The principle on which that settlement was made, was to claim as the share of Government two-thirds of the net rental. But the fraud and chicanery opposed to our revenue officers generally caused them unwittingly to *fix the demand at more than this share*."‡

* Return on the Revenue Survey (India), 1853, p. 121.

† Fourth Report on Colonization and Settlement (India), p. 205

‡ Mutinies in Oudh, p. 72.

On the whole then, does the "Times" Calcutta correspondent, writing on the 9th October, 1858, exaggerate, when he says, generally and sweepingly, but probably having an especial eye to Northern India: "The rent, if you will have it a rent, is a rack-rent. . . . Can a taxation screwed to the last possible point of endurance, and really levied exclusively on food, be considered light?"* Or are St. George Tucker's words of 1832 become obsolete: "Our lightest assessment is perhaps too heavy"? †

But let us take from Mr. Gubbins,—not only the latest witness, but surely one beyond cavil on such a point,—the following picture of the effects of an excessive land-tax, which shews how far they extend beyond the mere economic region, deep into the heart of public morality:

"Even in England it should not be difficult to understand how an exorbitant, or unequal, and ill-adjusted land-tax necessarily saps the foundation of all public prosperity. Nine-tenths of the population [of India] be it remembered, are agricultural. *If then the burthen of land-tax imposed upon the country be excessive, nine-tenths of the people suffer.* All improvement is checked; a general squalor and low style of living and conduct, never in India too high, prevails; and crime is multiplied. ‡ *The people are in want; and steal and*

---

* Times, November 13, 1838. † Selections, p. 10.

‡ It is difficult for us to realize the fact, that there is a *pathological diagnosis* of over-assessment familiar to the Anglo-Indian official. "What are the usual signs of over-assessment in India?" it was asked, with special reference to Guzerat, of Mr. Williamson, who had been Revenue Commissioner in Bombay, by the Cotton Committee of 1848: "A falling off of the cultivation, a want of spirit in the people, arrears of revenue, and the necessity of remissions after the settlements are concluded." "When you say a falling off of the cultivation, do you mean that portions of the land are left wholly

rob they will, however active may be our exertions to prevent them. Numberless illustrations could be given of this state of things. I was once collector of a district, where the native revenue officials were known to request that payment of revenue might not be pressed, saying, 'that *it would soon be collected when the dark nights returned;*' that is, the people would acquire then, by theft, the means of paying it. In another, I remember some villages where the assessment pressed heavily, the head-men of which were constantly getting into trouble from the thievish habits of their people. One of these men happening to visit Agra some years later, came to see me. 'Mobarick,' I inquired of him, 'how are the thieves of your village?'—'*Sir,' replied the head-man with an offended air,*—'*we do not steal* NOW; *our revenue payment has been made easy.*' He proceeded to tell me of the large reductions that had been made, and assured me that the neighbouring villages to his had, for a like reason, given up their malpractices."*

We hear much of Indian robbers,—of the efficient measures taken to suppress Dacoitee. Here is proof positive, from the experience of an Indian civilian, that apart from its hereditary, professional elements, Indian robbery is in a great measure artificially made and kept up, is a fruit of our revenue system; that the native revenue official connives at it, that the Government treasury fattens upon its proceeds, that the "crack collector," whether he know it or not, is practically but an accomplice of the native decoit.

We may trust that that race of "crack collectors" is extinct. We may learn from Major Wingate's evi-

uncultivated?"—"I mean, owing to land being thrown up less is cultivated."—Report on the Growth of Cotton in India, p. 149.

Imagine the Duke of Bedford's land becoming uncultivated by reason of his rack-renting it!

* The Mutinies in Oudh, pp. 429-30.

dence how, in Bombay at least, remissions of revenue have invariably been encouraged of late years.* But we must not suppose that the mischief of a "crack collector" disappears with him. A name, which I need not repeat, will long be spoken of with execration in Bundelcund. And so, I suspect, in Chingleput must be that of the collector of whom St. George Tucker tells us that he proposed the *confiscation* of hereditary tenures, "*as a means of compelling the ryots to cultivate their lands!*"† Was ever anything heard of so brutally absurd? Nor dare we forget that the necessities of this very rebellion tend to reproduce that state of things indicated by the same writer in 1832, when he said: "Our collectors are too prone to exact the uttermost farthing, *because their credit depends upon the amount of their collections.*"‡ Certain it is that, within the past year, the revenue has been exacted in certain districts of Madras during a period of scarcity amounting to all but actual famine. And with such a pressure upon them as that of the military operations of the North, it is utterly impossible that the local Governments should not have viewed those officers with most favour who sent in the heaviest specie-bags.

And now we may judge how much depends for the Indian peasant upon one word of the proclamation being made a reality:

"Subject to the *equitable* demands of the state."§

* Fourth Report on Colonization and Settlement (India), p. 58.

† Selections, p. 31, *n.*

‡ Selections, p. 10.

§ The subject of the Indian land-revenue has been treated of in detail by Mr. J. B. Norton in his "Topics for Indian Statesmen,"

LETTER XXIV.

HOW THE PLEDGE OF RESPECT TO NATIVE PROPERTY IS TO BE CARRIED OUT.

I THINK I have shewn that, beside and before the policy of annexation properly so called, there has been at work in India on the part of the British Government, not always consciously, what may be called a policy of absorption,—a course of proceeding tending to absorb the land, the wealth of the natives, to destroy native rank, influence, and industry. And these two policies,—which are in fact but two separate sides of our national sin of covetousness—have reacted perpetually upon each other. The prospect of the absorption process has intensified the terrors of annexation. The sight of annexation has made the sufferers under absorption more desperate.*

And thus it must never be forgotten, that with each

ch. viii. p. 175 and foll.; by Mr. Mead, in his "Sepoy Revolt," chs. 24-9, p. 309 and foll.; by my friend Mr. W. E. Forster, in his lecture, "How we tax India." Mr. Norton's work is especially remarkable as a defence of the ryotwar system.

* "I cannot refrain from mentioning to you the excitement which prevails universally, owing to late resumptions, not only among the chiefs, but zemindars and landed proprietors. It was extremely bad policy, in my opinion. And forbidding adoption, against the most ancient practice and usage of the Hindoo chiefs, and in direct breach of treaty-faith, was certainly a most injudicious and suicidal measure. It has alienated the confidence of all classes, from the prince to the peasant. I, who mix with them all, in the most intimate and familiar manner, can safely bear my testimony to the above."—Extract of a letter from Central India, dated 23rd May, 1857. Observe the date—just before the outbreak in that quarter.

new annexation the perils of every future annexation became greater. The value of the native states, as a refuge for the restless and the discontented, was long ago pointed out by Mr. Elphinstone and other great men of a great epoch in Indian history. Rebellion is surely the last resource that men seek, who can find ease in change of place. Whilst if, as I firmly believe, the temper of our Indian fellow-subjects generally has been a smouldering discontent, to bring that discontent into contact with the fiery smarts of recent annexation must always have tended to precipitate explosion.*

For the preservation then of our Indian empire, I believe that the annexation policy was not given up one hour too soon.

But let us remember that both the policy of annexation and that of absorption have been once already given up. Once already, now nearly three-quarters of

* The following further extracts from letters by the writer I have just quoted (and whose opportunities of judging are peculiar) may here be inserted.

"They may try, if they please, to mislead the people of England by saying that disaffection is confined to the army, and that the naturally evil-minded and dissolute are taking advantage of circumstances to plunder and devastate; but let them be assured that the disease lies much deeper . . . . You cannot know the intensity of the fire that is burning in every Mussulman bosom against us . . and there are not a few of the Hindoos of certain classes who are just as inveterate."

In presence of such facts as these, the enthusiasm excited by the Queen's proclamation is most striking. The almost frantic joy which the advent of what is expected to be a new policy has brought forth only lights up the more fearfully the gulf which the old policy had been scooping out at our very feet.

a century ago (1784) the English Parliament (with more right feeling indeed than grammar) proclaimed that "to pursue schemes of conquest and extension of dominion in India are measures repugnant to the wish, the honour and policy of this nation."* It went further still, and enacted that "whereas complaints have prevailed, that divers rajas, zemindars, polygars, talookdârs and other native landholders within the British territories in India, have been unjustly deprived of, or compelled to abandon and relinquish, their respective lands, jurisdictions, rights and privileges, or that the tributes, rents and services required to be by them paid and performed for their respective possessions to the said United Company, are become grievous and oppressive; and whereas *the principles of justice, and the honour of this country require that such complaints should be forthwith inquired into and fully investigated, and if founded in truth effectually redressed*" — the Court of Directors should forthwith "take the said matters into their serious consideration," and should "adopt, take, and pursue such methods for inquiring into the causes, foundation and truth of the said complaints, and for obtaining a full and perfect knowledge of the same, and of all circumstances relating thereto," as the Court of Directors should think "best adapted for that purpose;" and should "thereupon, according to the circumstances of the respective cases . . . give orders and instructions to the several Governments and Presidencies for effectually redressing," in such manner as should "be consistent with justice and the laws and customs of the

* 24 Geo. III. Sess. 2. c. 25. s. 34 (Pitt's India Act).

country, all injuries and wrongs which the said rajas," &c., might have "sustained unjustly" as before mentioned, "and for settling and establishing, upon principles of moderation and justice, rules by which their respective tributes, rents and services" should be "in future rendered and paid to the Company."*

Nothing can be nobler than the spirit of the above enactment. But we all know it proved a mere flash in the pan. And for the simplest of all reasons. The Company, the really guilty party, as the one that ultimately profited through every act of extortion by its subordinates, was made the judge of those extortions. Could you seriously expect justice from it?

Still, I believe, in 1859 as in 1784, "the principles of justice and the honour of this country *require*" that the complaints of princes and landholders—aye, and of peasants if they will speak out—"should be *forthwith inquired into and fully investigated*, and *if founded in truth effectually redressed*." Past experience shews that the Government of India cannot be entrusted with such an inquiry. I have claimed before—I claim now the appointment of a Royal Commission for the purpose, as the necessary complement of the transfer of the Government of India to the Crown. Such a claim has been urged long ere this, by those who best know India. It was put forth before the Cotton Committee in 1848, by my uncle, Mr. F. C. Brown, a Malabar landowner. It has been insisted on once and again by the Madras civilian Mr. Smollett. The glorious band of Bengal Missionaries, in 1856-7, prayed it in vain at the hands of the Lieutenant-

* 24 Geo. III. sess. 2. c. 25 (s. 39).

Governor of Bengal, of the Government of India, of the Parliament of Great Britain. Mr. D'Israeli—when he was not in office—treated it as indispensable; Mr. McLeod Wylie, the Calcutta Judge of the Small Debts Court, agrees with the "Native of Northern India" in demanding it. Listen how weightily the latter pleads,—and I have reason to know that he is the exponent of the general, I might almost say the unanimous desire of all that part of the native population which is best affected to our rule:

"First of all, let us have a Royal Commission,—unless India is so fortunate that Sir J. Lawrence is appointed Governor-General with the powers of the President of the Board of Control, or her own Council, or the Court of Directors take it into their heads to select at once Commissioners who may be found even better than Sir John. The Commissioners must be experienced men, well acquainted with the languages of the country, not very old, active, sharp, stout and bold, who can bear the fatigues of long journey, and are unreservedly disposed to mix with the people. They must not travel like the Governors-General to cut down the burs and peepuls which give such a cool shade to the weary traveller, to consume the wood, grass, and earthen pots which take the poor peasants months to prepare, and to fill the coffers of the burkundazes (policemen) who invariably pocket the price of all such things for themselves; nor remain shut up in the big tents surrounded by secretaries like the Governor-General; nor content themselves merely with, or waste much time in inspecting the records; be prepared to travel by dak (post), with one or two secretaries, through the length and breadth of the country, and collect their information from the people, and the people only, corroborated, of course, by the records of the offices. They must not put up with the local authorities, for by so doing the people will be overawed to give any correct information—though the Commissioners must see, and hear also, the local authorities, and have many references to adjust with them. The party which is against the Royal Commission and wants to keep the public of England in perpetual darkness about this country may object, and say that such a Commission will put the Indian Government in a great jeopardy. But ask them if the annual tours of the Commissioners of Revenue or the Governors put the magistrates in jeopardy, and do the people set at naught their authority? *All the other reforms must depend on the inquiries of these Commissioners.*"

But until the appointment of such a Commission, other steps may be taken to shew the firm adherence of the Government to the policy of the proclamation. The recognition of the right of adoption, which I have urged ere this, must avail the poorest inam-holder as well as the most influential of native princes. The Inam Commissions must, I believe, be abolished, if the tranquillity of the Deckan is to be preserved; Government, in the prosecution of its claims for revenue, must place itself within the pale of the ordinary law, must submit to the jurisdiction of the ordinary tribunals. To go into more detailed suggestions as to the improvement of the real property laws of India would be beyond my province; but I feel assured that a policy which, without attempting to start from "first principles" of universal state-ownership, like my Lord Harris, without riding a hobby to death like Munro and the ryotwar school, or like Bird and the village-settlement school, would simply set before itself the duty of maintaining all existing rights of property, not in themselves immoral or anti-social, of developing such rights where they are not yet recognized or fixed, according to the special "laws, customs, and usages" of the different portions of our vast Indian empire, would, ere long, discover means of remedying all the main evils complained of,—the sudden displacement of the old landowners, the insecurity of tenure of the new,—the frequent shiftings of the rights of property, with little or sometimes no increase in their value,—in

Madras, above all, that deadly check upon agricultural enterprize, the fear of seeing Government come into the market as a land-purchaser, the knowledge that its fiscal powers,—alarming in themselves, as Mr. Gubbins shews them to be,—are capable of being used directly to bring estates under its ownership.

And in order that the pressure of the land-revenue itself may not continue to be a means of destroying native property, or hindering its creation, I feel satisfied that an expansion of the currency is one of the measures most urgently required. How that should be done, whether by the adoption of gold as a standard, or (temporarily at least) as a joint-standard with silver, or by a bank note circulation, as urged by Indophilus, involves many a difficult question, which my ignorance of finance would not suffer me to attempt.*

* Although specie shipments are now habitually made, not from but to the East, the effect of the home-charges must not, I conceive, be overlooked, in detaining specie in England, which would otherwise be sent out. That India has the capacity, when her resources are duly developed, of amply providing for those home-charges, I have no manner of doubt. But until that point is reached, is it not a question how far the burthen might be lightened by an equivalent expansion of the *English* paper circulation? For instance, the deficiency of 1859 is estimated at 8 or 9 millions. More than 2 millions of these would at once be covered if the Bank of England were allowed to advance the Council the amount of the home-charges, such advance being guaranteed by the State. Would not such an expansion of our circulation be a real benefit to this country, where sooner or later the staunchest supporters of Sir Robert Peel's Banking Bill will probably have to admit that a fixed primary circulation, so to speak, of 14 millions of paper, is not compatible with the ever-expanding wants of English society? How far the process might be facilitated by local issues of paper would next have to be considered.

LETTER XXV.

THE AMNESTY, AND THE DISARMING ORDERS.

I HAVE nothing to say on the subject of the amnesty announced by the proclamation. It is large, generous, royal; it supplies its own comment, in the surrenders which it at once called forth, and which are thinning the ranks of the rebellion far more rapidly than even the doughtiest blows of our officers.

I cannot, however, refrain from remarking upon a late proclamation of Lord Clyde's as to disarmament, which appears to me to go counter to the very spirit of the amnesty. To deprive the Oude talookdars of anything in the shape of ordnance is but natural. To deprive the population of its arms is surely far more questionable. The right to possess arms—guaranteed to us Englishmen by the Bill of Rights—forms, so to speak, part of the very character of the military classes of India, and every Rajpoot's hereditary pride must be stirred to the quick by its withdrawal. But the possession of arms is far from being a mere matter of pride

I suspect that if paper is once made a legal tender for revenue, the natives will not be shy of taking it. Indeed, I should think the refusal hitherto to accept Government paper as tender for Government purposes (revenue, deposits on purchases, &c.) has been one of the main causes of the local depreciation of Indian securities.

Nothing, however, as it seems to me, can be more injudicious than the making dividends on Indian loans payable in London, as has now been done. This tends directly to increase the drain for home-charges, and to shift the debt from native to English hands, reducing by so much the native stake in the maintenance of our supremacy.

and social dignity. It is one, for the greater part of India at all events, of absolute necessity, for protection against the wild beast, against the robber. Let us not forget that India is not a mere island garden like England, in which scarcely a wild cat remains, and it is a point of honour among country gentlemen not to kill a fox otherwise than in the orthodox manner, after giving him a run for his life. It is a land where the tiger haunts the brake, the alligator the river; where the wild elephant in the South sometimes stops the traffic on a post road; where wolves follow every corps on the line of march, dash into villages and even cities, and tear infants from their mothers' sides; where whole tribes live by the produce of the chase. Nor let us forget that it is also a country where, in spite of the presence of the European, robbery is committed not only by the craft of single thieves, but by gangs of armed men, and with much of the planning and of the discipline, of the conflicts and of the surprises, of regular warfare. The danger—say rather the futility—of disarmament under such circumstances, (which must necessarily be aggravated by the rebellion, since warfare and its attendant carnage and desolation invariably multiply the number of beasts of prey, both four-legged and two-legged, the dismissed or fugitive soldier having almost a natural tendency there to become a brigand,) has been ere this pointed out by experienced officers.

"Some magistrates and local rulers," wrote Colonel Sleeman long ago, "have very unwisely adopted the measure of prohibiting the people from carrying or bearing arms in their own houses, the very thing which, above all others, such robbers most wish; for they know, although such magistrates and rulers do not, that *it is the innocent only, and the friends to order, who will obey the command.*

The robber will always be able to conceal his arms, or keep with them out of the reach of the magistrate; and he is now relieved altogether from the salutary dread of a shot from a door or window. He may rob at his leisure, or sit down like a gentleman, and have all that the people of the surrounding towns and villages possess brought to him, for no man can any longer attempt to defend himself and his family."*

So Colonel Alves, in the Supplement to his "India and its Dangers," written in view of the very measures now proposed or being carried out:

"The honest man requires protection against the rascal, who, it may be feared, will always find arms; many have no other means of livelihood;† and every village requires protection against the ravages of tigers, hyenas or wolves, to say nothing of gang or other robbers. To many the loss of arms would be degradation, to others starvation, while their retention by good men would prove an aid to our police. This advantage is quite attainable by rendering our Government acceptable to the people, and it is no trifling one. *Let us draw the sting from the mind rather than the hand.*"

He deprecates even the indiscriminate dismantling of private forts in Oude itself:

"The chiefs who own them pride themselves on the possession of those ancestral castles, with which the histories of many of their families are interwoven, and will view any attempt to dismantle them as degradation of a very humiliating kind. . . . . India has ever been more or less obnoxious to internal commotions, and walled villages and peaceable armed inhabitants have constituted mainly the defence of the people and their property; *and had our subjects of Bengal been thus able to defend themselves they would not have been plundered or killed in hundreds, during the late Santal outbreak.* Moreover, the possibility of an invasion from the North-west at some future time cannot be left out of consideration.

---

* Rambles and Recollections, vol. i. pp. 319-20.

† I am informed that the insurrection in Candeish arose from the attempt to disarm the hill Bheels, who live by the chase, and must plunder if they are deprived of their weapons.

. . Both Sikhs and Ghoorkas in our pay have tasted of the spoils of Delhi and Lucknow; and Jung Bahadoor's men have shared largely in the booty of the latter capital. These men on their return home will display their wealth, and talk over their deeds of arms; and the tale may pass throughout Tartar land. . . . It is but reasonable to suppose that hordes still exist who might, under the influence of some combination against us, pour down upon India at some future day, when we might possibly not have friends on our own Northern and North-western borders. But disarmed, dispirited, and their fortresses dismantled or thrown down, of what assistance could the once warlike chiefs and inhabitants of Oude be to us, unable as they would be to protect themselves, their families and property? What alone, in all human calculation, would prevent such an attempt being ever made, would be a knowledge pervading the world, that our rule in India was popular—therefore morally strong—and that our physical means were everywhere such as to baffle, not merely conquest, but even extensive plunder and rapine."*

What adds to the weight of this reasoning is the physical configuration of Oude,—and indeed of the Gangetic valley generally—a vast alluvial plain, in which few of the rivers even have precipitous banks, and of which consequently the whole system of defence must be mainly artificial. Such a system of defence, adapted most admirably to the nature of the country, is supplied by the jungles, and jungle-circled fortresses, of Oude and the adjacent provinces, in the former of which the population can easily take refuge, whilst in the latter a handful of determined men can hold out, against anything but shell practice, long enough at all events to arrest the march of an invader. Let us beware then, in dismantling Oude, of making all Northern India one Grand Trunk Road for a foreign enemy to Calcutta.

* Supplement to India and its Dangers, pp. 22-5.

Nor can I forbear here to say a few words as to the position of these Oude talookdars themselves, who have given us so much trouble. It is easy, after the first sickening perusal of Sir Wm. Sleeman's "Journey through Oude," to condemn them wholesale, to deem the annexation of the country justified by their crimes and those of the sovereigns whom they opposed. And yet, when one examines the book a second time, when one studies it, as I have endeavoured to do, in its details, when one considers the conclusions to which his experience led the writer, his own character, more recent events, a very different set of impressions rise up in one's mind. How is it that he who saw all these things, he who describes them at first hand, did not view in them that justification for annexation which suggests itself to us in his narration, but on the contrary strenuously opposed that measure? Then one recollects that the narrator, worthy man though I trust he was, was the most experienced of thief and murderer-catchers,—one of those men endowed no doubt with a genuine hunger for justice, but who seem to relish it especially in its coarser forms; whose appetites for it are whetted by crime, whose nostrils snuff villainy from afar. If such a man, invested with high rank, surrounded by a military retinue, exempt from all superior jurisdiction, open to receive all manner of complaints, were to travel through England itself on a tour of inquiry, would he not be likely to produce such a report as would make Englishmen's hair stand on end, as to the state of their own country? Would not every crime and vice rise to the surface before our eyes in his pages, till there should seem to be nothing else?

Might not his account, though true in every detail, prove essentially false as a whole, if we took it as a picture of the real condition, moral and social, of the country? Should we not, if otherwise ignorant of that condition, have to seek it in the side glimpses which the report afforded, rather than in its fuller delineations?

If we apply a little of this caution to General Sleeman's book, it is wonderful how the picture changes before our eyes. Follow his track stage by stage, and you will be struck by two features, which would not attract attention in themselves, but which become striking in the long run; the extent of cultivation over a large portion of the country (except within the limits of Rughber Sing's ravages), and even where the soil lies waste, the almost constant occurrence of "groves" and "trees." The cultivation he explains by statements such as this, that "tillage is the one thing needful to all, and the persons from whom trespasses on the crops are most apprehended, are the reckless and disorderly trains of the Government officials."* But the abundance of trees is a far more remarkable circumstance. In his "Rambles and Recollections," Sir William Sleeman had himself specially dwelt on the absence of trees in our North-Western provinces, through revenue mismanagement. "Our Government," he said, "has in effect, during the 35 years that it has held the dominion of the North-West provinces, prohibited the planting of mango groves, while the old ones are every year disappearing."† In his "Journey

* Journey through Oude, vol. ii. p. 219.

† Rambles and Recollections, vol. ii. pp. 176-7.

through Oude," he insists repeatedly on the value of trees and groves to the people, on their abundance in Oude, on the security with which they are planted and enjoyed; saying expressly that they "are more secure in Oude than in our own territories, and the country is in consequence much better provided with them."*

A single fact like this tends of itself to shew that the distractions and miseries of Oude, however dreadful, were not of those which go to the very vitals of a nation's existence. And when this light once breaks upon us, we begin to see elements of order warring on all sides against disorder; sometimes a well-meaning Government officer, sometimes a kindly revenue contractor, but foremost of all and almost universally, the talookdars. The grievance of the crown against them is avowedly, not that their estates are not flourishing, but that they are flourishing and do not pay revenue, or not revenue enough, the Government's chief resource against them being "to prevent the cultivation of the land."† On General Sleeman's route, you will find the country almost invariably flourishing, in the exact proportion of the talookdar's strength. To instance one of our present enemies, the estate of Benee Madho was "admirably cultivated," "covered with a great variety of crops," the people seeming "very happy."‡ These talookdars were indeed men of two classes. Mr. Gubbins says, that "the greater number of them were hereditary heads of rajpoot tribes."§ The ancestors of Benee Madho had been settled in Oude for about 25

* Journey through Oude, vol. ii. p. 31. † Ibid. vol. i. pp. 56-7.
‡ Ibid. pp. 253-5. § Mutinies in Oudh, p. 62.

generations.* Others were new men,—bankers, or government officers, or contractors,—who had gradually taken root in the soil. Such was the Brahmin Maun Sing, of whom and of whose family Sir William Sleeman states, that though they had acquired their property in the land by abuse of authority, collusion, and violence, they kept their faith with the cultivators, effectually protected them from thieves, robbers, their neighbours, the king's troops; that under them the landholders and peasantry seemed "all happy and secure," the people "strong and well made, and without any appearance of disease;" hardly a beggar was to be seen, and the residence of religious mendicants was "especially discouraged."†

Putting all these facts together, I think we are led to the conclusion that, great as were the miseries of Oude at the time of annexation, they were those of a crisis. Power was changing hands; it was passing, by the very laws of human society, from the imbecile sovereigns to the stronger land-holders. Better would it have been surely on all accounts to have abstained from meddling with such a state of things. But having meddled with it, our only chance lay in taking it as it was. "We ought," says Mr. Carre Tucker, late Governor-General's agent and Commissioner at Benares, in a valuable letter on "Oude and its talookdars" which has been privately printed, "to have acted on the principle of accepting the existing status." What has followed on the adoption of the contrary principle we all see. Many of the Oude talookdars are still in arms,

* Sleeman's Journey through Oude, vol. i. p. 245.

† Journey through Oude, vol. i. p. 149 and foll.; pp. 162-5.

and the people have apparently in every direction sided with them. The long persistence of the Oude rebellion is surely the best answer to those who would treat the talookdars as a class only as so many hateful tyrants.

If I sought for evidence that the state of Oude could never have been so bad as we are prone, from a hasty perusal of General Sleeman's book, to imagine it, I would seek no other than that of Mr. Martin Gubbins, an avowed apologist of the annexation. At the date of the rebellion, he tells us, "all those numerous dacoits,"—who at our entrance into the country were "reckoned by hundreds,"—"had become peaceable and quiet subjects." "The single proclaimed robber who had given us any trouble, and whose previous deep-dyed offences under the native Government had excluded him from pardon, had been destroyed. There was in Oudh no more of heavy crime than was found in the best managed districts of the North-Western Provinces." "For fourteen months," he says elsewhere, "Oudh was fully as tranquil as any of our older possessions."* What! in 14 months, "*all*" the dacoits of Oude become "peaceable and quiet subjects" —and Bengal still full of them! What! in 14 months "no more of heavy crime" than in our "*best managed* districts" of the North-West! the country during *all* that time, "fully as tranquil as *any* of our older possessions!" Are we speaking of plain facts, or of the fabled waving of an enchanter's wand? No, no, Oude can never have been the den of brigands, the

* Mutinies in Oudh, pp. 429-31; p. 69; p. 89.

almost hell upon earth which we may have imagined it, to have undergone so sudden a transformation.*

Mr. Gubbins indeed attributes much of the good achieved to the curbing of the talookdars, to the forced restoration by them of their ill-acquired lands. He admits indeed that "in some instances, by the indiscretion of local officers, the talookdars were treated with undue severity."† But he maintains that "no doubt can be entertained of the moderation of the three years' revenue assessment;"‡ that the revenue system "certainly" gave satisfaction, "in so far as the limitation of its amount is concerned;" that the land revenue of two divisions, Khyrabad and Bareytch, had been "admirably settled."§ But let us listen to a couple of his civilian neighbours on the point.

Mr. Carre Tucker of Benares, for instance, while praising Mr. Gubbins's ability—saying he "reduced the settlement in numerous instances,"—states that Government followed "supposed political and financial expediency, instead of ascertaining and maintaining existing rights in possession." It imagined "that in the course of a very hurried assessment of revenue by officers, many of whom were inexperienced, it was possible to adjudicate properly difficult claims to former rights." Lord Canning has admitted that "it is too true that unjust decisions were come to by some of our local officers by investigating and judging the titles of the landholders." And they, as Sir James

* It is at all events little creditable to our long years of rule in India that Oude should have, as it were, leapt at a bound to their level.

† Mutinies in Oudh, p. 68. ‡ Ibid. p. 429. § Ibid.

Outram has stated, feeling themselves "most unjustly treated under our settlement operations," and "smarting under the loss of their lands," when they saw our rule "virtually at an end, the whole country overrun, and the capital in the hands of the rebel soldiery, with hardly a dozen exceptions, sided against us," the yeomanry following "the lead of their natural chiefs." Mr. Tucker himself, it would appear, wrote to Lord Canning, after Havelock's first retreat, "that if he would authorize the proclamation of a revision of the summary settlement upon the basis of upholding twelve years' clear and uninterrupted possession of all tenures existing at the annexation, Rajah Maun Sing and the other talookdars who had not then gone over to the enemy, but were wavering, would remain staunch." But his Lordship telegraphed back that the proposal was "totally inadmissible. Thus," says Mr. Tucker, "in Oude the sepoy mutiny *became a rebellion of the whole people.*"

Again, we have some invaluable side-glances supplied to us by the magistrate of Budaon in Rohilcund, Mr. Edwards, who at the height of the rebellion found the most generous shelter with one of the Rajpoot talookdars of Oude, Hurdeo Buksh, and his relatives. Although his experience is confined to a single tract of country, still it should suffice as a favourable sample of the whole, the tract referred to being part of that division of Khyrabad, which Mr. Gubbins describes as having been "admirably settled."

Now the first thing that strikes one in Mr. Edwards's narrative,—and it is a fact which can never be too often repeated,—is that the war in Oude did not begin with the talookdars. Mr. Edwards had been driven from his own district in Rohilcund when he sought refuge in Oude. Indeed so far from the rebellion having begun with the landholders generally, there is every presumption that they were forced into it, as much by the mere peasants as by any other influence. As he is leaving Rohilcund under the protection of a Mahomedan sheik, Mr. Edwards passes through a number of villages "literally swarming with men armed with swords and iron-bound *lattees*" (staves). They are "silent and not disrespectful," seeing the sheik, whose tenantry they were, but the latter had to send ahead to "prevent any attack" upon the Europeans.* In Oude itself, apparently by the middle of June, "none of the rajwarras, as the chief talookdars are called, had as yet joined in the rebellion, but on the contrary had stood quite aloof from the sepoys."† So essentially were the Oude talookdars an element of order and not of anarchy, that late in July, when the state of the British districts was deplorable in the extreme, while the villages were burnt and plundered daily, the roads deserted, and no man's life or property safe for a moment, but everything subject to fire and sword, the districts "in Oude under the talookdars and

* Edwards's "Personal Adventures," p. 28.—In the "narrative given by one of the ladies who escaped from Sultanpoor, and after finding an asylum with Lall Madho Sing, (of Amethee) reached Allahabad in safety," which forms appendix No. 9 to Mr. Gubbins's work (see p. 465 and foll.), it will be found that the first attack made upon the party was by the goreyts or village watchmen, and that they pursued it even beyond the residence of Golaub Sing, talookdar of Turole, the first protector of the fugitives.

† Ibid. p. 101.

powerful zemindars were calm and peaceful as a lake." Such was the report of Mr. Edwards' messenger: and he adds, "This is certainly the case with the extensive talooka of Hurdeo Buksh, and those of powerful chiefs immediately around us. The rebellion has not yet extended to these estates; the people go about their usual avocations, and all is quiet and peaceful within their limits."* "Everything," he repeats a little further on in describing the village of Kussowrie, "looked peaceful; the people were at their usual occupations; there were no external signs that war and rebellion were raging all around us."* Yet the quiet thus maintained was from no affection to British rule. The sympathies of all were evidently on the other side; and what will seem strange to those who look upon the talookdars as mere rebels against their own king, in favour of the deposed dynasty. A rumour flies about that the Governor-General is coming with the king of Oude, that Oude will be restored. The village Thakoors, uncles of Hurdeo Buksh, "seem quite delighted at the prospect." "They often speak to me," says Mr. Edwards, "about the annexation, and ask me why the Governor General acted on 'Sullivan Sahib's' advice, as they call Sleeman, who they assert was the man who ruined their raj." And then follows a remarkable passage, which I shall extract further on, as to the exactions of our native officials, and the pressure upon the village Thakoors. Despoiled talookdars, revenue assessments so high that they can only be paid out of property, sales for default impending, the in-

* Personal Adventures, pp. 141-2. † Ibid. p. 146.

troduction of the vilest conceivable set of native harpies, such are the elements of the picture,—which belongs, be it always remembered, to the "admirably settled" division of Khyrabad!

I take it, therefore, that the talookdars of Oude, if our enemies, are our *injured* enemies, and deserve that this should always be borne in mind. Nor dare we forget that, in spite of injuries received, they have for the most part conferred benefits upon our countrymen. Hurdeo Buksh and his relatives perilled their lives to save those of Mr. Edwards and his party. Roostum Sah, Mr. Tucker tells us, "*though deprived of almost all his villages, and reduced to sell his wife's ornaments,* saved the lives of my brother, Charlton, and the Sultanpoor refugees." "It is singular," says Mr. Gubbins, speaking of the same chief and another, "that Roostum Sah and Lall Honwunt Sing, in the Salone district, who had both been severe sufferers by the settlement proceedings, should have distinguished themselves by their kindness to British officers." * If, indeed, as Mr. Gubbins also tells us, other talookdars, "who had retained their villages with greatly diminished assessments, have been most active against us," may it not be that, on the annexation of their country by foreigners, the noblest specimens of the class were not those who would be most likely to welcome them, —the vilest rather were those who would soonest cringe to them and their underlings,—almost all-powerful as we see the latter to have been in Mr. Edwards's

* Mutinies in Oudh, p. 139. See also, at pp. 433-4 of that work, the list of talookdars who have remained faithful to us, or have signalised themselves by protecting our fugitives.

book? But as a rule, throughout the rebellion, to use Mr. Tucker's words, "the chiefs behaved like gentlemen."

Let us be careful that we do the like—and that, if need be, according to our own standard rather than by theirs. Let us not pour the vials of our wrath upon the Raja of Amethie because he may have prevaricated, after the manner of his countrymen, about a few pieces of ordnance, and forget in so doing that, as he himself reminded us, his fort had been a refuge to Englishwomen in their flight,—that the very guns which we claim of him must have been their main assurance of safety,—and that to protect fugitive women is at least the act of a true gentleman all over the world.

LETTER XXVI.

THE PLEDGE OF INTERNAL IMPROVEMENTS.

"When, by the blessing of Providence, internal tranquillity shall be restored, it is our earnest desire to stimulate the peaceful ministry of India, to promote works of public utility and improvement, and to administer its government for the benefit of all our subjects resident therein. In their prosperity will be our strength, in their contentment our security, and in their gratitude our best reward. And may the God of all power grant unto us, and to those in authority under us, strength to carry out these our wishes for the good of our people."

This again is one of those paragraphs which would

give scope to volumes of development. The details of the measures to be carried out belong indeed essentially, in my view, to the labours of such a Commission of Inquiry as I have spoken of. The three leading heads of improvement, however, in addition to such as I have already pointed out, seem to be those of judicial and police reform, public works, and education. As respects the first especially, the four reports of the Colonization Committee of last year afford abundant evidence of the present state of things. I believe indeed that, in the Punjab and in Scinde, a really efficient police has been established; that it has been greatly improved in Bombay; that steps are now being taken —after being long talked about—to improve it also in Madras. But still I find it impossible to doubt that throughout the greater part of British India, the radical corruption of the police, and the inefficiency—at least in all its inferior stages—of the judicial system, add an abiding, habitual source of insecurity to person and property to those which arise from the policy of the Government and the laws passed by it. And this has been, indeed, recognized by the Court of Directors itself. In their "Memorandum" of 1857 on the "Improvements in the Administration of India," they admitted, with charming candour, that notwithstanding "partial amendments, it cannot be said that the courts, in what are called Regulation Provinces, have yet been freed from their radical defects. The principal impediments to a good administration of justice are a complicated and technical system of pleading in the civil courts, and in the criminal courts the character of the police." But they almost immediately proceeded to declare that "the Non-regulation Provinces have had (generally from their first acquisition) the benefit of a cheap, accessible, and expeditious administration of justice, free from all such formalities and technicalities as either defeat justice or add needlessly to the difficulty and expense of obtaining it." And they pointed triumphantly to the Punjab as exemplifying this assertion.*

Now I am most decidedly in favour of a "cheap, accessible, and expeditious administration of justice." I am quite prepared to believe that the Punjab system, as a system, is better than that of the Regulation Provinces; that it has been, under Sir John Lawrence and his coadjutors, eminently successful. But I say that, to the confusion of all system-worshippers, the Punjab

* See pp. 33 and foll. Some surprise may be felt that the evils of the administration of justice and of the police should have attained so much more prominence in Bengal than in other Presidencies. I believe the real cause to lie in the truth, as applicable to moral and political as to medical science, that where there is suffering there is life. Bengal has life enough to cry out under its grievances; the other Presidencies have not. There is no judicial appeal, be it recollected, from Inam Commission injustice. I may, however, here refer to the Torture Report of Madras, and to the glaring instances of legal injustice before quoted in the case of landholders and native officials. Mr. Smollett tells us, and the fact is confirmed to me from elsewhere, that "in many Government ryotwar provinces there are positively no original suits in the civil courts, not because the people have no taste for legal strife, or dwell together like brethren in unity, but simply because *there is no property of the value of £1000 sterling to bring into the courts of law.*"—Civil Administration of Madras, p. 90.

An admirable plan of judicial reform has however been drawn up at Madras, which I shall presently refer to.

system, as a system, without *the men* who have applied it successfully in the Punjab, has signally failed; and I earnestly pray that we may not be deluded into fancying that it or any other system is to be the panacea for India.

For it was the Punjab system which Lord Dalhousie avowedly applied to Oude, seeing no reason to doubt that it would be acceptable. And if we would see what the "cheap, accessible, and expeditious" justice of that system became, when applied by those native underlings, whom it has been seemingly the privilege of British rule to create and foster, let us hear, through Mr. Edwards, the magistrate of Budaon, the testimony of those Oude Rajpoots from whom he received so generous a protection:

"They speak with the greatest respect and affection of some of our officers, especially of Christian, late Commissioner of Seetapore. . . . If they could always have got access to him, they say, they would have had no reason to complain of our administration; but he had too much to do, and was seldom visible. The native officials they describe as regular harpies, and a native deputy collector who had been stationed at Sandie, they frequently mention to me with expressions of the deepest hatred. This fellow, they assert, had a pair of slippers of extra size made on purpose for 'shoe beating' (the most disgraceful punishment that can be inflicted on a native), in open kutcherry [court], any one who refused to pay him what he demanded in the shape of bribes, or to sign any agreements respecting the disposal of their villages and land that he chose to fix upon, however unjust and ruinous to their interests these might be. Old Kussuree told me that *he had paid* 1000 *rupees* (£100) *in petitions alone*, not one of which ever reached Christian, and more *than* 6000 (£600) *in bribes*, notwithstanding which *he had lost the villages farmed by him and his ancestors for many generations, and had been assessed so highly for those he had left, that he had only been able to pay his rent the following year by the sale of some of his* *family jewels, and a mare he highly valued; and this year he said he would no doubt have been a defaulter and been sold up had not the rebellion fortunately occurred.* In the conversations I had with Hurdeo Buksh, who is a very superior intelligent man, he has given me to understand that the native omlahs (officers) who were introduced in such shoals, at and immediately after the annexation, were the curse of the country, and in his plain spoken phrase, made our rule to stink in the nostrils of the people. . . . To any native official under Government he declared he would as soon lose his life as go."*

As regards the police indeed—although the military system may be carried too far, and it would be insanity to place ourselves once more in the hands of a huge native army, by simply calling it a police,—still I cannot doubt that its character is likely to be greatly improved through the rebellion, by its being made more military. The smooth old police *burkundauze* seems to have been generally as much of a coward as of a rogue. A military organization will tend to call into the police service a new set of men from the military classes, with the point of honour about them of personal bravery and fidelity to their immediate chiefs; men who probably will be little else than plunderers reclaimed by government pay, and will often relapse into plunderers again if deprived of it, but who will generally be above the dirty daily routine of bribery.

As respects civil and judicial matters, I cannot help saying that I know nothing better yet than the reforms which are understood to have been proposed by thoroughly competent parties at Madras. One of these, with a view to put down the frightful existing amount of forgery and perjury adopts, if I am rightly informed, the principle of our English Statute of Frauds in requiring all deeds

* Personal Narrative, pp. 166-9.

connected with land, and money deeds beyond a small amount, to be in writing, parol evidence being inadmissible; but it requires also the prospective registration of all deeds relating to land, allows the optional registration of all money deeds, as well as all deeds relating to lands already existing; and requires all unregistered documents to be stamped, and the stamps not to be applicable to any other purpose than that for which they were procured. Another, —proceeding on the great principle that the Courts should be made *trustworthy*, so that they may be left with an easy mode of procedure, "unhampered by the extensive system of record now required, and which is called for to give the means of exercising an elaborate system of appeal, such system of appeal being requisite to keep in check Courts which are not trustworthy,"—takes as the proper mode of procedure that obtaining in the Small Cause Courts in India, or the County Courts at home. Under it the Small Cause Judges decide on an average 13 suits each per day on the merits, while the average of the moonsiffs is 20 per month. An easier procedure will allow of a great reduction of Courts in point of number, and the reduction of number will permit of raising the composition of the Courts. In all, it is understood there would be a plurality of judges. Suits for the most trifling amounts would go to village punchayets; those up to 1000 rupees in value to the Zillah or district Courts, composed of one European and two native judges, who should go on circuit within the Zillah, with power to employ punchayets to investigate and report on any matter connected with a suit; the Zillah Courts also to have criminal jurisdiction. Over every four Zillahs would come a provincial Court of three European judges, making six in all for the Madras Presidency; such Courts to have jurisdiction in original suits above 1000 rupees in value, and on appeal from the Zillahs; one appeal only to be allowed, on special grounds. Two judges would go on circuit to the Zillah stations twice a year for civil work, and one three times a year for criminal work. The Provincial Courts on the civil side would have power to make use of punchayets, and would have assessors on the criminal side; registrars would be attached to the Courts as a means of training judicial officers to a knowledge of their duties. It is expected that under this system the immense field for corruption that now exists will be swept away. It will be more difficult to bribe three judges than one, and every Court will have in it a European judge, ordinarily above bribery. The immense horde of isolated native judges, and the large and miserably paid establishments attached to them (most fertile sources of corruption) will disappear; and when a suit is decided from first to last in a fraction of a day, there will not be that opening for chicanery and bribery which exists, when a cause hangs on hard for months or years.*

Without pledging oneself to all the details of the above scheme,—without especially treating them as universally applicable beyond the Presidency to which they apply,—I think one may fairly say that a more thorough and genuine reform of a great evil has perhaps never been proposed in India.

* In the above sketch I have done little more than transcribe the words of one whose benevolence, ability, and experience may be relied upon.

Nor must it be supposed that this reform is less genuine, because it partly restores a former order of things.

"The Provincial Courts," writes one who has returned to Southern India within the last few years, "were abolished during my absence in England, and with them the circuits they held, and they were replaced by Civil and Sessions Courts. In England, I thought this a simplification of system, and thus far an improvement of judicial machinery. I had there before my eyes all the County Court Judges, all the Recorders of cities and towns, sitting singly, and earning the public respect and confidence. On arriving in ——, thus prepossessed in favour of the single judge, one of my first inquiries was to learn how the Sessions Courts were liked for their despatch, and whether they were giving satisfaction from bringing justice more cheaply as well as quickly to every man's door. Quite the contrary. I have not met with a solitary native who has not regretted the Provincial Courts, who has not spoken of their judgments with the greatest respect, and contrasted the authority due to them with the very diminished respect they express for the decrees of the Civil Courts. If I may use the expression, the majesty of justice seems reduced in their eyes to one half. Whatever Court costs least money is considered, they say, good enough for them, and the only thing considered. Such being their universal feeling, I cannot entertain a doubt that restoring the Provincial Courts is a step in the very best direction to the reintegration of English justice in native estimation."

We have little or no conception, indeed, how these hundred millions of thieves, forgers, perjurers, as we are sometimes pleased to call them, really long and thirst and cry for justice. The amount of purely *amateur* justice,—justice invested with no legal, often with no material sanction,—which is every day being called for, being exercised and being obeyed in India, is almost incredible. Every private European resident in the country districts is a judge, if he will only let the people use him as one.

"Hardly a day passes," says the writer of the last quoted letter, a planter in Southern India, "that I have not to distribute justice to parties who come to ask it, far and near. My rule is to confront the complainant and defendant, and first hear their stories, then examine them *vivâ voce.* If an issue is started on which I desire another judgment than my own, a jury is at once impanelled, from the bystanders ordinarily, and the cause is there and then completely threshed out, always to the submission of the litigants, if not to their individual contentment. I do not trust punchayets unless I know who presides at them, for otherwise they are apt to degenerate into a squabble for one or other of the parties interested, according as personal or caste influence prevails. An ordinary native thinks that he must take part for or against; the neutrality of an English juryman is hardly intelligible to his *caste* modes of thought; hence the indispensableness of close supervision over him in judicial investigations."

Take a most remarkable instance, from the same quarter, of voluntary, unofficial registration.

"On my return from England, I was quite horrified at the universality of the crime of forging land-deeds and money-bonds, just as if there existed for it no punishment at all in the Regulations. The first men in the country (Hindoos and Mahommedans) are openly guilty of it, and of the consequent subornation of testimony which it entails, without the smallest shame, or apparently without the smallest loss of character. A wealthy man has lately filed in Court a bond for 30,000 Rs. which all his own family, *without exception,* acknowledge to be forged; this sum is equivalent to £3000 in England. In order to stay the plague in this neighbourhood, I opened a public registry in February, 1856, in a large blank folio kept below stairs, charging a fanam or two for the copying and attesting each deed with my signatnre. Already the deeds enrolled number nearly 60, and not a deed or bond of any importance is now entered into without the stipulation that it is to be duly registered in my folio. It is further a registry of wills. I do all I can to encourage all castes to make wills, disposing openly of such real and personal property as they have the command over, executing and registering them publicly in the presence of all parties concerned. In a very few years, there will not be a land-deed or money-bond in force which is not registered; forgery, subornation, and theft of deeds will die out for want of hope of committing these crimes successfully."

Surely a people with all their vices so thoroughly amenable to justice deserve to have it secured to them.

The subject of education I shall wholly pretermit, as too closely connected with that of religion to be satisfactorily treated of in this place.* Nor dare I venture upon that most interesting subject of public works, which has at last, I trust, thanks mainly to the indefatigable efforts of Colonel Cotton, won for itself its due recognition in Madras. I trust indeed that the worst of that fearful process of absorption of native wealth without return, which went on so long, is now fairly over. The reverse action has clearly commenced in Bengal, chiefly, I presume, through the export of indigo to Europe, of opium to China, the former branch of trade having only been rendered possible through the security afforded by the Permanent settlement. There, specie to a large amount has for years been re-absorbed; prices of produce have largely risen; wages also, it would seem, in various districts. Elsewhere too, reproductive works, though as yet the merest trifle in comparison of the need which exists for them, are beginning materially to increase the actual yield of the soil. The Government of Madras has fully acknowledged (15th May, 1858) that they are "the most economical, because the most profitable, undertakings in which the government could possibly engage."

The improvement of the means of communication tends to increase the money-value of agricultural pro-

* I cannot, however, forbear from referring here to a Homily "On Theology and Government in India," by a very dear friend, whom I am not worthy to praise, the Rev. F. D. Maurice, printed (by J. E. Taylor) for the subscribers to the weekly issue of his Sermons.

duce, by opening up new markets, or facilitating its access to those markets which the suppression of duties both in England and India, and the repeal of the navigation laws, have thrown open already. The removal of the restrictions upon the settlement of Europeans, operates more or less to retain capital within the country. Lastly, the formation in England of Companies for the execution of public works, or the carrying out of certain branches of industry in India (which some fantastical city critic of the "Times" disapproves of), tends to restore to that country some portion of the capital which we have drained from it.

The Proclamation looks forward to the "prosperity," to the "contentment," to the "gratitude" of the Queen's native subjects. I am fully persuaded that one and all are capable of being realized. But let us beware, as I have said before, of endeavouring to realize them too much after our own fashion; let us beware lest a too great haste for English improvements bring with it a rough impatience of native ways and customs, and so restore the too easy tendency to an annexation policy.

I do not indeed doubt—what Englishman can doubt it?—that civilized and Christian Englishmen can govern India better than any of its yet unchristianised princes ever could or can do. Nay, I do not doubt that here and there some one Englishman or other, within his own limited sphere, is always doing so; is setting before the Indian races a pattern of administrative excellence which they never could have realized for themselves. I do not refer here to the civilizing of wild tribes by such men as Augustus Cleveland, in the last century, among the Hill-men of Rajmahal; or Dixon, in our days, among the Mairs of the west. I speak of the government of settled and populous countries by English rulers; of Richard Jenkins at Nagpore; of John Munro in Travancore; of rulers still living, as Cubbon in Mysore, and John Lawrence in the Punjab; and, on a smaller scale, Meadows Taylor in Shorapore;* to whom we might add, though as

* Captain, now Major Meadows Taylor's services as an administrator are so much less known than his talents as a novelist, that I am sure the following very brief sketch, from a reliable source, of his doings in Shorapore, will be welcome to my readers. The Bedars, it should be observed, are an aboriginal tribe of the Deckan, conspicuous for their bravery; (see General Briggs's Lecture on the Aboriginal Races of India—Journal of the Royal Asiatic Society, vol. xlix. p. 294.) the chieftaincy over whom has centered in the Raja of Shorapore, in the Nizam's country, but now included in the ceded districts.

Captain Meadows Taylor was appointed to look after the Bedar country in 1842. He found it in a state of anarchy and ruin. In less than twelve years he had paid off all its debts; and, without coercing the cultivators, had a full treasury for the young Raja and a revenue of £30,000, instead of £16,000 debt. When, by Lord Dalhousie's orders, the prince having come of age to govern, Captain Meadows Taylor placed him on his musnud and took leave of him, the young man falling on his neck and weeping, Captain Taylor told him, that if he departed from goodwill to the British Government, he would not be Raja of Shorapore five years. The prince was thoroughly vicious and cruel, squandered away everything he could, paid no debts, let the roads and tanks and all improvements go to ruin, and having 10,000 of his Bedars at his back, with Arab and Rohilla mercenaries, took occasion of the late rebellion to plunge into a war, where his little army was quickly routed, and himself, a fugitive, sought his life from the British Resident at Hyderabad. Colonel Davidson sent for Captain Taylor, who having parted from the Raja in a palace met him again in a prison, and it was himself who, while groaning and weeping, reminded Captain Taylor of his prophecy, fulfilled in four years and about nine months. In fear of

instances in many respects peculiar, Charles Napier in Scinde, and perhaps John Jacob but yesterday on the Scinde frontier. Instances like these shew, I think, in spite of all the alleged intractableness and savagery of the Indian races, not only that they are governable, but that they have a peculiar aptitude for being governed by Englishmen; and that Englishmen, worthy of the name, have a peculiar aptitude for governing them. But on looking through these signal instances of the success of English rule, they will be found to occur always under peculiar circumstances. Generally speaking—take the cases of Nagpore, Travancore, Shorapore—the Englishman is a mere temporary administrator for the native sovereign, during his minority or otherwise. He is, therefore, governing the natives, not for the benefit of England, but for their own. In the other cases—Scinde, the Punjab—the province has just been conquered; it is felt to be essential at once to invest the English administrator with almost unlimited powers, and to render his rule as acceptable as possible to a yet untamed people, so that pretty nearly the same end is reached; he is allowed still to govern mainly for the benefit of the natives, and not of England herself.

Now what does this amount to? To this—that where British rule has been seen to be, not merely

the gallows, he put an end to his own life. Captain Taylor, who had already in former days been at war with the Bedars and had reduced them to perfect obedience, was sent again to restore order in the country. Before he had been in Shorapore three days he received again their submission. When he entered the country he was hailed with joy; and at the entrance of the city his palanquin was filled with flowers, and his bearers loaded with presents.

Christian in name, but founded upon that principle of self-sacrifice which lies at the very core of Christ's gospel—so far as it has been the rule, not of a system, working through certain human instruments, but of some genuine English *man*, devoting himself to the welfare of the people committed to his charge—so far the blessings of English rule have been real, have been joyfully acknowledged by the natives of India. But so far as that rule has not been the rule of English *men*, but of English policy, founded not upon Christian self-sacrifice, but upon heathen covetousness—so far it has been that which well-nigh the whole of India has been heaving to overthrow of late, that which by fire and sword alone we have been able to maintain.

I am convinced indeed that our Indian empire is too large to be properly governed by us, and that one great cause of native discontent lies in this unwieldiness, which amounts in fact in many districts to a literal absence of government, and at all events reveals itself as such—in the North-West for instance—on the occurrence of any great crisis;—which hinders us utterly from supplying even men enough, let alone good men, for the work that is required of us.* The

* I have not dwelt here upon the claim of the English settler to be admitted to office under the Queen's Government, believing that in general he can speak for himself. Yet the day of justice has undoubtedly not yet come for him. In Madras it is boasted that 60 Deputy-collectorships are thrown open to him. But at what salaries? 500 rupees a month, for men full of age and experience; whilst a boy Assistant-collector within the covenant gets nearly 1000 after three years; the Deputy-collector's services being moreover placed at the entire disposal of the Collector, for whatever use he may think fit. It is obvious that no first-rate or even second-rate man will take office on such terms.

miserable failure of the Indian government hitherto, in a purely business point of view, is something absolutely ridiculous, if it were not so sad. Only conceive of a country so richly endowed as India not having been able, in the midst of the perfect peace which prevailed before the rebellion, to pay its own expenses! Only realize the fact, which appears in the evidence before the Colonization Committee of this year,* that the Presidency of Bombay, the one most open to European trade, the smallest and most manageable of any, has never paid its own cost! Only compare the condition of India with that of Ceylon, which, as Sir Henry Ward told his Legislative Council on the 28th July, 1858, has had "for five consecutive years" an increasing revenue; has "no debt;" "is executing large works out of its own surplus funds," which works, "as soon as completed, increase the revenues out of which they spring;" where "British energy and capital are creating in the interior of the island vast properties," which furnish "the readiest market for every article that the industry of the low country can supply;" where, to cap all, the hard work of cultivation is actually done by temporary emigrants from the coast of India itself! Why should not every one of the provinces of India,—often equivalent in population to Ceylon,—be as prosperous as itself?†

* Fourth Report, p. 66.

† For this purpose, it will not only be necessary, I suspect, to restore the separate Presidencies to at least the degree of autocracy which they enjoyed before 1834, as indicated by Mr. Bright's great speech of last Session. I have letters before me, from one now resident in India, and who knows the country well, asking why every province of India should not enjoy the same autocracy as

For the present, as it seems to me, our aim should be, so far as possible, to take the native princes, with increased territories and increased freedom of action, for our fellow-workers in all Indian reforms, retaining to ourselves so much territory as we can govern thoroughly well, leaving the future to take care of itself. "The three provinces of Bengal, Behar, and Benares," wrote St. George Tucker, "are of more value than the rest of our widely extended empire; and *insulated, or protected by an impassable barrier, we should be richer, by being confined to this our first great acquisition and best possession.*" These words were written in 1832,—and how much weightier are they now, when our empire is so much the vaster, and on the morrow of a great rebellion! Yet we need not, we cannot go so far, even if we wished it. The administrative talents of the natives have in general been crushed or corrupted, instead of developed, under our rule, and the hands are wanting to which we could confide many a province and district that we should be better without than with. But I suspect—for one instance—there is no adjacent British territory which would not be too glad to exchange our rule for that of Holkar and his minister Ramchunder Rao. By such contraction of our dominions we shall be able to concentrate our efforts upon internal improvements, and shew the

Ceylon? Carve India into twenty-five separate colonies, each independent of the other for all purposes of internal administration, federated as respects self-defence, customs' duties, &c., and you restore in the most healthful manner those local centres of wealth, industry and activity, which it is one of the great mischiefs of British rule to have destroyed.

natives of India the true pattern of what Christian Englishmen can do.

I do not indeed look to any hasty termination of the British rule in India; with all its faults I believe it to be essential to India's development; I believe no greater curse could befal India than its premature withdrawal. But all experience tends to shew that India never can be a British colony, in the same sense that the United States have been, that Canada, Australia, and the Cape are now. The Anglo-Saxon race cannot spread itself in layers over the country, or fix itself in masses within it. A few hill-ranges here and there,—the slopes of the Himalayas to the north,—seem the only localities where it can thoroughly take root, doing upon God's earth the rough work with the smooth. Elsewhere, it would seem, except through some exceptional units here and there, it can only direct, overlook, fulfil the easier, indoors labours, and that generally under the necessity of frequent absences for health's sake. It seems impossible to see here the elements of a permanent connexion between the pure Anglo-Saxon race and the native ones. How far the mixed race may supply the place of their fathers, remains to be seen. The experience of the rebellion seems to shew that, even physically, that race has been greatly undervalued. But the connexion must last till we have assured to the native races those blessings which they seem incapable of obtaining without us,—Freedom, which must always have Truth and Justice for its handmaids,—Christ's Gospel, the true source of freedom, the true sanctifier of family ties, the true leveller of the distinctions of race and colour, because the only power which can avail to raise the man to his true stature, as child of God, member of Christ, inheritor of the kingdom of heaven. Yet "a time," wrote Lord Hastings, forty years ago (1818), "not very remote will arrive when England will, on sound principles of policy, wish to relinquish the domination which she has gradually and unintentionally assumed over this country, and from which she cannot at present recede. In that hour it would be the proudest boast and the most delightful reflection that she had used her sovereignty towards enlightening her temporary subjects, so as to enable the native communities to walk alone in the paths of justice, and to maintain with probity towards their benefactress that commercial intercourse in which we should then find a solid interest."*

And though the above noble passage is empty of a Name which many would fain have read there; let us rest assured that we cannot truly enlighten our Indian fellow-subjects except through One who is the Source of Light,—we cannot teach them justice except through Him who is the Judge of all the earth.

I have treated the Proclamation, as I said I would, as a reality. I believe it was so meant. No set of men, I trust, in her Majesty's Cabinet would be so base as to put forth such a document without the will to fulfil it,—to forge the Queen's name, if I may so speak, to promises made only to be broken. Yet I cannot but repeat that, as I am assured, "the natives in every

* Private Journal, vol. ii. p. 326.

part of India are already remarking that, simultaneously with, and immediately after its publication, the acts of the Indian authorities are in direct violation of its spirit and its letter,"—that they speak already of the Queen's Government as likely seemingly to turn out merely "the old farce under a new name."* If this state of things be suffered to go on, "the most awful risk imaginable,"—to use the words of one who feels deeply on this matter,—will be run. For I firmly believe, that if the policy which the Proclamation nobly disowns be resumed,—the policy of annexation and absorption,—of all-grasping covetousness,—of insolence of race,—of special pleading with laws and treaties,—the loss, the deserved and ignominious loss of our Indian empire will come upon us sooner than we dream.†

* The appointment of the Inam Commission at Madras, as the *last* act of the Company's Government, and the *first* public measure following on the inauguration of the Queen's Government, has in particular roused the bitterest feelings in that Presidency.

† I had scarcely written these words (21st Dec. 1858), when Mr. Russell's letter to the "Times," dated Pursaidepore, Nov. 14, met my eye,—complaining of the parsimony with which copies of the Proclamation were supplied to our officers,—of the official translation being written in a fashionable Court Oordoo, which the common people in Oude could not understand,—of the repugnance shewn to the amnesty by "valued and distinguished servants of the old Company;" and stating that "a very distinguished officer of the Government, whose rank in the councils of the Indian empire is of the very highest, actually suggested to one of the officers charged with the pacification of Oude, that he should not read the Proclamation till he had battered down the forts of the chiefs."

Since the above date, however, we know that in spite of all obstacles the amnesty has worked its way, and has amply justified itself by its success.

APPENDIX.

As a sample on the one hand of the mode in which the Proclamation could be dealt with in India by one really alive to its worth,—on the other of the feelings with which it was met by the people in a part of the country which has been wholly undisturbed by rebellion, I venture to annex the following report by a near relative of my own, a landholder in the South, to the authorities of his province.

"Anjarakandy, 6 December, 1858.

"To G. R. Sharpe, Esq.

"Assistant Magistrate of Malabar.

"Sir,—Yesterday, pursuant to public notice given several days previous, the native inhabitants of these and of the neighbouring aneshums were convened, and Her Majesty's Proclamation, assuming the government of her Indian dominions, was read and made known to them. A very large number of persons, relatively to the population, of all castes and creeds, attended. All manifested the greatest and most respectful interest in what they were assembled to hear; and as the occasion furnished me with the opportunity of arriving unsuspiciously at the inner sentiments prevailing among peaceful and respectable Hindoos and Mahomedans upon a very important subject, now of engrossing interest, it is my duty to make known to you and to Mr. Grant, the magistrate of the Province, what occurred.

To introduce what follows I must premise that on my return from England I learned with infinite pain and surprise, in conversation with both Hindoos and Mapillas, that it is a settled belief among the people that there exists a desire on the part of the Government to make them renounce caste and creed and adopt Christianity; not of course by any demonstration of force, but by gradual and covert means, by prepossessing the minds of their children and offering temptations to their temporal interests. I state the naked fact. My individual assurances, repeated on every available occasion, have proved powerless in combating this erroneous and fatal impression. I therefore gladly availed myself of the occasion of the Proclamation, to shew to the people that the disclaimer they had heard from me was repeated in the most marked and emphatic language by the supreme head of the state, and was by her commanded to be published throughout the length and breadth of the land. Accordingly, after the Malayalim version of the proclamation, carefully adapted to the comprehension of the persons who were to hear it, had been slowly and deliberately read, I, invited question and comment upon it, by asking whether all present clearly understood what they had just heard; if not, that I was ready to explain its meaning, and resolve any doubts. An ancient Mapilla in the midst of the crowd made response that some parts he understood, some he did not. I asked him forward, and on questioning him before all as to what he did not understand, I perceived plainly that his doubts were fixed upon the real meaning of that passage of the Proclamation, in which Her Majesty declares in the clearest language that no proselytism of the natives is designed, that no interference with their religion or usages will be suffered without punishment, and no bar be raised, by reason of creed or caste, to the right of all to public state employ. I saw unmistakably, in surveying the faces and the attitude of the listening crowd, that they participated in the doubt expressed by the Mapilla. I saw, in short, that they did not trust their own ears, and that on the bare mention of their religion and usages, so strong were their prepossessions running in the opposite direction, they feared nothing less was intended than a proclaimed interference with both. I therefore caused the Queen's disclaimer to be again twice read over, and assured the people that Her Majesty's commands would be the rigid rule of her Government. Not till then were they thoroughly satisfied as to what was intended. 'If that be so,' said a Hindoo, 'then the Padres will no longer be suffered to come to the festivals of our Pagodas, when we are peaceably met together, and hold forth and abuse our religion and usages to our very faces, provoking us to break forth into violence.'

But whatever the hopes of future good to themselves and their country, raised and encouraged by other parts of the Proclamation, whatever the approval, and it was a hearty approval, bestowed upon them, the touchstone of the merit of the whole paper was in the minds of the assembly the treatment to be dealt out by the new Government to their caste and religion. I record the fact as undeniable evidence of their sensitiveness upon these subjects, and as proof that the feeling is sunk to the depth of their hearts. Sensitiveness to his faith is not held to be a disparagement to a Christian. The true Christian will never hold it to be a disparagement in a Mahomedan or a Hindoo.

I have the honour to be, &c. &c.

F. C. BROWN.

P.S.—A Bramin present asked for a copy of the Proclamation. have sent another to the Mapilla sheikh of Kalye.

"F. C. BROWN."

I add the following details from a private letter from the same writer:—

"One Mapilla said, they had had scores of Proclamations upon every conceivable subject, but never one so wise and sensible as this. 'That is true,' rejoined another, 'but the Maharanee is in England, a very long way off; who will see to the execution in India?' The very same feeling as here was manifested by all classes at Tellicherry. 'That is an admirable clause, the toleration clause,' said to me the *Protestant* moonsiff. 'What an excellent passage that is in the Proclamation,' said the *Roman Catholic* sheristadar of the Sessions Court. As for the natives, there was among them but one burst of satisfaction. . . . By the way, the Government Malayalim version of the Proclamation would have been so much Greek to my neighbours. I had to prepare a corrected one of my own."

ERRATA.

Page 186, line 10 from bottom, *for* "the Sepoys," *read* "our Sepoys."

Page 190, line 6 from bottom, *for* "heirs," *read* "heirs male."

NOTE.

In considering, at pp. 41 and foll., the legal value of the word "successor," the use of that word for fiscal purposes by the Succession Duties Act, 17 and 18 Vict. c. 51, should perhaps have been referred to. The positions laid down remain however wholly unaffected by the omission; for on the one hand, it is as true now as in Sir E. Coke's time, that the word "successor" creates no fee-simple (Co. Litt. 8 *b*.), and on the other, the sense in which the word is taken by the Act goes far beyond the construction of it by annexationist officials, and approximates closely to its use as a term of international law.